GO HIRE YOURSELF
AN EMPLOYER

Richard K. Irish is vice-president of TransCentury Corporation, a Washington, D.C., based management firm. For twelve years he has specialized in international executive search. For the past five years, he has conducted clinics for job-seekers and employers alike on the whole employment process. He is the author of *If Things Don't Improve Soon, I May Ask You to Fire Me!*

RICHARD K. IRISH

Go Hire Yourself
an Employer

A Revised and Expanded Edition

ANCHOR BOOKS

ANCHOR PRESS/DOUBLEDAY

GARDEN CITY, NEW YORK

An earlier version of part of Chapter Eight was published in the October, 1976, issue of *Glamour* magazine, as was most of Chapter Nine, which appeared as "Survival Guide for Washington Bureaucrats" in the April 16, 1972, issue of *Potomac* magazine of the Washington *Post*. All of the last chapter appeared in *The Graduate* magazine for 1977.

Go Hire Yourself an Employer was originally published in 1973 by Doubleday & Company, Inc.
Revised Anchor Press Edition: 1978

DEDICATION

This book is dedicated to everyone who at one time or another is told, "You're too young, old, qualified, unqualified, experienced, inexperienced, beautiful, plain, expensive, educated, uneducated, or too damn good" for a job. . . .

CONTENTS

ACKNOWLEDGMENTS

Thanks to a number of people, this book evolved into what you're holding in your hands.

Credit for the title goes to an old friend and colleague, Fran Buhler, who, in his southern staccato once said to me: "But . . . Dick, ole Buddy, . . . seems what, er, you're trying . . . to say is . . . "Go hire yourself an employer." Well, thus are books christened! I'm also especially indebted to Warren Wiggins, president of TransCentury Corporation (where I ply my trade) for his encouragement and assistance, and to Lila Ballendorf and Rebecca Dembs, both of whom typed the manuscript with the tender care they invest in everything; other associates—Colin Walters, John Coyne, Bill Josephson, Dirk Ballendorf, Bob Gale, and Tom Page all read and criticized the manuscript. Theresa Bradley and Tom Hebert made original contributions. To all of them, my thanks.

The book bears the influence of some other writers I respect: Bob Townsend, Peter Drucker, and Bernard Haldane. But, of course, I'm responsible for all that's written here.

Portions of the second edition were written at Christmas Cove, Maine. I'm especially grateful to Mrs. William Seipp for the use of her summer home there. And the fine meals and companionship too.

It would be impossible to acknowledge the names of thousands of others who made a contribution—whether they know it or not —to the book. By those, I mean all the unemployed who have shared with me their travail, frustration, and victories over the past fifteen years.

Finally, a special *Te Deum* to my wife, Sally, whose patience, loving care, and humor were as necessary in writing the book as pen and paper.

September 16, 1977
Marshall, Virginia

FOREWORD

From where I sit, it's a puppy-kickin' world.

If a doctor is someone who thinks everyone is sick, I'm someone who thinks everyone is unemployed.

It's because I'm in the people business. A body broker. An employer, and lately, a counselor to the unemployed.

I hear that there are more employed people in the United States than ever before.

But from the number of résumés that cross my desk, not to mention the swatch of pink phone messages from the anxiety-ridden jobless, to the excessively deferential unemployed waiting to see me in the reception room, the whole job scene strikes me as a tragic scene from *King Lear*.

So, every working day I'm reminded of what it's like to be out in the cold without a job.

Back in *circa* 1958, I was unemployed for the first time in my life. It wasn't always so. Before 1958, that is before my "blue" period, I had the usual stop-loss, grunt, or, as they say today, counterculture jobs. I was a dishwasher, a tour director, a traffic checker, soldier, bartender, camp director, salesman—all of which I enjoyed because these jobs were a means to an end: financing a college education, a European trip, my fiancée's wedding ring.

But, like you, I'd been carefully taught to despise "interim" employment. Parents, peers, and placement counselors stress *career*—professional employment. To this day, I've developed a lively prejudice for the word "career." It strikes me as the phoniest word in the lexicon.

For me, this six-month spell of unemployment was easily the most painful period in my life. I blamed my woeful condition on everyone but myself. The President of the United States. The educational system. Sputnik. Capitalism. The Labor Trusts.

But, of course, the real blame was my own. Every mistake I excoriate in this book, I committed. Cubed. And I learned, then, that no one learns from his mistakes—unless he *wants* to. Most folks repeat mistakes the rest of their natural lives.

Not just job-seekers. Everyone. Mistakes are patterns of behavior, learned to cope with conditions (usually as a child), which are no longer appropriate or effective as an adult. For illustration, some chronic job-hoppers:

— have problems coping with authority
— can't focus on personal objectives
— require rigid supervisory guidelines
— can't work within lateral structures
— hesitate and finally postpone making decisions
— back off from conflict situations
— are invariably aggressive, never yielding, or vice versa
And so on.

Now, it doesn't matter who you work for, what you do, for how much, or where. Invariably, these so-called character weaknesses or mistake patterns will follow you into every job, through marriage and divorce, into child-rearing, and on into senescence.

Nobody likes to change. Personal change is tedious, hard work. But nobody likes to continue making mistakes either. A beginning, a big beginning, is admitting your mistakes and *wanting* to change. Until this crossroads is reached in your head, you cannot find happiness on or off the job.

It was years before I stopped believing there was something wrong with the "system" and, in bluer moments, with me—all because of my clumsy, outdated, and naïve job-finding strategy and my apparent need to fail.

The symptoms of the unhappily unemployed are obvious to everyone, particularly employers: hostility, self-pity, wanness, and a predilection for apocalyptic solutions.

At least I showed all the signs: I developed a lively hostility to personnel people (an animus not yet overcome); systematically studied scientific socialism; sought consolation in Tchaikovsky's *Pathétique* symphony; ate repeated meals of yogurt and garbanzo beans; frequented public libraries and stock-brokerage houses (warm spots for job-seekers wishing to come in from the cold); and developed a fine existential philosophy.

Finally, much to my distress, I was offered a job with a bank, a Mom-and-Pop operation in San Francisco known as the Bank of

America. Yes, believe it or not, I took a job as a management trainee. Thus began my chartreuse period, characterized by extreme self-pity, sullenness, boredom, and pathetic discontent. After a year wrestling with foreign-exchange rates and international remittances, on Christmas Eve I gave myself a gift and quit, leaving the world of international banking to the gnomes of Zurich.

Oh, it's a pity you weren't there; you would have heard those sweeping violins pick up the doleful theme from the last movement of the Sixth Symphony, seen my square-jawed, three-quarter profile outlined against the San Francisco sunset, thrilled to my rage against "The System." But, of course, what ailed me was not revolutionary fervor; rather, I was a hopelessly middle-class rebel with seemingly the tritest of causes: Job Dissatisfaction.

But in 1964, through a happy chain of events, I became an employer myself. Suddenly I was on the other side of the desk noting in the unemployed all the selfsame frailties of character and the same mistakes I had never seen in myself. The experience of seeing myself every day for the next twelve years (in the persons of all the unemployed who passed by me) was what educators call "a learning experience." It occurred to me that during my "blue" and "chartreuse" periods I was no exception, that all job-seekers take on a kind of gray hue of incompetence, ineffectuality, and sullenness. In a word, I began to study the whole people business: finding, keeping, and growing on a job. A lot of what I learned is in this book.

I like my work. Finding people jobs, helping people to re-examine their lives and reassemble themselves, and counseling the unemployed on the methodology of the job campaign are gratifying. Marriage brokers, realtors, psychiatrists, and other middlemen must derive similar satisfaction from their work.

This book began as an intracompany document to assist unemployed job applicants who were knocking down our doors, all of whom we couldn't possibly employ. Now it's a book for everybody who wants work doing what they *want*, or is thinking about switching jobs and/or changing "fields" (as they say in academe), or improving the quality of the job where they work now.

A cursory review of the abundant literature on strategies of finding employment, vocational-guidance manuals, and encyclopedias of potential employers yielded little of value. Most of them justly collect dust in libraries and are often worse than useless, since they give a *rational* picture of the employment process which is irradiated with irrationalism, whimsy, and sheer caprice.

Recently, however, even in colleges and universities (which are always the last to hear), there are signs of change: increasing emphasis, for example, on *counseling* rather than *placement* of graduates, a greater regard for teaching people how to find jobs *themselves*, and improved approaches to helping people focus on *ability* rather than relying on education and experience as the appropriate "qualifications" for employment.

But, even now, most how-to-find-a-job systems fail in understanding the peculiar chemistry between the hired and the hiring, the simple but still little-known methods on how to find judgment jobs—jobs where you're paid for your decisions; and the role that "luck" plays in the process. Worse, many books and "life planning guides" simply don't cope with the elementary fact that the point of working in the first place is because it gives pleasure. Nor is there sufficient appreciation that the aim of the game is not to get a job (*any* job!) but to *discriminate* between employers. And there is insufficient understanding of the role of the human will ("doing what we really *want*") in finding a job we love. The old saw is still true, of course, that finding a job is "a question of being at the right place at the right time"; but it's even truer that people who know what they *want* (and overcome subjective resistance or doing what other people *expect*) are happier and more competent in the job search and on the job.

The question/answer format is how I teach (and you learn) the art of finding a judgment job, all of which cover most aspects of the job-finding process. These questions are repeatedly asked by people I counsel. Agreed, the ping and the pong of question/answer can be annoying, but this dialectic is an ancient form of instruction and a practical way to highlight information necessary to every judgment job-seeker.

Therefore, this book is a teaching device: it shows you how to be the right person, with ostensibly the right qualifications at the right time and the right place. It is the product of some ten thousand interviews I have had with the unemployed, my own hiring experiences, and the success stories of a very few people who know how to find a job.

— This book can speed up your employment and ease the burden of finding a judgment job (or vice versa!).
— This book is for all the unemployed, not just young college graduates.
— This book is for "career" counselors.
— This book is for classes of people: women, teachers, specialists, forty-plus, veterans, minorities—all of whom have specific class problems in addition to the main problem of just finding an interesting job.
— Lastly, this book is for employers, who need all the help they can get!

Hiring authorities need to focus on candidate *motivation and ability*. Of secondary importance are education and experience. People who hire need to learn how to "screen in" effective people. Unfortunately, many employers "screen out" candidates by focusing on the wrong characteristics.

An able person is hard to find; someone who is able and *willing* is even more difficult to identify. Employers who grasp this elementary fact are miles ahead of those who believe a job is a gift. The art of picking effective people for judgment jobs is itself a judgment job, and savvy employers will "open up" the recruitment process.*

The theme of the book is how to become competent in the job hunt and how to make that competence carry over on the job. The thrust of my advice is how to identify contribution(s) you can make to potential employers and how to act on that information. The point is to make you self-aware, confident, poised, and prepared to *hire yourself an employer*.

Most of us think of our *need*, never our *desire* for a job. People, therefore, make the mistake of accepting a job because it's *available*. Following a conventional pathway to a job, the linear direction, is generally frustrating. Life is not a race with winners and losers. There are simply some people who love what they do (and

* My companion book, *If Things Don't Improve Soon, I May Ask You to Fire Me* (Anchor Press) addresses this issue in far more detail.

do it), and others who are in a mindless race leading lives of "quiet desperation" (Thoreau).

The methods outlined in this book are for people with strong egos (or who want them). But job-seekers who feel *powerless* self-destruct out of an inappropriate sense of insecurity (people must become their own security—nobody *owes* you a job). "Powerless" job supplicants need to address these problems before they "qualify" for judgment jobs: the only choice is to find a grunt job (*any* income-producing job) and start the painful, necessary, and finally fulfilling task of self-analysis.

At times I am irreverent. My biases are manifest and, I think, truer than Newton's laws. I make no apology for my iconoclasm; the world of employment has far too long been shrouded in a suffocating pedantry masquerading as "manpower development."

Also, my style, which is personal, brusque, occasionally ironic, and hopelessly self-assured, is designed to bully the reader, needle you into action. Of course, it won't work! I mean I can't *make* you find a job, but I can tell you *how* to do it. Doing it, however, is your responsibility. And, in the process, if you start feeling so good about yourself you can't *stand* it, do understand that changing oneself is the world's toughest and most important work. Far from losing your "incompetent" identity, you grow into your real self. And if friends and neighbors don't like the new you, then that's their problem, not yours.

Most people doubt their competence and ability to find a job. So they accept jobs on the basis of need rather than desire. They need bullying. They need to be persuaded to do what they *want* instead of what they *should*.

The self-directed activities in Chapter Two are designed to provoke action. As conscientious, adventure-minded job-seekers, these activities cause effective feedback about oneself: a sense of competent identity. Once this information is on paper, you "translate" what this information means.

And this book is not, repeat not, Dick Irish's strategy to finding a job. Competent job-seekers use these techniques; it's what makes them successful. The best job shrinks, too, advise the same approach. For years, these approaches have worked. The problem is, most people accept jobs they don't want and hate. And guess who's "blamed"? The "system," that's who!

I believe it is in your power to change the character of your employment life, to step out of roles planned for you by your mother, father, placement counselors, friends, and employers. My central point is to look upon employers as someone you hire to give *you* the means to develop into the person you *can* be.

As such, like books in the trade I deplore, this, too, is a "How to . . ." manual. Now, nobody of course learns to make love, repair a car, or hit a baseball by reading a book. But everyone can usefully supplement his skills with improved techniques and self-knowledge. Learning on the job, I believe, is the only sensible way to learn a trade; looking for a job is the only way to find a job. (And never quit a job until you have a job. It's the oldest axiom in the employment game. Use your current job as a base, as a means toward what you want.)

This book is not restricted in the kind of readership it seeks: not the unemployed alone, or women, or the problems of Vietnam War vets. Rather, the book is restricted to the kind of jobs it recommends: so-called "judgment jobs."* (That's what Bob Townsend calls them in *Up the Organization.*) These are jobs where the whole human being is required to exercise his mental muscles, where a high premium (i.e., a good salary) is paid for your intelligence and intuition, where "good solid judgment" is your qualification for the job. Whether you work in a pickle factory or the CIA, most of the jobs are uninteresting. Ten per cent of the jobs, however, are "judgment jobs." How you get them is what this book explains.

This book is for those unhappy in their work, people who want to change their occupations, people who are competent who want to become more competent, people with strong egos that need important work for self-expression, people who *do* things and *do* them very well.

This is not a book for "losers." There is an abundance of "success literature" available for them. This book is intended for winners, or people who want to be. Those who need jobs—any job—are invited to read elsewhere.

Finding a judgment job you want, which you might have to

---

* Peter Drucker calls them "knowledge" jobs; in my second book I call them "growth" jobs.

create, or even "sell," is going to take time. Maybe longer than accepting the first job that's offered.

Use the house-buying analogy. If you and your spouse bought the *first* house you could afford, chances are you would buy it within a month. But looking for the house of your dreams is going to take lots of work, time, and reflection. And it's something you might build yourself.

Same with a judgment job.

So use this book as your script to psych out the "system," to master uncommon methods of finding interesting jobs.

With this disclaimer—there is no substitute for ability and proven performance—no "hustle" or employment "techniques" are going to solve any personal or psychological deficiencies. All this book pretends to do is make you understand yourself and make the "system" work for you. There are even, if you disapprove of the "system," some crude hints on how to change it.

Now, before we begin, let's review some assumptions on the job market which are true and important, but not really worth mentioning (except #9) more than once.

1. Job-finding is tough on everyone these days: the rich, the poor, the skilled and the unskilled, the high salaried, and even—Praise God!—the Beautiful People (whoever they might be). The country is still in the worst spell of unemployment since the thirties. So? You slash your wrists and wait for a flood of sympathy cards? Of course not. (Besides, thirty years hence, you can spin fireside tales of the Great Depression: "What was it really like, Grandma/Granddad?")

Even in the best of times—1968, for example—the unemployed were, from my vantage point, even more abundant. Good times bring out the impatient job-jumper in us and millions of otherwise satisfied job-holders start sniffing about for even better opportunities. A kind of inflated job psychology develops, and turnover in executive employment (already incredibly high in our dynamic society) takes on cyclonic proportions.

The point to remember, in good times and bad, is that there *are* good jobs. New firms are forming, new life is breathed into a thousand old-line endeavors. Like the stock market, the job market goes up and down. And like the stock market again, most

stocks might be going down, but some are going up. Even in bad
times, there *are* jobs opening up. It's harder to find them; judgment jobs are always elusive. But new jobs are developing every
day in response to forces and problem areas in our society. Whoever heard of space technicians, environmental-systems analysts,
cross-cultural training experts, family-planning specialists twenty
years ago?

Not you or me.

I wager that 20 per cent of all jobs currently filled in our country today did not exist fifteen years ago, and that many jobs we
perform now won't exist ten years hence. This is what some manpower experts, in a romantic paroxysm, call the "job-market revolution."

2. My guess is that never before has job relevance to society's
real needs been more evident. This is true not only of young college graduates, but increasingly of middle-aged job-seekers. And all
of this is happening at a time of increased organizational tempo,
more sophisticated and finite divisions of labor, and souped-up,
computerized decision-making processes. The nature of "work" itself is under grave scrutiny.

Hannah Arendt writes profoundly on this problem; other
scholars know the nature of modern work to be central to many
other problems. The main reason for worker dissatisfaction
(whether blue or white collar) is that specialization has ushered in
an age when men and women are separated from the fruits of
their labor. Our assembly-line culture, our highly specialized and
esoteric job functions—no matter how important—leave us alienated from the purposes and the final product of our work. Accordingly, I hazard, 90 per cent of all employment—no matter how
well paid and prestigious—leaves most modern men and women
longing for simpler, less remunerative, and more satisfying work.
Almost everyone I talk to wants a job "working with people." It's
the most hackneyed cliché on the job scene. And "relevance" and
"meaningfulness" are close seconds. But most jobs can be *made*
into what you want.

3. The ideal job doesn't exist. The dream job of all our imagin-
ings is a figment in the minds of thousands of college grads
dumped on the economy each year. That's the bad news. The

good news is how any job within this 10 per cent judgment-job category can be changed into "your dream job."

And fewer folks look for jobs when times are tough. Your competition for judgment jobs is the employed, not the unemployed. Ergo, fewer people looking for good jobs means more chance for those who are. Q.E.D., search out good jobs in tough times when job-holders are watching the grass grow in the streets.

Once I prowled the halls of a government agency; a fellow I knew slipped his résumé into my hand on the elevator; five minutes later, a colleague of the first, cornered me near the water fountain and asked if I knew of any jobs; a third person, the boss of the first two, called me that afternoon saying his résumé was in the mail.

As a headhunter, nobody in fifteen years didn't want to at least *talk* about a new job. So on your next job, carry a résumé around. You can't tell who you'll meet on the afternoon shuttle to Boston.

4. Don't ask me why, but it's a truism of the marketplace that employers are a breed who offer a job to someone who already has one. Employers are naturally suspicious of the unemployed; they are unenthusiastic about long hair; "Why," they ask, "did you major in archeology instead of business administration?" Contemporary dress and life styles still appall the fifty-plus employers, many of whom have the crew-cut mentalities they sported in boot camp back in the forties. And the manners of the young, the democratic informality of the hired hands, is still not welcome in banks, insurance companies, trade associations—in a word, wherever institutions need to convey "images." In the past five years there has, however, been improvement. But the young still find little reason for cheer in some current employment situations. However, I know an older chap—an industrial-management consultant turned down by an *avant-garde* architectural firm (a client of mine)—who was rejected for a lot of reasons, the main (unadmitted) one of which was that he didn't have a beard!

So, if you're young (or "old") and "inexperienced" (something, by the way, we won't let you admit in this book), or "overqualified," be prepared to take some jolts during your job search. Employers are openly skeptical about your scruples and your causes. Your ego, already large, is cruising, as we said in *my* youth, for a bruising.

5. And if you're young, let's face it; the best job you're going to find in the next forty years is being institutionalized. It might exist in some people's heads, or on the planning boards of university think tanks, or in a management consulting firm's files. But society is inventing the institutions that serve as instruments for tomorrow's needs, all of which await another generation's assumption of the levers of power and finance.

Institutions seem to be curiously behind the times, like the law. The job of people, no matter what their line of work, is to make the places they work (whether it's the post office, a university, or a government agency) more in touch with the times.

6. Another hard truth found here is that while you'll learn methods that improve your ability to find a job, most employers still practice employment techniques found in *The Pickwick Papers*. Either that or "scientific personnel management." It's still the name of the same game.

Understanding how luck, caprice, and whimsy affect you, the job-seeker, is like playing a ball game. There are rules and boundaries to finding a job. It's the extra effort, the spirit, and the way the ball bounces (and how you bounce back from disappointment) that judge your mettle and success. Disabuse yourself of the fiction, therefore, that employers necessarily *know* what they are doing when they hire (or don't hire) you.

The central problem of *homo sapiens* is the question of human *will*. Don't kid yourself; if job-seekers have enormous difficulty focusing on what they *want*, so do employers. Employers stand on one foot, then the other; establish desirable criteria for a job candidate and call it essential; or establish essential criteria and then call it desirable. Employers, like job-seekers, have problems focusing on objectives. So, if you are looking for a job, take an employer under your wing and help him clarify what he *wants*.

So looking for a job is "crazy." And that means keeping your head while other job-seekers are losing theirs!

There is a myth about in the land that ours is a free enterprise "system." There is free enterprise, of course; but the reason it works is that it's *not* a "system." This drives social scientists, plan-

ners, economists, and policy makers bananas and causes job-
seekers to feel buffeted about on an ocean of uncontrollable
forces. No, the job market is not rational, but, insofar as the government doesn't distort its natural workings, it meshes people
with jobs. What the job-seeker needs to know is that, although
the system is crazy, it works. However, someone wanting a job
needs to be rational. That is, the job-seeker needs to plan and organize his/her time, money, ideas and emotions to achieve what
he/she wants, not what he/she perceives the "system" demands.
Pay no attention, therefore, to *trends* in the job market. Instead
of looking for what you think is *available*, focus on researching
yourself. That's how to make job-finding rational.

7. Since you all want figures, for your information, if you are a
newly graduated job-seeker, it normally takes about nine to twelve
months to find your first entry-level "professional" job. That's *too*
long. If you apply the methods written up here, it should take you
no longer than four months to choose between a couple of good
offers, although waiting out *the* job could take a year. That's because people who know what they want (and find it) know how
to find the means (and the patience) to wait for a judgment job.

And if you're in mid-career and jumping fields, count on a couple of months' intensive preparation before launching into the job
market. And don't quit your job first. You've got to eat, feed your
kids, and make the mortgage payments. Who said you have nothing to live for?

8. Uncommonly effective job-finding methods are necessary in
finding the job *you want*. But that's only half the problem. Figuring out what you want is not easy either: it involves finding out
who you are, what you've done, then learning the methods to
match your strengths against the job market. It makes no sense to
learn *how* to find a job, land one as a drop-forge operator, then realize you hate iron foundries. It's not enough knowing *how* to find
a job, although not many do. That's why you'll have an advantage
over your competition. But if few people know how to find employment, even fewer know what they want.

What happens, sadly, is that most job-seekers want what the
media, peers, friends, parents—in other words the "world"—want
them to want. This is true of many major decisions we make in

life. My point is that it's you, not your fraternity brothers or placement counselors, who must judge what you want. Whether you're just out of college or in mid-career (in a job you find hopeless), it's not too late to rethink what makes Sammy run.

Most effective people reading this book will have four or five "careers" in their lifetime, even if they work for the same organization. "Career" counselors are nincompoops if their abracadabra leads someone to think they should become a landscape architect because of some "life planning" exercise.

It's better to focus on a job, and (after you have the job) on each serial *assignment* within the job, than to fantasize about some hypothetical career path carefully charted for you by career counselors, college professors, or fraternity-house soothsayers. Chances are, at the end of your life—looking backward—your occupational character will have a design and a logic unrevealed in your youth. That's because a *rational* approach to "career development" takes into account the marvelous surprises, fascinating *culs de sac*, unusual involutions life has in store for everyone. To plot, at age twenty-three, your life from graduate school to cemetery plot is truly irrational, *crazy*.

9. Easy, right? Do what you want. Wrong: it's tough work coming to terms with yourself, grooving on the human *will*. Erasmus, Luther, Schopenhauer, and Freud are read today because of what they wrote about it. So don't give up if you don't know what you want to do. Most people, and mostly all young people, don't, especially those who seem like they do! Figuring out what you want to do, however, is child's play compared to overcoming the anxiety and self-doubt that knowing what you want will cause. And this matter of *will* and *work* is something everyone needs to address at the beginning of every workday.

10. One aim in looking for a job is, yes, bread. But we do not live by bread alone. So finding a job which is self-fulfilling is important too!

11. That's right, your education won't help you to find a judgment job. But nobody's education ever did, unless they were looking for a job in education.

12. Employers, properly, want to know how you can help them,

not how they can help you. That doesn't mean they won't help you!

13. Lastly, you need to hire yourself an employer. You'll be spending as much time with this person as with your wife or husband, and you'll want a good marriage. Hiring yourself an employer means you are a peer of the employer's, and that you treat each other on a parity rather than a petitionary basis. This is not the nineteenth century. We defer to no one except, possibly, cardinals of Mother Church, expectant mothers, traffic cops. The last person you want to kowtow to is your employer. What he wants (although he often doesn't know it) is your sense of independence and perspective. Yours is a judgment job, right?

So let's go hire yourself an employer.

GO HIRE YOURSELF
AN EMPLOYER

ONE

To Drop Out, Stay Put, Sell Out, or Buy In

What do you mean by the job-market revolution?

Simply, that every year there is a 10 per cent turnover in jobs—job-seekers must stay *au courant*. Skills, aptitudes, and experience gained in one field have a definite crossruff in newly coalescing fields of work. And plenty of jobs simply disappear from the scene because the work performed is no longer necessary or practical. This means we must be fast on our feet and learn the art of job-jumping. Switching fields two or three times in one's occupational life is usual and sometimes necessary.

Good jobs are always changing. What about static jobs?

People and institutions are not static. But there are shelf-sitters. These are people who go to work in order to finance other activities: people with active off-the-job lives who could not maintain those lives without the benefit of salary. They do, off the job, what they really *want* to do.

Isn't the job-market revolution responsible in part for the whole-sale "dropout" culture?

Well, there are a lot of reasons unrelated to work that are responsible. The nature of work in modern society, the sheer industrial repetitiveness—no matter how complex or specialized—has caused a psychological rebellion among many people, not all of them Americans, by the way, or especially young. But it's the

young who launched the attack, because they were a new generation coming of age without parental memories of the Great
Depression. More than a decade of economic expansion, fueled by
the Vietnam War; chronically unbalanced federal budgets; the
space program; and the war on poverty, fostered the antithesis to
nineteen-fifties' materialism.

Jobs were plentiful.

And there are no "dropouts" in a depression.

*Has the recent employment depression dampened the move-
ment's momentum?*

Yes, but the communal syndrome—the "back-to-the-land"
movement, the stress on "working loose"—hasn't run its course; I
wager it's as permanent a part of the seventies as soup lines were
of the Depression of the thirties, war-production work of the forties, expatriate living of the fifties, and social-service involvement
of the sixties.

The most crippling factor in "working loose" at "what you
want" has been inflation. It requires more stamina and desire these
days to productively "drop out," because each year the financial
costs of doing so go up. With the exception of doctors, corporate
lawyers, petroleum engineers, and "federal regulators," it's hard
to think of other groups whose standard of living has significantly
appreciated during the seventies. Running faster to stay even is
the common lot of most working people today.

Nevertheless, as the economy, deflected from its expansionary
nature, resumes speed, the chances are good that more refugees
from the working world will drop out into occupations more novel
or traditional and less remunerative. So, for anyone who is looking
for his first job, or re-evaluating his whole occupational life, ask
yourself whether "work"—the 6:30 A.M. commuter train, the office
politics, the rat race—is worth the price.

*Isn't it true, however, that there's a vast and growing number of
educated proletarians to be kept off the job market?*

A lot of authorities maintain that American society in its com-
plexity and dynamism builds in the kind of "dropout" reaction so
many feel today. They see the adolescence of the young as deliberately prolonged, grad schools as headstart or transition centers for

the professional classes, and "alternative" jobs as a temporary expedient to keep millions out of an already saturated job market. Accordingly, our economy is protected from vast numbers of the young, overeducated specialists, and, increasingly, millions of dissatisfied and well-educated women.

Because of a no doubt shallow depth-perception level, I don't share the sinister "establishment" conspiracy the above analysis suggests. But if you believe just half of it is true and can't settle on what row you want to hoe, maybe the best thing to do is "nothing."

There's nothing stopping you.

What do you mean, "Do nothing"?

People need to buy time to think through and accomplish what they want to do. Sometimes it takes a decade. Becoming a psychiatrist, for example; accumulating capital to buy a small business; marketing a complex idea or project; raising money for some wacky business scheme—all are examples of people with realizable objectives, people who care enough about themselves to spend money, time, and emotion on the number-one person in their life.

But, really, far from it, these people aren't doing "nothing." They are, however, paying their dues, coming to grips with reality, accepting the terms and conditions of what they want to do, and that's the major "qualification": understanding and coping with reality.

How can I be sure I really want a job?

One way is to imagine you've struck it rich—say, you've won a million dollars in the state lottery. Chances are you'd quit your job. If people don't *have* to work, they usually *don't*, which says something about work in America.

But, of course, many very rich people (who don't *have* to work) *do*, and are very successful, i.e., happy. Because *working* is natural, like playing, sleeping, eating.

So the point of the exercise "if I had a million dollars" is *not* to discover how you would spend it, but what you would *do* now that you no longer *must* work. This is a tough exercise and your answers (or lack thereof) say a lot about you. Another example of why the human will is the most important factor in human happiness.

Of course, dropping out is okay for the young; but what about the middle-aged?
It depends on your definition of "dropping out." You should drop out in response to feelings, instincts, desires, and in search of satisfaction.

Middle-aged people have *less time;* all the more reason to reassess lives which are heading into the home stretch. Many, thus, unsatisfied with what they are doing, in mid-to-late career, knowing time is no longer on their side, will "drop out." An executive who quits his business to become a tomato farmer in southern Virginia . . . a professor who is a ship's broker . . . a businessman who runs a ski lodge . . . a social activist who sells real estate and travels: these people, employment and career experts will tell you, are on the increase. But inflation is biting into their pockets. And it's tougher to be a "middle-aged" dropout today than it was a few years ago.

Is it suicide for a man or woman to jump jobs in mid-career?
No.
It might mean a rebirth of enthusiasm, drive, and a quest for accomplishment.
But there are dangerous shoals.
Before you jump from your present position, or leap into the job-finding stream for the first time, you should understand about "job shock." Those who've jumped jobs and "career fields," as well, know what I'm talking about. Say you leave your present job as production manager, become a journeyman printer in your home town, and take out a union card.

This means a pronounced change in life style, received opinions, friends you make on the job, and attitudes you generally assume without knowing it. For your family and yourself this can be a traumatic and cathartic experience—like moving to a foreign country or becoming a religious convert. For some, a new job in a different field releases energy they didn't know they had. It's an experience too few people in life have.
For other people, generally those suddenly forced into an un-

wanted job, the experience is grim. Divorce, debt, despair are "job shock" companions. So, if you want to make a stab at a new field for the first time (and every first-time job-seeker does), be ready for the electric-shock treatment. But a new job—like a new girl-friend or boyfriend—generally has salubrious effects on your per-sonality. Whereas most job-seekers are sullen, ineffectual, and in-competent, the new job-holder has a brisk gait and the certain knowledge that he has chased a falling star and caught it.

What are the chief reasons middle-aged people stay at jobs they hate?
— the pension-plan trap
— lack of capital
— fear of failure
— familial disagreements
— inability to focus on desire
— debilitating "obligation" syndrome
— inflation
— physical disability
Of all of these (and perhaps ten more compelling reasons), the need to "stay put" and "do one's duty" is the worst. Feeling "obli-gated" to do a job one hates is a plague (worse than the Colorado Potato Bug) on mankind. Deprograming people from going to work at jobs they hate is my foremost mission in life.

So what you're saying is that there's a cultural revolution going on side by side with the job-market revolution?
Actually, I don't like the word "revolution." It's a loaded word which conceals lots of natural evolutionary change. What's hap-pening in this country is the product of a post-modern society try-ing to cope with technology, social change, urban decay, and a score of other major realities. But the nature of work—where, how, and when we work—is conditioned by the kind of society that great collectives of people want.
So, whether you're a barefoot boy with cheek, new on the job market with college diploma clutched in sweaty palm, or a some-what aging middle-class dissenter to our Babylonian value system, now is the time to study your soul, gird your loins, and conclude whether the young might be *half* right.

There was a time in the great long ago when we went to college to find the job to keep us in the suburbs and safely in the middle classes until we spun off this mortal coil. In case you weren't around in the sixties, there was a counterrevolution compounded of equal parts affluence, politics, new leisure, and social concerns. This new sentiment abroad in the land is watering the arid occupational plains traversed by our fathers.

The signs of these times are the self-awareness revolution, the ease and informality of dress, the informality of the new manners, the liberation of women and minorities, the urge to be oneself at all costs, and the requirement—in any job—that it be relevant to the times and our personal needs. And as for middle-aged people, the professional dropout classes, the evidence abounds that many men are foregoing the chances of the mandatory coronary, the suburban rat race, and the pace of consumer competition to carve out a more satisfactory and elementary existence.

Whether managing a ski lodge in New England, or a bicycle repair shop in Troy, New York, a lot of older folks are turning their backs on the "system" and the life styles it engenders. And the economics of this decision, while becoming more complex, is still possible. How much money, for heaven's sake, do we really need to feel comfortable? What, in fact, as the sales manager is wont to ask, is our comfort zone? Two thousand dollars per month? Twelve thousand dollars per year? One hundred and fifty dollars per week?

The point here is not for me to develop a long exegesis of how one makes it in a capitalistic society on relatively little, but to make all you incipient job-finders and job-jumpers face up to a question you should answer before programing yourself for the executive suite: Do I really want a job?

This cultural revolution affects how we work . . . and where. People are stressing callings, not careers: self-growth in meaningful work with real problems. The release of energy makes people intolerant of many institutions that do business as usual. So, your real *calling*—whether in the straight or the alternative culture—is where your future lies.

The Puritan work ethic has been turned inside out. The United States, once the pleasure-hating culture of the West, is positively Epicurean these days. Babbittry survives in small pockets of the country, in the board rooms of old-line organizations. And huge organizations whine continually about the problem of finding and, more importantly, keeping good people.

What about "dropping out" using unemployment benefits?
First a few facts:
— *Employers*, not working stiffs, pay for it.
— It was established to finance *re-employment*.
— Unemployment insurance was never designed to trap people into lines of work no longer needed or to keep people in places where there are no jobs.

The unemployed in the seventies are unlike their fathers of the thirties. Most use unemployment insurance not to find a job but to *avoid* looking for it. The whole system has become a national disgrace and fiscally unsound. (Many state unemployment insurance programs are now funded from general revenues—that is, your tax dollars and mine.)

Unemployment insurance, particularly for the young, has become a trap, another government scheme that prolongs adolescence ("I'll find a job when my benefits run out"). It destroys self-esteem—the beneficiaries are not required to *earn* their benefits. And it prolongs and increases the chance for continued unemployment because it provides the *means* to *avoid* employment. If unemployment benefits were cut back 50 per cent tomorrow, the rate of unemployment in the United States would drop two percentage points.

Ask yourself, therefore, if you are an unfortunate beneficiary of the dole, whether you *want* this kind of help. Savvy job-seekers who know what they want don't spend unemployment benefits to finance a fortnight in Sarasota.

Surely there are alternatives between "straight" and countercul-ture life styles?
One of these, I don't have to tell you, is staying in school. Experts tell you graduate schools are the product of an increasingly complex society which requires trained manpower to manage the machines of modern life.

I'm not so sure.

Almost everybody but me thinks college degrees are important on today's job market. But I've hired a thousand people, and (unless they were specialists) the particular thrust of their education concerned me not . . .

Degrees (and the unhappy obsession with them) are a childish manifestation of our certificate-mad culture. Degrees are increasingly unimportant the further from school you are (particularly for B.A. generalists).

Before the military draft terminated, grad schools enjoyed an enormous popularity among students which educators mistook for an unappeased lust for knowledge. But, of course, as any grad student admits—his arm twisted ever so slightly—the Vietcong encouraged this postgraduate boom in education.

If you intend to go back to school, think through the real reasons you're doing it. If going to school is for (a) scholarship, (b) sheer curiosity, or (c) specialized training in a field you truly love, fine. But if you return to school (a) to avoid a job commitment, (b) to stay dependent, or (c) because you don't know what to do next, you're making a serious mistake and doing permanent damage to your psyche.

I've talked to thousands of graduate students, most of whom were on the job market because school simply blew their minds; a few brilliant eccentrics and scholars loved the experience. *The rest looked like beaten people.* "To get a good education, find a judgment job."

What do you mean when you say, "To get a good education, get a good job?"

Career education is a bust. Training is a bust. To be more effective, learn on the job. To get a good education, work! A job is educational. In fact, education is self-growth. Our society has become, not educated, but "overschooled."

What is an "overschooled" society?

There's too much money in education: a huge business, a bureaucratic monster, a seventy-billion-dollar turkey. Students are overcredentialized; people are being prepared for jobs which don't exist. For young people "unschooled," but willing and able to work, a job is the best education.

But most young people see education as "Catch 22": without a graduate degree, they feel unemployable. With a graduate degree, they feel "locked into" a "career," and both those with and without degrees complain that employers want "experience." But what needs repeating is (a) that no one is "inexperienced" (we possess many "skills," most of which are portable from one "field" to another) and (b) that the purpose of education is not to prepare someone for a job.

OK. What is the purpose of education?
The purpose of education is not training a person for *a* job; the classical aims of education are preparing men and women for *leisure*. There is, however, plenty of room for *trade* schools. Law schooling is *trade* education; so are medicine, hotel management, computer science. They are *not* education; they are *skill* training and have no more to do with education for life within *civil* society than R.O.T.C. has to do with esthetics.

A liberal education, which is training students for leisure, at the same time teaches people how to *think, write, speak* (in more than one language), and acquaints them with the principles animating the physical and human universe.

Don't misunderstand me: barber colleges, schools of pharmacy, conservatories of music are important. But people who attend them need to know they are acquiring skills, not wisdom. All the more reason, in choosing *trade* schools, to focus on your accomplishments, strengths, achievements as a *base for a trade*.

But most people are schooled for the *wrong* reasons (they *need* a job) and become trapped (in their own minds) to a career path which is not of their own choosing. Students feel *unfree* (thinking that schooling predetermines what they will *do*). And nobody who feels *unfree* is going to be particularly impressive on the job market.

But can't schools train people to fill certain jobs?
Trade schools do. Computer programers, for example, have been largely trained by private, non-university establishments. But state-supported schools and many private academies graduate every year thousands of journalists, economists, lawyers, and political scientists who must seek work wholly outside their "profession."

That's no way to run a railroad or an educational "system." But the rub, of course, is that schools are designed mainly to give employment to educators, not students. Thus, many "professional" schools continue to educate young people in "disciplines" for which there is little or no demand. Our overschooled proletariat needs training on how to adapt their education to other "fields." For example:

— Librarians could become Information Retrieval Experts.
— Political Scientists should become Policy Analysts.
— Journalists need to become Technical Writers and Proposal-development Specialists.
— Foreign Affairs Specialists need to focus on domestic problem-solving.

At all events, whether your education does or doesn't help you find the job you want, you need to focus now, and ten years from now, on your own will to work and the *skills* you bring to it. Education which trains you chiefly for leisure was never meant to strait-jacket you into a "career" you no longer want or one (because of lack of demand) impossible to pursue.

"Professions," like commodities, obey the law of diminishing returns. But motivation is the greatest qualification in finding a judgment job. Searching in troubled fields, or in those with low demand, all comes down in the end to the motivation of the job-seeker. The few jobs available will go to those who really want them and know how to find them.

But aren't diplomas admission tickets to jobs?
Certainly for lawyers, C.P.A.s, engineers, operation research types, B.S.s in civil engineering, and court stenographers. Certainly not for business people, diplomats, management consultants, public administrators, marketing people, etc.

Going to school or going back to school to "acquire additional hard skills" is often a chimera. Thus, the obvious failure of man-power retraining programs and professional schools which don't take into account the fast-changing labor market. (Do we really *need* any more urban planners, architects, linguists, teachers, librarians?)

Look at further education, therefore, as something you *want*, because it improves your generic skills, sharpens your self-perception, and refines what you *want to do* upon graduation. Finding a good judgment job can cost $500 to $5,000. To acquire another M.A. could set you back $20,000 to $30,000. Which route is more cost-effective?

Are employers complaining about how schools train people for the world of work?
I don't know.
I do know that educators, themselves, are terribly confused.
If I were a college president or a dean (may the gods be deaf), I would focus not on curriculum, faculty, research facilities, or physical plant. Rather, I would *zero in* on admissions and press to know the *motives* of a prospective student for choosing my school.
Too many students use schools to evade life.

What schools are doing the best job in preparing young people for the working world?
Generally, *small, private, academic* (rather than career-oriented) schools. I've been impressed with graduates of Kalamazoo, Berea, Hamilton, Middlebury, Grinnell, R.P.I., Georgetown. Other serious schools like MacAlester and Carleton, aim at developing the full person.
Graduates of smaller schools with tough technical and liberal curriculums tend to be grown-up and less afraid of failure, rejection, and grownups!

Any tips on who should go on with graduate training?
The folks who should *do nothing else* except go on to school are invariably those who have something original to contribute. Dancers, scientists, economists, medical researchers—every "field" —people who are not so much students as thinkers, not passive receptacles of learning but active progenitors, men and women intending to add to the sum of human knowledge.
Yes, it's best for people with this special flair to continue schooling; they are clearly in touch with their talent.
The problem with genius is knowing it when you see it (particularly in oneself). And overcoming the resistance such self-knowledge causes. I wager most men and women of undiscovered

genius are recognized first by other geniuses. Another example of
our inability to establish our life's work *alone.*

Genius is rare, talent more abundant, aptitudes universal; the
trick is finding out what your genius, talent, or aptitude is—and
acting on this information. In my work I've found discovering
talent relatively easy. The most difficult task is wrestling with the
human will in overcoming subjective resistance to practicing our
talents.

Finally, I know few people of "genius." A dead giveaway to
your lack of "creativity" (surely the most abused adjective in the
job-finder's lexicon) is the comfortable and nonreflective use of
the word to describe *yourself.*

But won't grad school get me a better job?
So you want a job, but need more training?
Fly that proposition by one more time. Is it really true?
Or are you avoiding coming to grips with finding a job?
If it flies straight the second thinking-through, chances are you
should go back to school.
I make a modest suggestion:
Avoid all graduate programs long on shape and short on con-
tent. My humble opinion is, You could do worse than graduate
business school.
Why?
Because many organizations need good managers. And business
school graduates bring a sadly lacking orientation to all organizations: good business sense.
For example, in the human-service field.
Business school graduates are a natural for assisting minority-
owned enterprises, developing jobs for the hard-core unemployed,
beefing up organizational practices of well-intentioned but
inefficient community organizations.
At business school you learn sound accounting skills (which
help wherever you work), acquire certain expertise valuable in
managing "systems" and people, and develop a flair for the prag-
matic.
Women, now integrating the bastions of male hegemony,
should knock down the doors of business schools and *insist* on admission.

If you already have a business orientation, know something about double-entry bookkeeping, and *like* managing for effectiveness, skip business school altogether.

Do business schools teach management savvy?
That's what they advertise. My hunch, however, is that the better business schools are better at graduating potential specialists, particularly operation research types, rather than managers, as such.

Effective managers, like teachers and ball players, are born or acquire their skills on the job. If you have leadership skills, forget business schools at the outset of your "career" and focus on a job, acquire an M.B.A. in mid-career (at your organization's expense and on salary!), and use the time as a well-deserved executive sabbatical.

Savvy on the job, instinct for success, is a subtle talent nurtured generally in the family womb, gestated on a score of grunt jobs, and brought to birth on the line in a judgment job. Schooling will never replace "experience"—that is, the "feel" certain talented people bring to managing for effectiveness.

But don't grades predict success?
Grades are important, but unless the graduate is going into education, grades are a poor way to predict on-the-job performance. Grades measure how well we take examinations; but how many jobs require us to take exams!

Some people believe that grades in "elective" subjects are important. That's because electives are *freely* chosen by students and reflect will and motivation.

Do many corporate employers back off from young people coming out of graduate schools?
Studies show that most young men and women quit or are terminated from first "professional" jobs within three years. Plenty of savvy employers, thus, let the big banks, accounting houses, and Blue Chip industries do the hiring and then "raid" or pick off those younger people who truly want work—say, as a food-packaging engineer for United Brands.

Big business buys young people by the boxcar the same way it buys raw materials: a lot goes on the "scrap heap." And younger graduates themselves, innocent of what they want, become disillusioned. This is particularly true of those who believe academic achievement predetermines success in business, government, and the professions.

Moreover, so many "entrance level" jobs are simply highly structured screening sieves (i.e., industry is screening-*out* those who don't "fit") that the best and the brightest grow bored with the lack of "challenge" on the job and look elsewhere. That's when "second-tier" market-oriented companies hire them and give them real work.

Finally, younger people are searching for "mentors" on the job and rarely find them in octopi organizations. Indeed, middle managers in large organizations are hostile to and threatened by the young. Particularly younger people strong on theory and short on "line experience."

What about young M.B.A.s especially trained for business?

Turnover is cyclonic the first five years. Expectations of success are greater and disappointment sharper for both the young M.B.A. and his employer. Those who leave first employers do so, not so much to "job-jump" to a better job, as to "job-hop" to a similar disappointing position. And job-hoppers rarely move up the salary ladder compared to job-jumpers. The best-compensated young men and women are those who remain with the same organization and job-jump *within* it.

What's the major reason some people succeed in judgment jobs?
People.

How well you lead, enlighten, praise, chastise, judge, accept, reject, understand, and learn from people is the chief factor in being successful in judgment jobs. Schooling people for trades, skills, and occupations should take this central fact into account. (It might be the most *practical* justification for a liberal education!) But test scores and examinations never reveal this ability.

That's why, if I were a business school dean, I would query intelligence tests, SAT scores, and academic standing, and focus on student motivation, real achievements, and self-management potential.

So what you mean is the importance of starting at the bottom?
Yes, down in the boiler room.
That's a view of the organization too few managers see. Without it, many managers are unschooled in how to deal with superiors and subordinates and do not know how to *lead* or *follow*. I remember once reviewing one hundred applications for admission to a business school. Ninety-nine of the applicants freely admitted leadership potential! One applicant, however, wrote: "I'm not a leader, but I'm an excellent follower." He was the first student admitted!

Down in the pits young people learn how to cope with resentment and frustration and take on real responsibilities. All of which is schooling in "interpersonal" behavior—so important in reaching top management.

Don't most organizations train on the job?
Some do—and most that do, fail. The best "training" is a real job with staff and line responsibilities where you are *accountable*, where what you do is easily distinguished, where the organization rises or falls (if only a micrometer) because of what you *do*.

The important things in life we teach ourselves: how to read, swim, make love, play parcheesi, balance the petty-cash fund, raise money, spend it, teach, talk, and haul for lobsters.

Same on the job: "To get a good education, get a good job."

What about doing your own thing?
A sentimental, pervasive, and largely self-destructive national delusion.
The dream of every American over the age of fifteen.
But few of us—in isolation—"do our own thing."
Oh, sure, there are independent lawyers, consultants, and myriad professionals. But they are no more independent than their big-organization counterparts.
Why?
Because independent men depend perforce on clients, and clients are heavy taskmasters. So think twice about running your own business—whether it's a string of hardware stores in Westchester County or a candle shop in Vermont. There's nothing wrong, of course, in running your own business. But don't think you will be

"independent." You'll be more dependent than ever on the need for business.

Going into business for one's self, becoming self-employed, becoming your own boss, is the American Dream. Most corporate hotshots would trade places with the successful self-employed *if they had the confidence.* And that's the kernel of the nut: Do you have the ability, conviction, and the *will* to do what you want? Do you give yourself a vote of confidence?

The self-directed activities outlined in the next chapter should help you measure your "self-employability" quotient and establish whether you have the confidence of your own convictions.

OK. *Think carefully before going to work. Beware the snare of grad schools. Don't think running your own business is easy. What's worth doing in the job mart?*

That depends on what you *want.*

And focusing on what *we* want, putting ourselves first, understanding that our feelings are more important than those of employers, parents, friends, *and* enemies is rare.

"Putting one's own feelings first" is a phrase repeatedly used throughout this book. I use it often because most job-seekers suffer from a bad case of the disease to please—putting the employer's interests before their own. A small voice in the back says, "But isn't that a selfish attitude?" There is nothing at all selfish in a good business relationship. In good relationships all parties are always productively co-operative. Relationships of every kind break down when the equity between people is destabilized, when the interests of justice are sacrificed to those of Mammon or individual egos. Look carefully at every employer as someone whose interests you would be glad to serve because his interests serve your own.

What are some examples of "putting one's feelings first"?
Item: Finding a great job, knocking yourself out, sizing up the competition (and finding them wanting), and a month later . . . asking for a raise! "Putting one's feelings first" means employers come in first too! If your goals and the organization's are congruent, then both parties are winners.

Item: Rejecting a cool job offer everyone envies you for, because you *want* to do something else.

Item: Investing your emotions in a job (that's a definition of a judgment job) and welcoming more responsibility, never shying away from leadership, visibility, and public recognition, and being comfortable with increased self-esteem. No joke: most folks feel *terrible* when they do an outstanding job; they feel a loss of identity!

The trick in "putting your feelings first" is knowing, in the first place, what your feelings *are.* How can you invest emotion in a job, feel good about your performance, and welcome the gratitude of your superiors, the respect of your peers, and the admiration of your "subordinates," if you don't know what your feelings are?

Tricky, what?

The toughest work in the world is "mounting a positive self-image," as the academics are wont to describe it. But for judgment job-seekers who "make it" (find what they want), it's the only game in town.

Isn't it absurd to talk about judgment jobs when budget cuts, expensive energy, rising unemployment, and civic bankruptcy face the nation?

Quite the opposite.

Crises, problems, bad times create the *need* for *other* judgment jobs. Think about the millions of new jobs created by the energy crisis, the rising crime rate, the environmental movement, the urban catastrophe, New York City's near-bankruptcy.

It's ghoulish, but the judgment jobs of tomorrow, if you can read between the lines, are advertised not in the want ads on the last page but on the front pages of the paper. If judgment jobs are problem-solving jobs, and if helping an employer solve a problem is the best strategy in finding a job, then it follows that smart job-seekers will, in addition to selling motivation, ability, training, and experience, sell *ideas* and *solutions* to *problems*—i.e., the Proposal Development approach to dream jobs.

Know thyself. (Plutarch)

Knowing your strengths means, by implication, that you know your weaknesses. That means you fend off grateful employers who want to reward you for jobs (with more money and prestige) for which you have no flair.

Tough: Turning down a job when you sense your strengths don't match. And be sure it's not because you can't stand the heat *in* the kitchen, increased competition, augmented visibility; after all, what we mean, really, by a "challenging job" is being *pushed*, tested, asked to perform at peak proficiency.

But employers (who can't know you as well as you know yourself) will promote you to your level of incompetence. Best to have a long chat with your boss, your on-the-job best friend, a disinterested outsider, before saying yea or nay to the most important decision in your occupational life.

That's how to avoid being victimized by "the Peter Principle."

What matters is the job itself. The *quality* of your work vastly exceeds in importance what most people regard as central to employment—i.e., salary, organizational identification, fringe benefits, promotions, etc.

Most people are unhappy in their jobs. (I think most jobs are something to be unhappy about.) But in nearly every line of work about 10 per cent of the jobs are judgment jobs.

Judgment jobs are jobs where you're paid for your decisions. This means taking responsibility: you hire (and fire) people, you spend and account for money, your work is easily evaluated, you become a "key" man or woman in an organization.

Judgment jobs aren't just management and administrative jobs. Teaching is a judgment profession, so are community action, counseling, and social planning.

The more complex society becomes, the more *kinds* of judgment jobs develop. This field is where the so-called unskilled, B.A. generalist maneuvers best: he knows how to learn on the job (his skill *is* learning on the job), he has the imagination to change jobs, *and the good judgment to know whether a job is worth doing in the first place*. Which is the difference between an intelligent "generalist" and a bluestocking "expert."

Do "specialists" have more difficulty than "generalists" in finding judgment jobs?

Yes . . . and no.

Specialists, if demand is fair to good, have no great difficulty finding jobs within their specialty. But if demand is poor to non-existent, they have enormous difficulty.

Most specialists lack imagination in understanding how skills relate one occupation to the next. Like students, specialists feel "locked into" their training and perceive a dim future, or no future at all, if their training/experience doesn't fit precise employer specifications.

All the more reason for specialists to give up explaining themselves by way of degrees/jobs and focus rather on skills and accomplishments. More on this vital subject later.

Isn't there a case for job security?

But remember, there is no such thing as a permanent job.

Still, some jobs are less insecure than others. And folks with large families, elderly relations dependent on their earnings, or essential financial obligations (e.g., school debts to repay), search out jobs that guarantee more stability than others.

Again, it depends on what you *want*, your *free will*. Maintaining a vacation cottage on the Cape, socking away funds for a child's education, moonlighting at a second job to pay off your second mortgage, are clearly not abstract obligations. The tricky factor to resolve is separating out (in our own mind) what is obligatory and dutiful and what is desirable and pleasurable. And supporting our children or our elderly parents, if that is what we *want*, is not a duty to perform but a joy to fulfill. The resentment begins when we feel responsible and unfree.

Solving problems takes time; you can't do it alone. Someone besides yourself must help you think through what you *want*. And the outcome might mean divorcing your spouse, kicking your children out of the nest at age eighteen, giving up friendships based on obligation (rather than desire). Or the outcome might be the opposite: reinvesting yourself in your marriage, planning a future to take into account money needed for your daughter's law school education, renewing friendships based on desire rather than habit.

Not *easy* decisions; but impossible if you can't focus on yourself. How can you, finally, tell what it is you *want* if you don't know what you're *feeling?* Knowing what we are feeling, and acting on it, is the only *real* security.

Could you give me a breakdown of types of judgment jobs?

There are five kinds of judgment jobs that constitute judgment jobs in general: (1) general management jobs, usually held by people a long time in the same or similar outfit, who run the place; (2) technical positions, in which one functions as a specialist; (3) company men and women more concerned with employment security and stability; (4) entrepreneurs, the enterprising self-employed; and (5) consultants, who often come closest to getting what they want in their occupational lives: money is secondary; time is compensation; and quality of work is essential.

All judgment jobs require talent or skill. Estrangement from that specialty makes you uncomfortable. Skills are your strengths. Know your skills and you'll know what you can do. Knowing what you *can* do is knowing what you *want* to do.

Another way of looking at judgment jobs is in terms of four generic categories: (a) design, (b) marketing, (c) management, (d) evaluation. Whether the objective of the organization you work for is retailing mutual funds, managing real estate ventures, publishing a scholarly quarterly, or electing the next President of the United States, every job supporting that objective can be analyzed according to the above terms.

More on this important subject later.

How about money rewards? Which of the five judgment-job categories pay best?

Well, it's in order of the jobs named. The general manager's position pays most; the maverick consultant earns *least.*

Specialists are well-paid but usually hit a salary ceiling in mid-career. Entrepreneurs do well but never have any money because they plow it back into the firm! Company men and women are paid adequately to very well, but it's the pension program and job security that keep them punching the time clock.

But doesn't everyone want a judgment job, and isn't the competition cutthroat?

Yes and no.

Everyone wants a judgment job. But only about 10 per cent of the professional work force knows how to go about it. Working with ten thousand or more unhappily employed or unemployed

people in the past few years has led me to stereotype the typical job-seeker. If you are anything like him, you
— are incompetent in creating job leads.
— often excessively deprecate nonwork experience.
— find it difficult to "get up" for a job interview.
— are acutely uncertain about job goals.
— rarely understand the connection between undertaking a successful job campaign and making what you *learn* work for you on the job.
— are downright ignorant of the job-market revolution.
— tend to be hung up on titles, careers, and position.
— fail to translate real experience into meaningful occupational terms for the job market.
— are uneducated in how to negotiate for salary.
— are shy about "taking people's time" and interviewing them.
— are especially concerned about the relevance of work to society.
— are "fired" on "principle" from your first job.
— are skittish about using perfectly acceptable sales techniques in upgrading job-finding capability.
— are bored to tears with "straight" employment situations.
— are especially enthusiastic about special-situation, nonestablished, short-term jobs of social consequence.
— like and expect a culturally diverse and cosmopolitan work environment.
— are "shook up" and nervous about America's problems.
— want a job where you feel a sense of accomplishment for the public good.
— want (as opposed to your father's) less authority and wish to participate co-operatively in reaching decisions.
— are intrigued about new job opportunities in public health, ecology, drug education, housing, energy, and minicomputers.
— are cloudy about long-term "career goals."
— want to know where you fit in the contemporary job market.
— whether young or middle-aged, are hung up on your lack of "experience" and ignorant about breaking into new fields.
— are unsure of your best talents.
— lack the self-confidence every job-seeker must generate.
— are unable to focus skills on a particular field.
— panic at the thought of being "fired" from the job.

— hate the idea of being economically dependent on parents, spouses, Uncle Sam, or even employers.

— secretly envy people who do what they love for a living.

— like working for authorities who are not authoritarian.

— inwardly feel "unqualified" (compared to other candidates) after accepting a job.

— believe that politics is more important than performance on the job.

— often "blow" interviews for jobs you *need*, but don't want.

— clutch and feel intimidated in interviews when the matter of experience surfaces.

— feel an unaccountable sense of elation and a loss of identity when you are truly effective on the job.

— practice Masonic secrecy when you start looking for another job.

— privately believe all employment interviewers are powerful people you must *appease*.

— become accustomed to being miserable on the job, since that is, you believe, the nature of life and work.

— don't try to "qualify" for judgment jobs, the top jobs.

So go after the "top job"?

If it meets half of your criteria or more, yes. It's a cinch you will make a better impression. Don't compromise and go second class when going first brings you closer to the captain's cabin. You'll feel greater self-esteem, which carries over into your interviews.

Isn't aiming too high a certain invitation to failure?

It's an invitation to disappointment but never to failure. Failure is the state of mind of people who never took aim or aimed too low. And my intuition is that most successful people tend to think themselves failures. That's because they cultivate the happy habit of doing what they want, satisfying objectives, developing new agendas, breaking new turf. But finally they conclude their lives unsatisfied. Probably a definition of civilized man: his reach exceeds his grasp.

Discontent, dissatisfaction, and unhappiness are common character states for every man and woman. The difference lies between those who try and fail (and try and succeed) and those who don't. The latter are *always* discontented, dissatisfied, and unhappy.

Why is there less competition at the top?
Most people don't want responsibility: more risk, more chance of being fired. People prefer job security rather than challenge and adventure. They want safe jobs. To go after the top job is to "qualify" as a risk-taker.

Also, it sets you up to be considered as the number two man/woman.

Is there a special age when you should stop accepting deputy or vice-presidential positions and aim for the top?
By the time a person reaches thirty-five in this country, one is considered able to fulfill the utmost executive responsibility: presidency of the United States. At thirty, or certainly by thirty-five, you are ready to be accountable, responsible, visible, and available for the highest position. Chances are you won't get *that top job*, but by aiming beyond your reach, you stand a better chance of snagging the golden ring the next time around.

I don't like "ambitious" people, but they do seem to succeed at whatever they try. Or do they?
I don't like the word any better than you. For a lot of complex reasons, most of us have come to suspect the ambitious. Something about our hypercompetitive culture makes ambitious people monsters.

At the same time, to lack ambition is a curious and impotent characteristic (frequently found among the unemployed). So when I write of ambition, I mean it in the sense of being opposed to bigness and growth as such, the use of human beings for inhuman ends, and the philosophy of the fast buck and the main chance.

What you need (instead of ambition) is a sense of potency. And if you don't have it, you are in deep trouble. Potency is knowing *who you are and what you want and acting on that information.*

Ambition or self-potency (which is a quick way of saying *you know who you are*) is the first block you lay in building self-confidence. Remember, you now *know yourself*. Or at least you know yourself better in terms of employment. But still, you might lack the gumption to wade out into the job stream. Ideally, of course, if jobless, you should (a) fall in love, (b) inherit money, (c) see a good shrink. The reason for your continued blues—despite your new self-knowledge—is plain: there's no bread coming in . . . so you're holding back. You look, act, and think poorly. You still think that you're "unqualified" or "inexperienced" for a job.

So straighten out on one important point. So-called "inexperienced" people are unusually competent and effective because they haven't had the brains bred out of them. They are usually flexible, work well with people, and learn on the job. And training on the job is far more important than skill education, which often prefigures how "experienced personnel" do things. Only the inexperienced take a fresh view of a situation. Properly mixed up, experienced and inexperienced people prove the best workers for an organization. The hallmark of the inexperienced is enthusiasm and drive. If you convey this, it can't help helping.

What's the problem with success?

Finding and doing and succeeding at what we *want* causes interesting problems. I wager as many people see psychiatrists because of good fortune as bad. And the reason seems to be tied into our sense of self-esteem. If a person's sense of self is poor, which is usual, sudden acclamation, success, riches, or fulfillment triggers guilt. This condition is intolerable. As children, guilt was the character state we despised; it's no different when we're grown-up. People who feel guilty switch out of this unbearable state and welcome unhappiness. Being unhappy is a "normal" state for folks with low self-esteem. But it is a *tolerable* state compared to the strong feelings of guilt suffered by people who succeed (where their parents failed) and/or become richer (when disappointment and resentment are "natural"), and the result is a confused sense of identity. The "successful" person suddenly feels he/she is losing his/her grip on his/her "true self." When, of course, precisely the opposite is the case. We feel we are *betraying* our heritage, rising above our station, turning our backs on the past. And successful people *do*; they are becoming the kind of person they want to be. The usual feelings of resentment normally directed outward toward "the system," parents, spouses, and employers, boomerang and haunt us in the form of *depression.*

Many authorities talk about people's *need to fail.* But, it's far truer to say that nobody *wants to fail.* It's just that success is a new character state and needs some getting used to! So watch out for a purple funk if you find and do and succeed at what you *want* (may everyone know whereof I speak). Like adolescence, your first day at school, the honeymoon shakedown cruise, the new environment of your own creation takes some coping with: another rite of passage too few people experience.

But doesn't it depend on what each of us defines as success?
That's right.

My definition is being happy, productive, self-expressive, and fulfilled in whatever line of work you do; I've found it working on a loading dock, starting a business, teaching, writing this book. And that seems to me *the difference* between potency and success (according to my definition) and self-serving ambition, or selfishness, which seems the popular definition of "success." In other words, doing what we want, protecting our own interests, becoming self-reliant, fulfilling our talents, help me and *you* at the same time. Whereas the merely ambitious are always looking out for Number One. Naturally, people unable or unwilling to be self-directed unwittingly take on the coloration of their environment; they have no "goals" except those professed by the "system"— money, power, status. Poor substitutes for a sense of self. And a definition of "An American Tragedy."

So looking for a job means being assertive?
No man or woman is ever assertive enough. It's a glittering half-truth that women fail on the job because they aren't assertive. That's true of men too.

And assertive people are never aggressive—i.e., disagreeable, pushy, autocratic, domineering: defective characteristics. Being assertive, on the other hand, means persuading other people that you want the job, and showing them you can do it!

How we admire people who know what they want; it frees us to say what we want! But employers and job-seekers who *can't* are confused. Neither party, in this often hilarious transaction, is in touch with his feelings; neither party is putting himself first. Neither one knows what he *wants!*

Why isn't job-seeking a rational process?
It should be, but usually isn't. It's irrational because job-seekers don't know what they want or what they do . . . a lost sense of direction. It's psychological dispersion. The result is frustration and greater incompetence.

My advice is to do a market-research survey *on yourself.* Find out what you *want,* and then seek to find where your want can be satisfied. It means dollars and time. And usually the ideal job won't be found the first time around; one simply accepts the second or third best. Even the best among us must "create" our dream job on the job.

What about the trade-off between what you do and where you work?
Big question.
I generally shy away from job candidates who say, in effect, "Who I am is where I work." Still, in mid-career especially, plenty of people are backing off from judgment jobs if it means a drastic change in living location.

If young, however, I would go *any* place to do what I wanted and let considerations of *place* become central in *mid years.*

Who is the happily employed person?
The happily employed person is one who feels a sense of partnership with his boss instead of subordination. That person says, "TGIM!" Work is something to look forward to, not be apprehensive about.

The good job is never stagnant; it's always changing, and so are the lives of employed people. They *like* themselves and their jobs. They don't always know what they are doing. They do know they are accountable and manage time, money, and people as contributing factors to an organization's progress. They can be fired at any time. But they work out of wish or desire—not out of duty or obligation.

Every morning the happily employed person gets out of bed "unemployed"!

Every morning when I get out of bed I'm unemployed?
That's right: whether you're the Executive Vice-president of Ingersoll-Rand or six months unemployed.

It's because "work" is simply a series of assignments which must be satisfied before a job can be said to be done. And every morning, whether we are "employed" or looking to become employed, we must identify what our objectives that day *are*.

More reason to put personal objectives up front on your job search, understanding that people *with* jobs are unemployed if, of a morning, they are unable to match personal objectives against organizational goals.

TWO

Will and Work

OK.

Let's look at some ways people who want to mount a self-directed job search, identifying hidden talent and using this information, answer, "What is it I want to do?"

The *best exercise* is to list those positive activities that gave you a sense of fulfillment.

This exercise should take three days. It means listing, not necessarily in chronological order, those positive experiences (when you functioned at maximum effectiveness) which gave a sense of self-satisfaction.

Randomly, what follows are ten achievements I recall from talking to hundreds of people I required to take this exercise. (Parenthetically: I've noted what jobs they eventually took and the relationship between who they *are* and what they *did*.):

— I touched Joe DiMaggio on the back during a spring-training match in Clearwater, Florida, in 1955, while he was playing center field for the New York Yankees. (Told to me by a young lady who now works—the only woman—in the sports department of a national news magazine.)

— I changed a flat tire on my mother's automobile when I was eight years old. (Told by a twenty-four-year-old failed journalist now editing skill manuals for a Job Corps camp.)

— I taught my retarded brother to read. (Told by a young woman now the director of a school for autistic children.)

— I managed the campaign of a shy boy in our school for the office of school secretary—he won the election. (Told by a political consultant for three successful candidates for Congress.)

— I always completed the income-tax forms for my father. (Told by a self-educated accountant, now the controller of a major U.S. company.)

— I managed a successful lawn-cutting business at age ten. (Told by a successful landscape architect with offices in three cities.)

— I learned French at an early age without schooling. (Told by the managing director of a French-language summer camp for children—all of whom must speak French.)

— I broke the U.S. Infantry record for cross-country hiking. (Told by an instructor at an Outward Bound School.)

— I managed Ethiopian secretaries in an East African office situation. (Told by a woman managing a large office in England for an American firm.)

— I failed every college course except art, where I got the highest grade in the history of the school. (Told by the director of a major American art gallery.)

Why not make a list of weaknesses as well?
Simple.

If both of us sit down and start listing our disappointments, misfires, incompetencies, and plain old-fashioned ineptitudes, both of us would be filling out "blue books" until the return of Haley's comet. And the whole exercise would destroy us.

If an interviewer should ask you, "What are your weaknesses?" answer as follows:

"I find myself growing impatient with ineffective people."

"I increasingly spend too much time on the job, forgetting personal needs."

"I often daydream in meetings with no agenda."

"I sometimes hurt people's feelings on the job by asking them to go faster than they are prepared to drive themselves."

Surprise, surprise: most interviewers won't push you further on this matter; the trick is not to blush plum red.

It makes absolutely no sense to study your weaknesses except as they are the reverse side of your strengths. Nobody hires you because you can't learn new math or jump rope or were court-martialed for not rising for reveille in the Army. What these experiences tell you, however, is not to become a banker, a recreation director, or a worker in a large and regimented organization! And if you have real weaknesses, the chances are good that you have real and recognizable strengths. You drove a Maserati convertible nonstop across Utah's salt flats for twenty-four hours, you were the operations clerk for a dump-truck company in the Army, and you worked your way through college as a taxi dispatcher. Chances are you should work in the transportation field.

Rather, make a list of what you've done *right*.

How do you learn to know yourself? Simple.

Take pencil and paper, take the phone off the hook, turn off the TV, and warn everyone in your household to stay away. Go back as far as memory allows, and list every accomplishment, achievement, contribution which made you feel proud deep down in your tummy. Spare yourself not—no matter how modest or otherworldly, everything listed has relevance to the job you *want*.

Study each "accomplishment"—i.e., that positive activity which gave you a sense of self-fulfillment—and give this experience a "name." At this point, take a pair of scissors, cut out each accomplishment and stuff it in an envelope marked "Management" or "Mediation" or "Agricultural"—"categories of skills" are as infinite as your accomplishments. Now examine the contents of, say, the "Agricultural" envelope and rethink whether the skills are strictly "Agricultural" or, rather, "Agricultural Planning."

If you can *identify* and *name* fifty accomplishments or more, you'll establish five or more generic skills. Again, the point is to clarify your skills, asking yourself again what you "call" them.

Now you have the raw material for your résumé. Think through each category, mesh it with more appropriate categories, and establish no more than five (no fewer than two) distinct generic skill areas. Now review your work *by category* and discard every accomplishment (or category) which does not, repeat *not*, support what you *want* to do. Plenty of people's strengths are weaknesses if they don't support the job they want. Singing in your college choir is a strength (if you want to be a Performing Arts Manager); a weakness (if you are trying to qualify for a geological expedition to Patagonia).

Now you have two to five generic categories and from three to fifteen accomplishments within each category. Establish which *category* is most important in being considered for the job you want (and which is *least* important). *Rank* the other categories in between. Whether or not you know it (and you won't), you have the guts of an extremely effective functional résumé.

Human activity in the world of work is broken down into the following: data, things, people, money, and nature. Of the four categories, where do your skills lie?

Answer that question inductively. That is, beginning with a list of your accomplishments, giving them a name, segregating accomplishments by genre, ordering each category in accordance with how it supports jobs you want—having done all of this work—it's duck soup figuring out where your talent lies. And it's ambitious folly to think about jobs outside your *abilities*, no matter how romantic or well-paid or highly regarded. (My secret ambition is to be the fireball relief pitcher for the Phillies. The reason my ambition is secret is I squint at distances over fifty feet and my "fast ball" resembles Rip Sewell's blooper pitch.)

Now, these are just examples. And selection *is* editorializing. By no means do all accomplishments exactly relate to the jobs you want. But the habit of analyzing your past in positive terms—seeing where you've been a potent human being—is the secret to understanding who you are and what you do well.

What about those who have no real experience?

There is no such thing as a degree in "experience." Rather, there are degrees of experience!

The point of these activities is to compel you to come to terms with those events in your life that made you feel effective. Those events *predict* how well you will accomplish certain jobs, because achievements which gave you a sense of self-fulfillment are *translated* into *skills* which *predetermine* job objectives.

So no one reading this book is "inexperienced," any more than they are "unable." But job-seekers will continually put themselves down by citing a lack of experience when what they are really telegraphing is an impotent human will.

So knowing oneself and what one wants is the key to finding a judgment job, but that's just common sense.

Right on . . . and common sense is the uncommonest element between heaven and earth.

The point is not just to find a job—no matter how well-paying or prestigious. Rather, it's to know what job it is where you're going to have the best chance to fully function as a human being and where you can make the most satisfying contribution. This means sweeping away cloudy goals, adolescent illusions, and worldly standards which don't realistically apply. It means embracing the idea of self-fulfillment as the real objective of "work."

Pity the poor chap who went to law school because his father expected it of him; the salesman who hates selling, but acted on the standards of a Greek-letter fraternity; the artist who really wants to be a shoe salesman!

After this exercise, you have a handle on yourself and are able to represent strengths and weaknesses to potential employers. Remember, however, that a strength for one employer is a weakness for another. You might, for example, feel comfortable and productive working in an analytical capacity, and bomb in a job where you must meet many people face to face—and vice versa.

Our occupational strengths and weaknesses are opposite sides of the same coin.

Knowing what it is that you've done, quarterbacking your past for real successes and not just for those accomplishments people were proud of for you, is the name you eventually give your job. Once you've successfully thought through this list, you've arrived at the point where you feel the first stirrings of ambition.

A second exercise—aimed at putting you in touch with your desires—is projecting yourself forward into time and fantasizing what is happening to you.

The way to go forward in time and see yourself the way you want people to see you, is to write your obituary.

Pretend that we are well into the next century and that you have just expired; the New York *Times* is writing your life history. Your obit will be a legit version of events up to the time of your writing it; everything henceforward is fantasy of what you *want* your occupational and personal life to become. The operative word is *want*. The aim of this exercise is to put you in touch with your fantasy life, ignite the old dream mechanism, freeing yourself to imagine the impossible, making yourself aware that "in dreams begin responsibilities."

Writing your obituary, as if this were the year 2010, is a way of seeing yourself the way you would want the world to remember you. And it's an exercise in reviving those grand goals and glorious prospects that made adolescence worth the rites of passage.

For middle-aged and elderly people, writing one's obituary is a way to recover the confidence of youth, ignorance, and innocence. It makes you want to *dare* the gods and furies, and it reveals, as nothing else can, a job-hunter's hidden agenda.

For many, it's difficult writing an obituary; they can't face the prospect of their demise. However, for rich imaginations stimulated to think deeply enough into the future, this exercise exposes your dreams . . . and wishes are the fathers of deeds. The problem, of course, is that our wildest dreams often come true (with apologies to Oscar Wilde). That's a subject for another book!

But aren't employers required to hire people for their qualifications?

The word "qualifications" means, in this order, the following:

1. Motivation: "Does this guy or gal *want* the job?"
2. Ability: "Does this person have the talent?"
3. Experience: "Has this person ever done anything like this before?"
4. Training: "Does this person have any training to prove he/she can do it?"

"Qualifying" for a job, therefore, means really wanting it, being able to do it, showing that you have done it or been trained to do it. Few candidates for any job will be able to muster affirmative answers to all four questions. The one question you must say "yes" to is #1: "Do I want this job?"

It's no surprise, but those who say "yes" to the last three, usually for excellent reasons, can't say "yes" to the first. That's because they have accomplished the job—it no longer *tests* them. The job, therefore, is no longer challenging. What's so strange about that?

Developing realistic job goals, sweeping away manifold self-delusions, therefore, requires a hard look at yourself. Here again, putting yourself in the employer's shoes, asking yourself *why* you should be employed, what you offer an employer, is your exercise in realism.

Your worst step forward (and the commonest mistake of the first job search) is *not* defining goals in comprehensible, realistic, and concrete terms. This fact surfaces early in an interview situation. "This guy doesn't know what he wants or what he does. And he wants *me* to give *him* a job?"

Since I've done a fair amount of employing myself, I fancy I can see the *process* (whereby one person offers another a job) from both vantage points. The central truth of the whole process is that nobody is hired for his weaknesses—it is his strengths, his capacity to make meaningful contributions to an employer, that decide whether he's offered the job.

During the past decade I've also worked for about ten variously remarkable people, men and women, effective and ineffective. The striking characteristic of all employment relationships is that there is no such thing as the *wrong people*: there are only people matched with the *wrong jobs*. And that's fundamentally both the employer's and the employee's responsibility and loss.

Your aim is to make you aware of what your strengths are, and to fashion those functional talents into a résumé, an interview presentation, and a job campaign that advance you farther than you can go using conventional and ill-productive job-finding strategies.

But can't you be too specific?

No . . .

Every judgment-job candidate should have *three* or *four* job goals. Each *goal* will relate in terms of *function* to the next. Not to reveal your goals causes employers to think you don't know what you *want*. Moreover, revealing what you want causes employers to confess what they need. By being particular, a jobseeker frees an employer to be specific. Another reason why the human *will* is central to the employment process.

One happy result of establishing what you want is that you may qualify for hidden jobs, because an employer has more knowledge about you. Hundreds of judgment-job candidates have told me about finding great jobs which they did *not* define in their résumé but which fit their skills and their objectives because they took the pains to discover what they wanted and let employers describe similar jobs which were also available.

Is there anything else I can do to discover what I want?

A third activity is to put yourself in the employer's shoes and imagine him writing a "want ad" that meets most of your needs in a job.

Write three longish help-wanted ads as they might appear in the trade press or the daily newspaper. Pretend that you are a chief executive officer of an organization writing up the requirements for a position you want to fill. List the "qualifications," training/experience, and kinds of personal motivation you are searching for in a candidate. Make sure you write up the essence of what is to be *done* and something about the work environment, salary, etc. Zero in on the special contributions successful candidates must make to the organization, the strengths the employer seeks in people he will interview, the flair or talent required for the job.

The aim of this exercise is to make you focus on the contributions you make to an organization by doing a job you really *want* to do and which some organization wants done. A secondary objective is to acquaint job-seekers with the jargon of job descriptions, taking the words employers use to describe *jobs* and transmuting these same vocabularies into a description of who you are, what you can do and—above all—what you *want* to do.

Writing your achievement list suggests what you *can* do.

Writing your obituary suggests what you *want* to do.

Composing three or four job advertisements indicates what is *realistic* to do.

But each exercise must be done in the above order. Otherwise you'll become confused.

And it's only after you've spent a goodly amount of time and heart-searching that you're ready to interpret what all your homework means.

What if I want to do what I've done?

If you *want* to do what you have done, great! If I, as an employer, must choose between two people—one who is motivated and able, and one who is motivated and "experienced"—I'll go with the latter every time. But the major point is: all of us are "experienced."

Why?

Talent, ability, flair—what we mean by "experience"—are rooted in our childhood. These roots are our individual accomplishments, "experiences" which made us feel effective, potent. All of us have too few of these positive activities to be proud of, but nobody has none. If, as a job-seeker, you can demonstrate some examples—in the interview and your résumé—of being a "self-starter," a decision-maker, an entrepreneur, then it's not necessary to *proclaim* that you are; let your accomplishments speak for themselves. Back off, therefore, from sweeping generalizations about your abilities. For example, how many job applicants are "self-starters," "decision-makers," or "problem-solvers." Far better to give examples of decision-making, problem-solving, and "creative" accomplishments.

Showing that you are "experienced" is your responsibility to the employer, who will push you, as he should, very hard on this point. So if you are experienced and able in a line of work you still love, sell *both*.

Yes, but isn't it true that some people with little or no talent succeed?

Remember what Leo Durocher said about Eddie Stanky, the old Brooklyn Dodger second baseman: "He can't hit, he can't run, can't field. What he can do is beat the hell out of you!"

True, but most people feel most pleasure and are most competent doing something *well*. Straying too far from one's ability is risking disappointment and failure. At the same time, not straying far enough risks not being considered for judgment jobs. Again, the onus is on you: What do your *instincts* tell you about a job? Try to quantify and qualify those instincts; gut reactions are great, but we need to rationalize, know the reasons *why* we accept or turn down a job. If you hate exercising authority, are shy of visibility, back off from competitive situations, chances are better than even that those are the *wrong* reasons; if you don't feel comfortable about a new job's responsibilities, feel more pain than pleasure in the prospect, sense you can't *grow* on the job or will rarely exercise your abilities, chances are better than even that you should nicely say no.

Is talent God-given or acquired?
Damned if I know.
My hunch is Freudian; we acquire our flair, talent, ability—call

it what you will—somewhere in early youth in the family nexus while acting out our parents' desires (or *reacting* against them). Otherwise, how do you explain the uniformity of success among the Strauss brothers (music), the DiMaggio brothers (baseball), the Kennedy family (politics)?

What I *do* know is that everyone has "gifts"—hundreds of skills, in fact, and all of them transferable into many lines of "work." Often, those who have the most talent are least aware of it.

What about what you said in the last chapter about not needing to work?

A fourth exercise (and the toughest) is making you think about "work," not as something you *must* do, which makes for certain job dissatisfaction, but focusing on "work" as something you want to do.

"If I had one million dollars I would . . ."

Write out what you would do if tomorrow you were the recipient of a fat inheritance. Most people work out of a sense of obligation and constraint; hardly anyone, from a sense of joy and desire. If the monetary restraints on your doing *what you want to do* no longer exist, what would you do with your life?

Freedom to do what you want is a frightening experience. It's why so many people in the flush of retirement collapse psychologically and physically. It's the reason the rich are often more interesting than the poor—they have the *means* to make or break their lives.

If you can't figure out what you want (now that you no longer need to work), *don't worry*; most people can't. It does mean, however, that you'll want to change into the person you can be. And it might take years to free yourself from doing what you *ought*, to doing what you *want*.

Anything else you recommend?

Another activity is understanding that a good growth or judgment job is working at what touches your emotions. To be 100 per cent effective on the job, more than your intellect is required. No one will be truly potent until he does what engages his emotions. The passionate response to jobs is a certain satisfier—the whole man and/or woman is engaged.

Therefore, list those things which make you feel angry!

The aim of this exercise is to make you list those things that *adversely* affect your emotions. In doing so, you unconsciously list characteristics you want in a job. This exercise identifies a passionate *caring*—so obviously absent in the psyches of most job-holders.

A sixth exercise is writing a biography of someone you admire. Three one-paragraph "biographies" of people you admire could suggest why you want to become like them.

No one really knows why we learn *this* and can't learn *that*. But if we simulate what we admire, chances are we become the *someone* we admire, thus having the potential to be as effective.

Also, interviewing five admirable working friends to find out their *career paths*, identifying the key switches, the out-of-work times, the smooth transitions, what they like and dislike in what they do, is another way to get inside your own head.

A variation on this activity is listing public people, living or dead, you admire.

"Gee, I could be like her too!"

Everybody is a hero-worshiper. And staking out people we would like to be says to our secret selves that we could be like them!

Reading the biographies of celebrated achievers in any walk of life puts you in the shoes of men and women, usually long dead, who continue to mold the future through the dreams of people like yourself.

Still another activity is keeping a file of *advertisements* or *news stories* you read. Unconsciously your psyche is self-selecting what *interests* you. Tearing out and filing every advertisement you find yourself reading identifies products, services, problems, and populations which suggest certain lines of work.

If you keep a file of articles and advertisements, don't ignore want ads. A file of dated help-wanted ads reflects a *pattern* of occupational preference. Clip every ad that you reread—don't worry about the reason. Research these jobs, talk to people in this livelihood, trade, profession. Why are you *intrigued*? Relate these jobs to your past accomplishments. Is there a connection between these jobs and your skills?

Another activity which is fun is making a list of the characteristics you seek in an organization:
— like working in small, task-oriented groups
— especially welcome working for an authority or expert
— love working late and on weekends to meet deadlines; hate "busy work" and water hauling
— require recognition for work well done
All of which should be included within your "Job Objectives" in your résumé.

As part of your general accomplishment list, or as a separate exercise, focus on every "job"—paid and unpaid, no matter how rotten, and identify one, two, or three aspects of the job you *liked*. Is there a pattern of *likes* that threads itself throughout all your jobs and experiences? What is the genre? What do you call it?
"What I really loved as a . . ."
— soldier
— student
— teaching instructor
— bartender
— babysitter
— door-to-door salesperson
What places do you want to live? What foreign countries do you want to travel to?

Part of who I am is where I live.

But it's less important than what I *do*.

Once you know three or four things you want to *do*, where you do it focuses and disciplines your job search. Once you know *what* you want and *where* you want it, you can begin to zero in on *how* to get it. That's comparatively *easy!*

If nothing else works, try listing everything that gives you pleasure . . .

Plenty of bright people can't bring themselves to do any of these exercises. Thinking about themselves seems *sinful* to them. But nobody hates pleasure, although we often act as though we do. Listing what we *like* to do gives us keen insight into what we (if you'll pardon the expression) *should* do.

Finally, some people who want to investigate the mainsprings of motivation can skip the previous exercises and simply write out their life story in prose. A close reading by yourself and by intelligent outsiders reveals a wealth of undetected skills and talents occupationally applicable.

This exercise is particularly recommended to people in midcareer and those making a radical jump in "fields." Write up your background as if for publication, as an anonymous journalist would for a news magazine profile.

The aim of this exercise, like listing your accomplishments, is to make participants focus on real feelings, true accomplishments. The aim of the exercise is to show you how the past is never past (Faulkner), and that the future is now (George Allen).

So these exercises are what you mean by putting your own feelings first?
Yes.
That's the toughest chore of all. Focusing on our own feelings *first*—knowing ourselves and what we want—is especially difficult for all of us who have been carefuly trained by school, church, and state to put *organizational goals* before *personal objectives*. Moreover, this indoctrination is so effective that millions of people are unwilling to separate the two.

Will these exercises help me to choose a graduate school or trade program?
Sure . . .
It means you build on strengths, skills, accomplishments in choosing a trade or graduate program. The chances of your returning to school for the "right" reasons are much enhanced.

How do these exercises differ from aptitude testing?
These activities are less expensive and time-consuming, and they measure *motivation as well as ability*. Moreover, nobody in a long white coat is going to declare, chapter and verse, that your fortune lies in "restaurant management, organizational planning, or probate law." It leaves the *interpretation* to you (and your friends), not to a machine or an "expert."

If these activities help me to decide what to do, will they help me answer any more questions?
Studying your work should reveal answers to the following:

— what level of responsibility you want inside an organization
— what kind of surroundings you desire
— what consequences you expect from your work
— what philosophy of work you bring to the job
— what kind of people you work with best
— where in this country or abroad you want to work
— what *kind* of organization you want to work for in regard to *your* and *its* objectives

Isn't it utopian to expect that you can always do what you want?
Only for those who think so. It's scary knowing you can become a self-directed, powerful personality, utopian! It's safer, less disappointing to believe you are *shaped* by your environment, determined by events; also, unhappier and unfulfilling. Yes, you are determined by *outside* forces, but you also shape your environment.

But doing what you want takes courage. And choosing to continue to do what you are doing might take the most courage of all. Not making a decision *is* a decision.

Not making a decision is a decision?
Sure.
Making up your mind to stay put *or* to find another job is a decision. Making a decision to stay is qualitatively *equivalent* to the thinking that goes into a decision to change jobs.

At all events, the decision is rational because it is based on desire and self-fulfillment, not on habit. Every working day I decide to buy, sell, or hold stock I own. If I hold it, *that's* a decision.

Same with you on the job. If you went to work today at the *same* job, you've made a decision.

Pity the poor chap, however, who stays at his job out of habit, not desire.

I buy doing what we want, but every job requires doing things we must.
Sure, every judgment job contains elements of pleasure, pain, disappointment, triumph, and frustration in about equal measures. That's what job candidates mean when they say they want a "challenging" job. But do they really mean it? A few thousand in-

terviews on both sides of the table have convinced me that most people *don't*. Most job candidates, in a word, are unprepared to accept the terms and conditions of tough judgment jobs. All the more reason for you to make a list of conditions you want in a job, in a boss, in an organization.

So judgment jobs cause pain?
Sure—painful, repetitive hard work and sweat. The kind of discomfort, frustration, and pain you welcome because overcoming it causes a sense of pride. Overcoming adversity is a characteristic of a good job. People want to be tested, pushed to their limits. That's what we mean by a sense of achievement. People with "easy" jobs often suffer from an acute lack of self-esteem, which is terminal to human happiness.

What do you do if you can't focus on what you want?
Do these exercises.
Ask for "editorial" help in psyching out what they "mean."
If all else fails, see a psychiatrist. No kidding. That's why we pay them fifty dollars an hour. Cheap, if it helps you overcome the resistance to doing what you want. And—without wanting to prejudice the verdict—not doing what you want will, ten to one, have a lot to do with Mommy and Daddy. (Old Sigmund Freud had an idea or two!)

What about the anxiety factor?
Anxiety is irrational; fear is rational. The fear of a gun at your head is natural and rational. But the anxiety about *doing what you want* (and the accompanying paralysis) is irrational and disabling. We haven't been trained to go after *what we want*. From parents to peers to professors, we are discouraged from having minds of our own. Job-seeking is an adventure. And the chances are good that the job either exists or can be created. And who's the winner then? But going after what you want will cause anxiety. Focus on *why* it causes anxiety. Then seek ways to reduce it.
The cause of anxiety in most people is "guilt." Doing what you want causes guilt. One way to avoid feeling guilty is taking jobs you don't want. Thus, you eliminate guilt and anxiety and live unhappily ever after.

Focus, therefore, on managing guilt and you'll free up in time to do what you *want*. It might take a lifetime, but it's all the time we have.

Are you saying, then, that effective job-seekers must have minds of their own?

Yes, and they will be better than their competition (who don't!). Most people assume employment objectives (as we do all objectives in life) on the basis of what other people want: parents, schools, churches, etc.; but it is your own mind that counts. This strategy makes the job-seeker more attractive and competent. And that's the advantage. Your competition don't know their own minds. Job-seekers who do are far ahead of the competition.

How do I know my own mind? How do I know if I have or can have a mind of my own?

Do the exercises.

A pattern of recognized accomplishments—fantasies, treasured experiences, etc.—will surface. This information is an encyclopedia of your *skills*. In those skills you are "expert."

How do you become an expert?

Start calling yourself an expert. And we are all expert at many things, but hesitate saying so.

People tired of being expert in one field need to stop calling themselves experts in *this* and start calling themselves experts in *that*. Once you understand that your skills are transferable, chances are excellent that you won't hesitate to jump into another line of work. "Education" and "experience" are terrible traps to self-fulfillment if we allow *work experience or training solely to* program our futures.

That's why, in a résumé, what you want to reveal are your abilities and accomplishments which support jobs you want. And why you want to downgrade experience and training if it doesn't support the job you want. And why you build on both ability *and* experience if you want to continue doing what you have done. Forward!

THREE

Le Résumé

Résumé? What's wrong with the one-page description of back-ground they told me to use in college?

Nothing, except you won't find a job with it.

A résumé is valuable for two reasons: (a) It makes you think about who you are, and (b) an excellent résumé can generate interviews and open up doors to the judgment jobs which a descriptive (or "obit") résumé can never do.

Can you show me an example of a descriptive (or traditional) résumé?

Sure.

This kind of résumé is used by 90 per cent of the people looking for jobs, and for all I know, is a product of the Eisenhower years when Ike wanted everything said "on one page."

Karen Lynn Mitchell
3766 Lanham Drive
Summit, New Jersey 32260
Telephone: 576-376-6661

VOCATIONAL GOAL
I enjoy working in a situation where I can be of assistance to the general public. I like the atmosphere of a busy office and am capable of making visitors feel welcome and assured that they will be helped in every way.

PERSONAL
Born: November 20, 1955   Health: Excellent
Marital Status: Single   Weight: 118

EXPERIENCE
Summers of 1973 and 1974
I worked in my father's automobile dealership. I helped out in the book-

keeping office, greeted customers, and did inventories in the Parts Department.

September 1974 to May 1975
I worked part-time at St. Bonaventure University as a language lab assistant. My duties were to monitor the students, hand out language tapes, and help out in any way needed.

September 1975 to May 1976
I worked part-time as a shift manager for a student-operated grocery store. My duties included supervising the cashiers, stocking shelves, keeping track of change, and dealing with customer complaints.

Summer of 1976
I worked as a front desk clerk for Ramada Inn. I was responsible for checking in customers, writing up reservations, operating the switchboard and reservations computer, and some filing.

EDUCATION
Georgetown University, Washington, D.C., School of Foreign Service. B.S.F.S. in U. S. History and Diplomacy.

St. Bonaventure University, Olean, New York. Fall of 1973 to spring of 1975. President of Women's Council, member of Campus Dorm Council.

HOBBIES AND INTERESTS
Flying, basketball, tennis, golf, cooking.

REFERENCES
References will be furnished upon request.

But I've read that résumés don't get people jobs.

Plenty of people ignore résumés altogether.

But these folks know what they want, know how to cold-turkey interview, have a knack of connecting with people, sense that jobs are hidden and become part of the hidden manpower pool. A résumé for these folks is a waste of time. And, in truth, the last three jobs I've bird-dogged I secured *sans résumé.*

But the point is still valid: a first-rate functional résumé, a product of three weeks' work and four "drafts," disciplines people to focus on answers to three questions everyone needs to know before inflicting themselves on employers: (1) Who am I? (2) What do I do well? (3) What do I want? Developing a résumé helps you to answer those questions. And the document serves you, with some alteration, the remainder of your occupational life. Moreover, a functional résumé generates more interviews. Interviews produce more people to interview. And people produce job offers.

At the same time, forget writing a résumé if you can answer

6

positively these questions and have no difficulty producing interviews. Congratulations—and, by the way, why are you reading this book?

Let's look at an effective *functional* résumé.

Same gal, same background.

Karen Lynn Mitchell
3766 Lanham Drive
Summit, New Jersey 32260
Telephone: 576-376-6661

VOCATIONAL GOAL
 Customer Relations Manager, Administrative Assistant, or Constituent Liaison Representative. Qualified in a position where use can be made of communication and management skills, and special abilities in effective organization and co-ordination.

SUMMARY OF BACKGROUND
 Graduate of Georgetown University; spent first two years of undergraduate study at St. Bonaventure University; one summer of intensive study of French at Laval University, Quebec City; worked at the Front Desk of Ramada Inn, often filling in for the General Manager; worked as a manager of the Georgetown Student Corp. grocery store—a position which entailed responsibility for the effective operation of a store servicing hundreds of students a day; Research Consultant for author; worked in the Customer Relations Department of a Datsun and Mazda Dealership.

SOME AREAS OF EXPERIENCE AND INDICATIONS OF POTENTIAL VALUE

ABILITY TO SOLVE THE PUBLIC'S PROBLEMS AND COMPLAINTS
 Evidenced by my work at the Front Desk of Ramada Inn where I was the first and often only contact the public had with the hotel. Made decisions and acted on all complaints received; helped customers to find alternate lodging when there was no vacancy; responded quickly in all emergencies—electrical fire, extensive flooding from broken water pipes, and quarrels among guests. Evidenced also by my solutions for customer complaints concerning products purchased at the Georgetown Student Corp. grocery store. And by my Customer Relations work with customers at Parkview Auto Sales: speaking with potential buyers until a salesman was available, ensuring the comfort of a customer waiting for car service, and handling complaints both in person and over the phone concerning bills.

MANAGEMENT SKILLS
 As a manager of the grocery store, was responsible for the inspection, acceptance, and payment involving deliveries; oversaw cashiers' accounting procedures for each shift; price-checking and customer satisfaction; apprehension of shoplifters; and the responsibility of making accurate accounting entries and locking up for the day. As Student Manager of the Language Lab, was involved in ordering supplies and new machinery, setting up employees' work schedules, hiring and training of lab instructors, and conducting demonstrations.

LEADERSHIP SKILLS
 While attending public schools, was elected president of my class for six

consecutive years; was selected from among 500 girls to represent my high school in the 1972 New York Girls' State Convention—a week-long seminar entailing in-depth study of local and state government; also captained three varsity athletic teams my senior year in high school: basketball, volleyball, and track.

COMMUNICATION SKILLS

Demonstrated ability in communications with peoples of diverse foreign backgrounds; while studying in Quebec City, was asked by the visiting Cuban Olympic Water Polo Team to act as their guide during their stay; also aided several French-speaking families in securing accommodations while working at Ramada Inn; proficient in French; possess survival knowledge of Spanish.

ORGANIZING AND CO-ORDINATING SKILLS

Organized the research process for a book about Charles de Gaulle. Co-ordinated the landscaping of an automobile dealership. Represented my high school at Empire Girls' State, was elected party chairman, and organized caucases and election campaigns. Co-ordinated the first fund-raising fashion show for Women's Council involving participation with several local merchants.

INGENUITY AND IMAGINATION

Devised an effective voting system for the Campus Dorm Council eliminating much time, effort, and wasted meetings. Wrote the commentaries for a fashion show with no previous experience.

COMPETITIVE SPIRIT AND PERSEVERANCE

Am an avid competitor in both athletics and academics. Have won several golf championships; hold two Section III-N.Y. State track and field records; have been a member of championship basketball, volleyball, and track teams. Have also competed in several English and journalism contests, winning DAR Excellence in History Award.

EDUCATION

B.S. in Foreign Service, 1977, Georgetown University; two years undergraduate study at St. Bonaventure University; one summer's study at Laval University; elected to Pi Delta Phi (National French Honor Society); elected Dorm Representative; Social Activities Chairman of Women's Council; Co-ordinator of Intramural Sports Program; over-all grade point average on a 4-point scale: 3.2.

PERSONAL DATA

GEOGRAPHICAL PREFERENCE
East Coast

POISE AND APPEARANCE
Have modeled in numerous fashion shows and seasonal collections; have appeared in advertisements in a national magazine.

DATE OF AVAILABILITY
August 1. Writing samples on request.

TRAVEL STATUS
Willing to travel for short periods of time.

SALARY
Negotiable

BIRTH DATE
November 20, 1955

MARITAL STATUS
Single

HEALTH
Excellent

How do you develop this kind of résumé?

It's clear that knowing who you *are* and what you *want* are the most important questions a job-seeker asks himself. "Getting yourself together" is fundamental before you inflict yourself upon the job mart. So, this is what you have to do:

1. Go back and review your list of *personal* achievements and job successes. A pattern emerges: What generic skills do you perceive? (See Chapter Two)

2. Summarize achievements proving your personal and professional *effectiveness* in one hundred words or less, and compress into a bare, hard-hitting analysis under a generic heading.

3. For *each* job—part-time, volunteer, vocational, and full-time —write brief descriptions illustrating your *effectiveness for the job you want*. If you've worked at a number of jobs within two or three years, compress these descriptions into functionally understandable terms describing *what* you've done (rather than for whom you did it) so long as it supports what you want. This is raw material for your "Employment History."

4. Inventory education—all of it—including the stuff you would rather not remember: the special training courses (no matter how inconsequential), recent reading, special conferences attended, and include under education *if it supports the job you want*.

Again, a pattern emerges.

(Are you following all of this! Remember, you'll be quizzed on this later!)

5. Note the vital facts of your life: age, health, family, hobbies. Study how these too can be presented in functional terms, how they can help your presentation.

6. Don't overlook military or volunteer service. Convert the terminology of these institutions into understandable non-jargon that laymen can read. Keep the facts believable: if you taught English as a second language, say something about techniques used, how many taught, and skills necessary to do the job.

7. Don't try to include everything in this list—only those facts which show you developing as a *personality* and *professional*, dem-

onstrating a pattern of success, a progressive upward spiral of occupational development supporting the job you want.

Combine the facts and assemble your résumé in this order:

A. *Vital Facts*—name, phone numbers (top right-hand corner).
B. *Job Objectives*—center page, near top—two-inch margins. Keep
   job objectives short, pithy, and transparently clear.
C. Use *Headlines* for each generic skill of your résumé; set them
   off at the side with plenty of white space surrounding. Strive
   for a good logo—don't jam up captions, descriptions, and con-
   clusions.
D. *Summary of Background:* Twenty lines gleaned from Item 3
   above show how your background *fits* your objective. Or, if
   what you want to do fits your "experience," write up your *Employment History:* Make it chronological and short, beginning
   with job title, name of organization, responsibilities, dates and
   earnings, and put it *after* your Vocational Goals.
E. *Personal Data:* Education, hobbies, qualifications, licenses, publications, travel. *But only if it supports finding the job you
   want.* Type it up.

Remember, wide margins, double-spaced, *headline* captions (obit
résumés are for the dead), making every word count.
   Edit.
   Edit again.
   Take it to a *stranger* (you respect).
   Remember, strangers are looking at it as an employer will.
   Take it to another. Act on their criticism.
   Don't show it to your friends.
   No pride of authorship, please!
   Now, look at your final document.
   Will this résumé win you interviews?
   Mail out a hundred and find out.

How do I identify job goals?
   It takes three days to think through the occupational implications of your achievement list. And another few days to pull together the body of your résumé. But the toughest part of your

résumé, the brain-buster, is establishing a series of related *job objectives*.

And I emphasize the *plural*. Nobody with a healthy imagination has only *one* job goal, except possibly poets, saints, and FBI agents. And only pedants in the Personnel Department will raise an eyebrow.

Do you have any examples?

I just happen to have a few lying about in my sample case. The first "job objective" is culled from some routine résumés I've reviewed recently; the second series of job objectives represents the same people *after* going through the self-knowledge exercise.

First: Seek human-involvement work utilizing my interest in applying community-development techniques.

Now, everyone wants work with human beings. And nobody can define community development, much less apply its techniques. Let's look at his objective *after* three weeks of hard work:

Second: Seek responsible, decision-making position with organizations fostering self-development in the fields of education and community control among American Indians, utilizing my skills in teaching and cross-cultural communication. Welcome adverse working environment, long hours.

This is an improvement. But he doesn't tell us what *kind* of organization he wants to hire (i.e., a tribal council, the Bureau of Indian Affairs). Moreover, he has but one job goal: teaching. Why not counseling, co-ordination, and curriculum development? And he mentions only one kind of population he wants to work with; why not Micronesians, Eskimos, itinerant farm laborers?

And what did this chap's homework reveal about him that improved the clarity of his job objectives?

Well, many of his "achievements" were accomplished in a minority context. He was the only gentile in a Jewish Boy Scout troop, the only Protestant in a Catholic boys' school, the only college graduate on a summer job, the only white Head Start director on a Mississippi assignment. He will feel right at home on an Indian reservation.

Let's look at another. A young, well-traveled lady who writes:

First: Seek position in suburban school system where my interest in music qualifies me for a responsible position.

No dice.

I'm *interested* in ballroom dancing. My problem is I have a peg leg.

Nobody hires anybody because they are *interested* in doing something. Are you effective? That's what you speak to in your job objectives.

Second: Educational research in Modern Languages and/or Music on an international scale (UNESCO, African-American Institute); Mass Media Communications and creative writing involving the dissemination of above educational materials and programs (VOA, USIA, and such organizations). Particularly qualified in education research of Africa, specifically East, Central East, and French-speaking Africa.

Much better. But again, she usefully could add two or three other objectives. Music-camp director? Editorial assistant? Publisher's representative?

And what did she find out about herself between her first and second effort?

That she was especially proud of "collaborating with Radio Malawi in producing several programs of cross-cultural music . . . performed in song recitals with the American cathedral in Paris . . . was the feature editor of her school newspaper . . . developed music exhibitions favorably reviewed in the European press, etc., etc., etc."

The point is that she was indubitably "qualified" for a European job in the field of modern languages (she speaks five languages!) and music. Maybe not "Director, Bayreuth Festival." But that did come up in 1994 in her obituary!

And, as for her original job objective (teaching harmonics in Darien), that's an outright lie. That's what she thought she should do, what Mom and Dad thought was *sensible.* Not what she wanted to do or what she *is* doing.

Now, how about a middle-aged scientist who suddenly drops everything, graduates from law school, and writes in his résumé:

First: Seek position in governmental organization utilizing highly professional background in physics and academic training in law.

Well, that's great. But most employers don't have the imagination to program such a rare job specimen. Look at his second effort:

Second: Seek to use my qualifications as a law partner or key member of private, quasi-governmental institution in advocacy, patent, or product-safety arena where demonstrated performance in management, general engineering, and applied science can be fully utilized.

Not bad. Nader's Raiders, the FDA, and a score of threatened manufacturers would like to have him on their side. A great guy to broker problems between technical and salespeople, or consumer advocates and producers, or an organization and its law firm.

So why doesn't he say so? That kind of info came out in writing up his job advertisements. And the fact that he's always been good at explaining technical problems to scientific illiterates surfaced in his achievements list. And his obituary reports that "a grateful American Government awarded him a plaque in the Smithsonian Institution!"

Great! But I'm sure having trouble translating my achievements into acceptable occupational lingo in the résumé. Can you give some examples?

Translating experience or achievements is making you work for yourself. No outright lies—otherwise you'll pass through some awkward interviews when your interlocutors ask for amplification; but résumés are advertisements for oneself, and some skillful embroidery won't hurt and probably will help as long as the product (i.e., you) is honest.

Savvy job-seekers are able to put their feelings first, focus on their real wants, and are especially able in representing what it is they do best.

Here are some examples:

Life: You were a fair field-hockey player in college.
Résumé: Enjoy intense athletic contests both as spectator and participant.
Life: You knew about fifty people on your last job.
Résumé: Co-ordinated fifty key program executives from every department to maximize efficiency.

Life: You stuck out two years in an impossible Peace Corps assignment in Africa.

Résumé: Initiated community-action program for a small hill station in Uganda, upgrading local marketing and administrative skills and expanding horizons of inhabitants. Received letter of congratulation from the Prime Minister praising me for my efforts.

Life: Tend to be stopped by every street beggar.

Résumé: Demonstrated ability to win confidence from total strangers.

Life: You can solve the London *Times* crossword puzzle in two hours.

Résumé: Commended by many supervisors for accurate recollection of miscellaneous facts.

Life: Tend to be frugal to downright stingy with your money.

Résumé: Prudent manager of organizational funds; able to account and justify all cash and credit disbursements.

Life: You fell in love with every male teacher from the eighth to eleventh grade.

Résumé: Am especially able to work under senior decision-making executives. Have been cited for loyalty and efficiency.

Get the idea?

Am I putting you on?

Well, a little bit . . .

The point is to represent your strengths and skills in the best possible way. If you feel comfortable with what you represent, you can defend and build on these skills in an interview; if your "skills and strengths" are untrue or exaggerated, this will surface in the interview too.

What about military experience?

Did you command a Signal Corps battalion in the Army? Don't say it quite that way in your résumé. Instead, "Managed a complement of one thousand men in developing communications system for brigade-wide organization using miniature circuitry, field telephones and radios, light airplanes, and carrier pigeons. Cited by unit commander for managing the best communications system in I Corps."

What are some other important items you shouldn't include in your résumé?

Some "facts" you need *not* detail in your résumé: hobbies and organizations. No employer needs to know you are a philately buff or a member of a Greek-letter sorority. If, as a member of an organization or in pursuit of a hobby, you truly *achieved* something (e.g., captained an intramural lacrosse team, integrated your sorority, or were elected national stamp-collecting champ), then functionally represent this information under *Summary of Your Background* or under generic headings.

At all events, like writing an effective research paper, what you leave *out* of your résumé clarifies your job goals and focuses on your strengths. This means that you leave a lot of interesting (but not supporting) material on the cutting-room floor. The aim of an effective functional résumé is clarity and brevity: you mean to focus on what you want and can do. Any information that *detracts* from this photograph weakens your "qualifications" for a judgment job. Moreover, the discipline of doing a functional résumé *compels* you to come to grips with the important questions in finding a judgment job. Here are some personal facts you should detail in your résumé:

1. BIRTH DATE: Extraordinarily important in the employment process. Generally an employer courts disaster if he employs someone in his twenties to supervise someone in his forties. So give your birthdate on the last page of your résumé. Generational conflict is real. Looking younger or acting older helps, but the plain truth is that age (rather than race, sex, education) is the *major factor* in employment discrimination today.

2. PHONE NUMBER(S): It's ridiculous, but at least 150 job candidates I've wanted to hire failed to give me phone numbers (or gave ones where they couldn't be readily reached). I never employed them, *because I couldn't reach them when I needed them.* Put telephone numbers up front on the first page of your résumé.

3. GEOGRAPHICAL PREFERENCE: Nine out of ten jobs are filled by applicants who live where they want to work. Don't try to find a job in New York City if you live in Anaheim. It *can*

be done, of course, but job-finding is tough enough right where you want to live—so start there.

If you won't work in New York City under any condition, flatly say so in your résumé. How many fruitful interviews (on the point of breathless consummation) abort because Johnny Jobseek didn't say—on his résumé—that his sinus condition precluded employment in a wet climate. This rules out every state but Arizona, John, babe.

4. TRAVEL STATUS: Sticky Wicket, Inc., wants Suzie Liberation, superwoman, to promote its Urban Action Program at three plants in the Northwest. She'll be traveling for three months. Suddenly, Suzie, mindful of her three tiny tots, says she can't go. (Can't go! She can't travel to Bethesda, for Christ's sake?) But she didn't put this in her résumé—and guess who's called a male chauvinist pig for not hiring her? Always level with your employer, in the résumé, on what your travel status *is*: some time, half time, full time? Do you like it? Say so! Abhor it? Say so.

I once hired and fired a woman for a traveling consultant's job because she forgot to tell me whether she was licensed to drive. Did she think she was going to use the Greyhound bus? At two hundred dollars a day!

5. SALARY: "Negotiable."
Or establish a range within which you'll consider negotiating ($21,000–$26,000). It's true you give away your salary requirements *before* you interview, but it's also true that you are "screening out" employers you can't afford.

Also, under "Daily Rate" indicate what you cost per day as a consultant: $75, $125, $182 (currently the U. S. Government's maximum), $500.

6. PREVIOUS EARNINGS: If yours is a progressively upward salary history, enumerate it. Personnel Directors breathe heavily, and operating people—who do the hiring—can figure out if your salary history is in their ball park.

7. NAME: You think I'm joshing? In ten years in this body-broker business I've received more than ten résumés in which the name of the applicant was *not* included!

8. SEX: If you happen to be called "Francis," "Leslie," "Carol," or any of a hundred androgynous Christian names, tell the employer—again, in the résumé—whether you're a man or woman. Once I wanted to hire a freight handler for our mailroom. I interviewed a person whose first name was Keith. She was a wisp of a woman, all of ninety pounds.

9. HEALTH: Because of a slipped disc, you can't stand on your feet more than an hour. So why are you interviewing for a census enumerator's job? So tell it as it is: asthma? (You won't work out as a research librarian.) Acrophobia? (And you want a job as a consultant—with all that plane flying!)

I'm planning to move from Utica, New York, to Los Angeles; should I wait until I'm in the Los Angeles area before beginning a job search?

My hunch is that you would be well advised to go to the library, check out the L.A. phone book, develop a list of five hundred or so possible employers, note addresses and phone numbers on 3" × 5" cards, send out as many résumés (without cover letters) addressed simply to "the President," write in your own hand on the résumé, "I'll be phoning you on my arrival next week in Los Angeles," sign your name on the résumé (at the top), hole up in a motel room in L.A. upon arrival, phone back everyone you sent a résumé to, and count on a 7–14 per cent response rate (which is very good!).

All of this presumes you possess a first-rate, printed, functional résumé.

At a minimum, after three days of phoning, you should have thirty-five interviews from about five hundred résumés, all of which you mailed five days prior to your departure for Los Angeles.

So a functional résumé will be read?

Classy, functional résumés, professionally printed and mailed in quantity, are "pass around" material. Oh, sure, most résumés are round-filed, but a first-rate functional résumé *will be read.* And mail from people who've read this book suggests that effective résumés are remailed! That is, people pick up résumés and put

them into the hands of someone who was asking only the day before yesterday about somebody to fill a job in New York City.
Yes, most résumés are junk mail. But the point about broadcast-
ing résumés widely is that it exposes more people to *you* and
arithmetically improves the chances of your being considered for a
job you want. That's why job-hunting is a "numbers" game, why
good jobs go to those who know how to find them.

*So a functional résumé helps you discover what it is you want to
do?*
Satchel Paige once said, "Never look back, they might be gain-
ing on you." Half true.
If you're going to learn who you are and what you do best, and
the kind of contribution you'll make to an organization that hires
you, you're required to study your past. But not your disappointments, failures, and misfires.

*How does this kind of résumé help me organize and plan my job
campaign?*
Simple.
It answers the questions, Who are you? What can you do?
What do you want to do? And it *disciplines where you look.* Another example of why doing market research on yourself is more
important than "researching the job market."
No longer dispersed, distracted, and discombobulated, knowing
your goals and abilities, *means* that you are ready to plan your job
campaign. A person who doesn't know where he is going cannot
read a map; a person who doesn't know what he wants cannot
wage a job campaign. A functional résumé is a road map to your
future.

*Is another purpose of the functional résumé to screen out em-
ployers I don't want to work for?*
Yes, indeed!
Employers screen out job applicants; why not turn the tables on
them and screen out employers who don't fit your job goals? Fair
is fair, and you don't want to waste time following-up on jobs you
might qualify for but don't *want.*
All the more reason to be precise about a *series* of different (but
related) jobs in your "VOCATIONAL GOALS."

Isn't the functional résumé risky?

You reduce the risk when you represent yourself by defining your strengths.

Plenty of people focusing on their strengths, putting themselves first for a change, are devastated reading the final draft of their résumé!

And friends, parents, and colleagues tend to giggle and put you down. (That's because they know your weaknesses and don't necessarily want you to succeed.)

Yes, employers can "turn off." That's why the functional approach takes a risk with yourself. But obit résumés leave neutral feelings and do not turn people either *on* or *off*. And that's the worst outcome in your job search: impressing people neither favorably nor unfavorably. And these folks, dull folks, take the biggest risk!

Risk-taking is OK, but isn't what you recommend really reducing risks?

That's right. People who take *no* risks are taking the greatest risk. But effective job-finding strategy means thinking on your feet, taking a few elementary risks (e.g., "being yourself"), all of which means better results.

The problem's in your mind.

The bio-sheet, the traditional résumé, is no reflection of your effectiveness. Real accomplishments reflect ability; arid, meaningless facts mean nothing. It is far *less* risky to rely on a functional résumé than the bio-sheet.

What do people who read this book and write you letters think of the functional résumé?

Many remain unconvinced. This is because people *don't believe in themselves*. They still want to rely on an employer's hypothetical crystal ball to match them with jobs in an organization. But employers have precious little time on which to base the decision "to interview or not to interview."

I have, however, seen hundreds of résumés of people who have read this book which are superb. Uniformly, people who develop an excellent functional résumé agree that the *process* is more important than the *product*. That is, the *thinking* that goes into a functional résumé "solves" a host of problems other job-seekers take for granted.

Why do I feel so bloody uncomfortable with this kind of résumé?

1. You sense that you are losing your identity because you come across as an able, effective, motivated human being!

2. You were carefully brought up to appear meek, humble, and unassuming.

3. Your best friend wouldn't recognize you.

4. You intensely dislike selling yourself, largely because you feel someone should "sense" your strengths.

5. You think it rude to "blow your own horn."

6. You feel you are "conning" a job.

7. Thus, you feel guilty of deception, which is intolerable!

8. Therefore, you won't be effective and find a job you want.

9. Then you can be unhappy and innocent and dissatisfied with your job, like all the other slobs.

10. You wonder if you shouldn't go to law school.

A functional résumé is a good advertisement for yourself and an acceptable *and* ethical document to promote employment in a line of work which will bring you self-fulfillment. *Not* writing a functional résumé is conning yourself into believing you are not as important as the employer.

Do you need both a functional résumé and a descriptive résumé?
Functional résumés reflect ability. Descriptive résumés reflect chronology. The obit résumé has its uses. If you generate an interview *without* a résumé and the interviewer wants a piece of paper, give him your bio-sheet, the descriptive résumé. Functional résumés are for your job campaign, your mass mailing; functional résumés are advertisements for yourself.
The major point, which can't be emphasized too much, is that a résumé has but *one* practical application: to generate interviews.

If you bag an interview *without* a résumé you either make or break yourself in the interview (see Chapter Five). To use a functional résumé in this situation is "Communications Overkill"; you already *have* the interview. Don't gild the lily by using an advertisement for yourself when you have already accomplished your objective.

So you need a functional résumé and a bio-sheet?
Yes. The bio-sheet is simply a list of schools attended, jobs held, names and addresses of people to contact. Use the bio-sheet to generate interviews through friends. The functional résumé is topical, analytical, generic, and a photograph of you that your friends will hate!

OK. Two résumés are in order: the bio-sheet (which I have) and the functional résumé (which I'm going to prepare). When do I use which?
Use your descriptive résumé for:
Headhunters
Friends
At the end of an interview ("Do you have any paper on yourself, Bob?")
Placement offices
Information interviews (if you don't know what you want)
Use functional résumés for:
Strangers
Mass mailings
Want ads
Bulletin boards
Cold-turkey interviewing
Information interviewing (when you know what you want)
Remember: If you need to *generate* interviews, use a functional résumé; if you interview without a résumé, use the bio-sheet. The practical purpose of a résumé is to obtain interviews; otherwise, it is useless.

What about a person who doesn't like himself enough to use a functional résumé?
For reasons not entirely clear to me, people who can't abide

functional résumés have far less of a problem taking the same accomplishment orientation using a blitz letter-writing campaign. It's easy to hire a secretarial service which can reproduce five hundred letters citing a series of accomplishments and aiming them at a generic population of employers.

Look at the following example:

Jonathan Scodoro
3778 Longworth Place
Washington, D.C. 20039

Dear Senator:

You or one of the Senate committees may need someone with my background in political public relations and media to promote news, write speeches, and manage other administrative needs.

As the assistant director of public affairs for a national association, I promoted legislative positions before Congress, which were in turn published in more than 150 newspapers. I generated national news from the association's annual meeting for the first time in 23 years, with a press conference on legislative issues.

As a department manager of a major metropolitan newspaper, I helped increase circulation almost 8 per cent in one year with my news and feature stories. Using an unprecedented format, I persuaded a local radio station to hire me as production assistant.

Wrote speeches which derived support for special-interest legislation passed in Congress. Publicized political rallies for seven candidates—all of whom were elected or re-elected.

Advanced, produced, and publicized nine regional presentations of the legislative positions of a public affairs council of corporations, and also answered several hundred consumer inquiries.

Persuaded 17 television stations to program free air time for a national campaign I worked on.

Look forward to meeting with you.

Sincerely,

Was this letter effective in getting interviews?

Sorry about that, no. The letter is terrific, but it's aimed at people who are swamped with job applicants. This approach could be useful, but this chap would have done better taking a "cold turkey" (see the next chapter) approach and using his round-robin letter for private industry.

Don't people long out of the job market feel at a disadvantage preparing a résumé?

Certainly a descriptive résumé which demands a chronological listing of recent employment, last job first, is a disadvantage. That would intimidate anybody who is recycling back into the work force. All the more reason to use the functional approach, stressing abilities (rather than recent work experience) and motivation (rather than college degrees).

How do I conceal how old I am?

You can't and don't want to. Doing so says more about your insecurity than stating the truth.

But you can conceal (without omitting), under Personal Data (last page), by *putting your birth date* rather than your chronological age. Surprise: many employers won't count up on you! So, "if too young" or "too old," give birth date, never age.

How do I tell an employer I never completed my M.A.?

"Completed all required course work leading to a masters degree in applied biochemisty (thesis pending)."

This is strictly true. How are they to know tomorrow, for heaven's sake, that you won't find time to complete it? This information is hard to *check up* on!

What kind of typeface, format, paper should I use for an effective résumé?

Go to a printer, a graphics expert, someone in the business of "images." Remember, so long as it's neat, grammatical with no misspellings, the content of your résumé is more important than its appearance. A printer can show you examples of résumés, typefaces, forms. Pick what you think "fits" your trade, craft, profession.

Do you need a different résumé for each job?

No. But you do need three or four objectives. The first one should be most important and the others alternatives, but don't write a new résumé for every job opening. Job objectives, when defined, will relate. And demonstrate how your "skills" qualify for different jobs in various fields.

What is the return on a mailing of one hundred functional résumés?

Of course, that depends on (a) the quality of your résumé, (b) the demand for your skills, (c) the clarity and precision of your thought processes. It's well to remember, if Albert Einstein were alive and well and looking for a job in applied physics on the East Coast, his response rate to a résumé wouldn't be much higher than your own.

But since you asked, I wager:

8–14 per cent of employers contacted may interview you.

40–50 per cent may send "nice" no letters.

10–15 per cent may send a signal: "Drop by and see me sometime."

30–50 per cent may not respond at all.

To augment your batting average, *follow up by phone!* Effective job-seekers could raise averages to 20 per cent. And that's damn good!

An obit résumé, however, with the usual cover letter, yields only a 1–3 per cent response. But if the cover letter is *functional* in nature, speaks to *real* accomplishments, and *zeroes in* on a real job, chances are better than even that your "score" can rise to 10 per cent.

Sending out five hundred résumés seems excessive.

Do you have any idea how many résumés arrive at Booze, Allen, & Hamilton; the Department of Health, Education and Welfare; General Motors Corporation every day? No lie: hundreds and hundreds!

Moreover, printing in volume is cheap (a thousand résumés is three times as inexpensive per copy as one hundred). A postage stamp is fifteen cents (or *was* when I wrote this paragraph; I wager it's more now, but still cheap).

Mailing in *volume* is how many charities, direct mail order houses, and junk-mail vendors make a good living. And all you want is one good job offer!

Again, I wager my next year's vacation, the reason you back off from a volume mailing is your own displaced sense of self-worth, your fear of striking out, and/or your fear that you'll succeed. No way you can possibly know of all the jobs you might want and are able to fill, let's say, within a five-mile radius of your downtown apartment. Reaching out via five hundred résumés to all those employers out there, one of whom may just punch your ticket, is a cost-effective, intelligent, grown-up way to find a job!

What about references . . . ?

Referees.

No, they don't have whistles around their necks and wear white caps.

It's a stately name for people listed as references on your résumé. While you look for a job, they are pretty important people. Choose them wisely, particularly those who know you in a work capacity, and those who speak to your strengths *and* weaknesses. Don't use former college professors as referees; schoolmasters are OK recommending you for graduate school, but are useless patrons in the job mart.

An able employer always *personally* checks out on the telephone—even when he's certain to hire you—the people who know your work best. That's why your references are important.

A nice note to people you want as references is always in order before beginning your job campaign. As an employer, I am suspicious of 90 per cent of all *written* references; referees are generally picked for social reasons: college chums, movement sisters, and drinking buddies. These are usually your best friends. The problem is, they accept you uncritically and couldn't care less how you function on the job. (That's what friendship is.)

But your referees should be objective, honest, candid, and able to analyze people.

It's not *who* or how important they are; rather, it's how able they are in taking an occupational "photograph" of you.

Without your halo.

But suppose I'm not bagging job offers because of what happened on my last job?

Generally employers are *too kind* to terminated employees. I've done a few thousand reference checks, and 99 per cent of American employers today hesitate to jeopardize the chances of someone who is looking for another job. That's what I mean by the lack of balanced reporting and its importance in choosing your referees. Almost everyone has two or three experiences in his occupational life which are sticky wickets. If terminating under less than desirable conditions, ask during the exit interview for a formal letter of reference explaining the organization's *reasons* for separating you. This puts the monkey on the right person's back at the right time.

I once interviewed a chap who had been fired *thirteen times!* And he succeeded in finding another job every time!

What about using third parties to check out your references?

Slightly devious but effective.

If you believe someone is giving you the double whammy, asking a friend to request a reading on your background is appropriate. This usually eliminates the paranoia bends if the referee's report is favorable. In the event it isn't, share the names of a couple of other people at XYZ, Inc. who know the *full* story of your performance with prospective employers. Tell him: "Look, Jake Muscatel, my boss at XYZ, Inc. has some pretty strong opinions about my performance. To get a balanced picture I suggest you talk, as well, to ———— and ————."

But won't my current employer cashier me if he discovers I'm shopping around?

You *are* a nervous nellie!

Maybe.

So,

1. On the face of your résumé, type "Current employer is not to be contacted."

2. Write "Personal and Confidential" on every envelope you mail containing your résumé.

3. Invent a maiden aunt with a congenital heart disease who requires your frequent attendance; this story covers your repeated absences from the office for a while, but it has a fishy odor. (I know one job-seeker who bumped off his grandmother five times in the process of finding five jobs!)

4. Slap a lawsuit on any prospective employer who *does* contact your current employer. It's an intolerable violation of your rights in your job search for employers to ignore privileged information.

5. Finally, ask yourself again, *Is all this secrecy really necessary?* It tips off future employers and tempts them to probe further. Moreover, the best way to keep a secret is to broadcast it widely. (For example, marking your correspondence "Confidential and Personal" or "Eyes Only" is no way to keep a secret!) Explain *why you want out* to the person who needs to know: your employer.*

What about concealing prejudicial information like being an ex-con?
An ex-con, having paid his debt to society, should, on a note in his résumé, detail the circumstances, penalty, and duration of his imprisonment. You cheapen yourself in your own and your employer's eyes when you omit information you perceive as prejudicial. It's the employer's responsibility to assess; whenever you confess to a prison record, a health problem, a spotty education, and so forth, you appeal to your interviewer's liberalism. If anything, he will hate himself if he rejects you; he can't be sure it's for the right reasons!
So don't be a dope; avoid mendacity and *never* apologize for not having a college education, or having done time for two months (at seventeen years of age, for God's sake!), or because you're separated from your spouse.

What about consulting?
Good jobs. Moreover, consultants don't qualify under any "personnel ceiling," are able to do interesting work for short periods of

* See *If Things Don't Improve Soon . . .* for a longer discussion of this problem.

time, have mobility, and develop connections to qualify them for additional consultant work.

A good consultant is always landing judgment jobs in a wide variety of fields. One of his qualifications is finding good jobs. A good consultant never grows stagnant on the job. The crossruff of his experiences gradually qualifies him for a whole host of special jobs.

One of your qualifications for a consultant's job is your availability. A consultant must have the confidence to face unemployment. There's no security in consulting work. Being a consultant is often a euphemism for being unemployed. But the work and life style are bracing and give the kind of exposure needed to learn where the hidden jobs are.

What are the strong and weak points about consultancy work?

PRO	CON
Varied assignments with many clients	Frequent periods of unemployment
Excellent pay for short-term assignments	Cash-flow problems
Chance for quickie vacations and stimulating "downtime"	Unwholesome boredom
No "boss" overseeing every nit-picking detail	Lack of structure: no boss to tell you how well/how badly you are doing
No political hassles	No real involvement over a long period of time
A feeling of freedom, independence	Enormous anxiety, guilty thoughts, unhappiness
No "career" progression	No "career" progression
No operational authority	No operational authority

Clearly, being a consultant depends primarily on what a person *wants*. Understandably, many consultants drop out to stay put on longer-term "jobs." And many operational types yearn for the freedom of the consultant. Without wanting to make too strong a case, those newly on the job market should eschew consultancy work; what young people want *fast* are responsibility and power. Middle-age and senior types, however, should give thought to consultancy work. It's a chance to make your "experience" and seasoning pay off and find time to do some salmon fishing in Iceland.

Does it make any sense to volunteer, for no pay, to work in a field you want where you have no qualifications?
You bet it does.
Half the political hotshots in the country started off as unpaid canvassers in some obscure campaign. And advertising geniuses often begin licking stamps for free in the mailroom.
Volunteer work—especially in glamor jobs such as the theater, communications, and politics—is useful training and makes the volunteer, especially if he becomes rapidly indispensable, highly visible to decision-makers who are quick to recognize and promote competence.

Just what do you mean by a "job campaign"?
Give yourself two or three weeks to assemble a first-rate résumé.
Give yourself another week to research the job market in "your field."
Find two hundred potential employers from the Yellow Pages, the public library, trade publications, and professional directories.
Your mailing service will print your résumé and stuff and stamp your envelopes. In a word, pay money for a grownup's job campaign. You have other things to do, like finding a job.
Fifty résumés generate about seven interviews. Each interview produces four other "leads."
Follow-up by phone—two weeks after every interview—if you *liked* the employer. He might not have a job, but he might have heard of a good judgment job in the hidden job market. So don't let somebody you like off the hook. Call him once a month and check in.
In a word, a job campaign is simply organizing your time to obtain the most exposure arithmetically possible. This means hard work. But the payoff is plenty of interviews, and that's where you begin to harvest job offers.

Do you have any tips on what not to do before embarking on a job campaign?
Don't send a mug shot with your résumé—it's cryptoracist.
Don't include your college transcript with your résumé. You

want a job, not a berth in a graduate school. And who the hell cares what you got in long division?

Don't bug a potential employer more than twice a month about a job for which you are being considered. Being eager is good, but salivating is gauche.

Don't say you want a "challenging" job "working with people." It makes sharp employers go glassy-eyed.

"Never apologize, never explain" (Disraeli). Deference is OK with agents of the Internal Revenue Service, but bad form in the employment process. So you were five minutes late to your interview? What was the employer doing that was so important?

Never, never drop names of important people in an interview. Over five hundred job applicants have thrown this pitch at me—and are probably still unemployed.

Don't knock your previous employer. Sour grapes is bad form.

Don't use intermediaries, i.e., third parties, to arrange job interviews. It's a half-assed arrangement all around. Call an employer direct and say, "Johnny Morris, your old college roommate, told me I should phone you about the job you have open."

Never send a résumé of more than five single-spaced typewritten pages. Honest to God, I've received résumés as thick as the Portland phone book.

Don't use the third person in preparing résumés. Only De Gaulle and Julius Caesar pulled it off.

Don't call yourself "Doctor" if you're a Ph.D. It puts off employers and starts an interview on the wrong step.

You say not to drop names, but can you avoid this in your résumé?

Not entirely, but you don't headline them either.

If you happen to be a direct descendant of Samuel Adams, don't say so in your résumé. And if you went to Princeton on a scholarship and played lacrosse, emphasize the scholarship and just mention the rest. Conversely, if you attended a barber institute, don't flout your populist origins. Snobbery *is* snobbery.

Employers are fickle: social-register caterwauling will turn off as many employers as it "turns on." And who wants to work for someone who hires you because you're a Daughter of the American Revolution?

What counts is (in order of importance):

1. Performance on your last job
2. What your references say
3. Ability
4. Attitude, enthusiasm, drive, and smarts

One footnote: if you worked your way through college, say so in your résumé. Almost anyone can pass from upper-primary through grad school if Mom, Dad, or the federal government foots the bill. But the poor chap working his way through Siwash U.—now, that fellow has character! And "Character is Fate" (Heraclitus).

How important is the job description?
One of the big mistakes many employers make is writing job descriptions on judgment jobs. Sure, job descriptions are important for PBX operators, hod carriers, and computer programers—carefully structured jobs where "time and motion" experts are necessary, where there is an industrial "piecework" objective. But in the job you want—where you are hired to make decisions—they are asinine.
Why?
Because judgment jobs are always changing. And in the best organizations change is positively encouraged because people are changing all the time.
So a job description does not account for occupational growth and change within people and organizations. Worst of all, job descriptions are prepared by personnel departments which know nothing about the organization.
So be leery of job descriptions—they rarely illuminate and often conceal a job's hidden agenda. The real art of matching a human being with a job escapes the authors of job descriptions. My advice is, if you meet but half the "qualifications," apply for any job you *want*.
Job-hunting is a crapshoot. And you might roll some lucky dice.

But my problem is finding out whether what I want to do is available on the job market.

A few years ago a slick publication, *Careers Today*, spoke to this problem. Three issues and a million dollars later the whole enterprise failed.

Why?

Because most "careers today" drive people to the brink of suicide, dope addiction, despair, or slow death. And the information published wasn't much better than pamphlets printed by most PR departments.

But there is a clear need for concise information on real jobs in thousands of fields. The trouble is that such information rapidly becomes obsolete and requires major capital backstopping.

There is a simpler way. And that's by "interviewing for information" in fields for which you feel "qualified." That means simply "dropping in" and discussing the investment field with a stockbroker; the "communications field" with a newspaper reporter, editor, and television producer; or if petroleum engineering's your bag, why not stake out a couple of vice-presidents at Standard Oil of New Jersey and take an hour of their time asking them about the business. Let each person you talk with refer you to four others, and build up a bank of people you can phone for advice about penetrating their field of work or giving you advice about other "fields."

Do this for a month and you'll reap a harvest of "inside" information; everything from job titles to salary levels at one end of the spectrum, to whether the atmospherics of organizations you interview fit your style. And there's no harm in learning that you *don't want* to be a patent attorney after you've researched this field and found out what the score *is*.

Three days discovering you don't want work in commodity investments sure beats taking a job as a trader trainee and spending three years trying to escape from a profession you despise.

The number of people who *drift* into jobs and organizations is incalculable. By taking charge of your job campaign—finding out what you want—you'll rationally direct the process of finding out whether a judgment job is available. And if it isn't, you've wasted only a couple of weeks of time instead of investing a lifetime in a career of frustration and self-disharmony.

More on "information interviewing" in the next chapter.

Swell. Where in the world are these judgment jobs you talk about so knowledgeably?

Eighty per cent of all jobs are filled through a grapevine, an "old-boy" network, a system of referrals that never sees the light of public day. No, you won't see them posted on a bulletin board, or registered with the U. S. Employment Service, or advertised in the Washington *Post*.

This is the so-called "hidden job market."

It is the market where good jobs are found. The reason there's a hidden job mart is because most employers fear—quite stupidly—the unwashed masses. Employers want men and women who are recommended by friends, business and professional associates, drinking buddies—almost anybody except someone off the streets!

You say this is nonsense! Undemocratic! Unjust! And you're right! But only foolish job applicants don't take the hidden job market into account.

FOUR

Go Hire Yourself
an Employer

OK.

Now that you've decided to buy in rather than drop out, first focus on what the nature of the job market is. There's the hidden job market where the good jobs are; second, there's the world of grunt or stop-loss employment, where you work to make money to wait out the job you want; and third, there's the illusionary world of permanent employment, tenured hire, where presumably one works a forty-hour week for forty years until death or retirement parts you and your employer.

A few homely, sometimes brutal, and occasionally cheerful "truths" about the job market you need to know before conducting your job campaign:

1. The most "qualified" people rarely find the job they want; the good jobs go to those who know how to find them.

2. Expanding your job search to include almost any kind of employer is defective job-hunting strategy. Far better to *restrict, narrow,* and *focus* on employers who provide the job you want (there are far more of them than you think). That way you are less likely to "quit" a job you don't like only to begin the dreary search again.

3. As a job-seeker you are as important as the job-giver. Most employers, like job-seekers, can't focus on what they want. If you

can, and what you want fits half what he needs, who is to say the employer has all the cards?

4. Personnel agencies, career guidance counselors, and executive-search specialists are the last people you want to talk to in looking for the job you want.

Personnel agencies work for employers—not you.

Career counselors charge you a fortune—better invested in your job search.

Executive-search types couldn't care less; they broker jobs for people not looking for jobs.

5. No one ever hired a résumé. Résumés are simply useful in obtaining interviews. Résumés which generate interviews augment the chances of job offers.

6. Judgment jobs are rarely advertised; if they are, it's because they have already been filled (affirmative action in action); if they aren't filled, candidates must possess a combination of rare skills which requires employers to advertise.

7. There are far more judgment jobs available than there are effective people to fill them. Finding *truly effective* people who have something to contribute is the employer's greatest difficulty. Focusing on ability and desire is the job-seeker's greatest difficulty.

How do you get around filling out all of those company forms—I thought a résumé was sufficient?

The application forms.

Nobody knows who invented the first one. Probably the same fellow who writes the fine print on the back of your homeowner's insurance policy.

A pain in the derrière, the delight of Ph.D.s in personnel administration, the most unnecessary form in any company, unless you are hiring data processors, hotel personnel, postal clerks—i.e., non-judgment jobs.

So what do you do?

I usually hire a secretarial service. I give them every conceivable bit of information any application might require: Social Security number, middle names of deceased grandparents, my M-1 rifle number in the Army.

I simply pass on the required forms to them. Then I'm free to do what I should do: look for a job.

If application forms are useless, why do organizations insist on using them?
Application forms are not useless to employers; they are useless for job-seekers. Employers use application forms to straight-arm the host of unemployed who park on their front stoop each working morning. That way, an organization proves it carefully "screens" all applicants. And personnel departments (who never do the hiring) justify their existence. So, if you are told to complete an application form, beware. That's "org-talk," meaning, "There is no job for *you* here." Remember, especially you folks who are new on the job market, finding a job is the *opposite* of being admitted to graduate school. There is no admissions committee, no rational process of selection, employment dossiers are *not* compared with each other. Does anyone over the age of twenty-one and with an IQ over 90 really believe that the key jobs in our society are filled the same way a Rhodes Scholarship is awarded? Shame on you! And if important jobs were filled *rationally* and democratically, you can be sure the whole process would be so time-consuming as to be unworkable.

Don't employers scan application forms and résumés for significant omissions?
Particularly in regard to earnings and dates of employment, all of which means a candid posture on your part. In other words, no fibbing. If you took a year off to go spelunking in Austria, say so. Did you accept a salary of $3 per hour to work with the nation's foremost semanticist and accordingly reject a college instructorship at $14,000? Say so. Were you nabbed by the police, booked, and charged for breaking and entering the second-story window of your college girlfriend's apartment? Say so.

Concealing information, or saying you have an M.S. in mass spectrometry (when it ain't so, Joe), is certain to land you in hot water and permanently wreck your chances of ever finding a judgment job. Because lying breaks the bond of trust which binds every successful business negotiation.

Don't do what a recent V.P. candidate of the Democratic Party did: conceal important personal facts. Fibbing about *facts*, covering up, playing possum, is a character weakness.

What does it mean to Go Hire Yourself an Employer?

Finding a job is a fifty-fifty proposition between a buyer and seller. The job-seeker is the seller offering talent, flair, or (a more conventionally used term) "qualifications." True, the employer provides a salary and a purpose to the employee; but the job-holder gives his life and time, something invaluable. Therefore, it is a reciprocal, parity relationship. The job-seeker needn't defer to prospective employers nor petition for work. You interview with the idea of *contributing* something valuable (your time) to some lucky employer, and the name of the game is not measured by the *number* of offers. Don't set the world on fire; start a flame in somebody's heart.

It's your responsibility, not the employer's, to identify what you *want* to do. This means understanding the nature of the world of work. The "system" is blamed rather than human nature. Employee goals should be congruent with those of the employer. When there is incongruence, there is certain job dissatisfaction. More reason why you must be competent in the job search. You must identify three or four of the most suitable "classes" of employers. The vast majority of employers don't want you, and you don't want them.

So look at the "big picture," both points of view: the employer's and the employee's. Nobody hires (or should hire) anyone for their *weaknesses*. Rather, people are hired for their strengths. And job-seekers must know their strengths, what they can best contribute. Otherwise, the transaction will be unsatisfactory. Employer and employee will be unhappy. And this occurs in two out of three job transactions and supports surveys which show gross job dissatisfaction in the work force.

Give me an example of job congruence.

It's simply when work conforms to desire. Look what this woman *wants* via her job objective:

Job Objectives:

Qualified for responsible Health Project International Management position in the Public Health, Family Planning, Medical

Delivery Systems, and Health Care evaluation areas. Desire Project Director responsibilities as a Planner, Manager, or Chief Evaluator for Health or Social Science oriented institution utilizing management, statistical, and report-writing capabilities. Particularly qualified to deal on a cross-cultural basis with indigenous target populations (i.e., retarded children or geriatric programs). Welcome a continuous assignment of two years or more.

Get the idea?

Now let's look at a job description and note what the employer *wants:*

> A contractor with the CDC seeks experienced research manager for metropolitan office to conduct study of venereal-disease incidence among inner-city residents. Qualified candidates should have five years project experience, an advanced degree in the social sciences, and strong evaluation and research skills. Report-writing skills a must; some quantitative orientation. Ability to supervise paraprofessional interviewers essential.

Our job applicant, having written out her three job advertisements, converting the lingo to describe jobs into her own professional objectives, focused on what she wanted and matched up against most of what an employer wanted.

Congruent job objectives means a substantial overlap between what an employer wants and what you, as the job applicant, want. There will rarely be an *absolute* identity of objectives, and there needn't be.

What exactly do you mean by the "hidden" job market?

Eighty per cent of all good jobs are concealed.

They're not listed with the Civil Service Commission or your State Employment Service, and the Personnel Department is always the last to know.

So, look for the good jobs in the hidden job market. These are the jobs which exist in the minds of those few people who make a place work. They have power and make decisions.

Don't look for any prepackaged job descriptions. Most operating people don't have time for such nonsense. And, like everything else worth hearing, you learn about hidden jobs through a grapevine of intelligence, an old-boy network, or in the specialized channels of your craft, skill, or field.

Do employers hire exclusively from the old boy/old girl network?
Not exclusively, but mainly: a mistake, because candidates who flow through this stream can never be sure whether their native ability and desire secured them the job . . . or the political connection.

Don't ignore networking as a source of jobs: it's the mainstream. But you'll feel better and do a better job for *a stranger.* That's right, *someone who doesn't know you.* Why? Well, it's because both you and your employer focus not on *the connection,* but on the *contribution* you would make to the organization. Keep this important fact in mind when you start hiring. The payoff in motivated and talented people truly "loyal" to you (after all, you showed good sense in hiring them!) is astounding.

Also, while it's tough resisting the temptation, contact friends, colleagues within the old boy/old girl network *last.*

That's right.

Try finding jobs from interesting strangers *first,* and save your friends (and friends of friends) for when you need them.

OK. So good jobs are in the hidden job market. But what do you mean by a good job?
Good jobs are "judgment" jobs. Jobs that pay off with something more than a paycheck: that allow you to grow on the job, face challenges, feel relevant, and function effectively.

On judgment jobs you are paid for the decisions you make.

There are all kinds of judgment jobs. Everything else is a nonjob. Proposal development, financial analysis, programing, evaluation, market research, are all judgment jobs.

Which function fits you best: design, marketing, management, or evaluation?

If you work in the *design* area, you would be a candidate for a design role with a mutual fund, an architect, developer or design-planner's job with a real estate venture, an assistant editor to a scholarly quarterly, a policy analyst on campaign issues with the issues section of a political campaign.

You say your real forte is marketing? Well, three to one, you might work out as a broker's representative for the mutual fund, a sales manager with the real estate venture, the circulation manager of a scholarly quarterly, and as campaign manager in a state assembly race.

But management gives you a place in the sun? Have you thought of being a securities analyst with the mutual fund, a project director with the real estate venture, a business manager for a scholarly quarterly, or a candidate in a political campaign?

What about evaluation? Well, in a mutual fund you might be a consultant evaluating a mass-mailing campaign; with a real estate venture, a quality-control expert weighing the quality and quantity of life in a new community; on a scholarly quarterly, the editorial gadfly paid to plan a long-term overhaul of the magazine's image; and in a political campaign, the chap who polls the public to see how the candidate's doing.

Savvy?

Judgment jobs are the only jobs you *want* unless you fancy clerking for ITT.

How do you avoid the blahs and blues in your job search?

Creative hindsighting, getting yourself together, is great. But be sure you stop thinking too much about yourself when you step out on the sidewalk and start to cold-turkey employers. Too much introspection is a bad thing, and unless a job-seeker keeps mighty busy, the blahs and blues tend to overtake him.

Hindsighting.

"Oh, if I'd only gone to law school, I wouldn't be in this job fix today!"

"Good grief, I should never have quit my last job without another job to go to . . ."

"Europe was great, but two years off the job market leaves me right where I was when I left."

Etcetera, etcetera, etcetera . . .

Quarterbacking your past on a gloomy, jobless Monday morning is my definition of purgatory. Suddenly, everything right about your life seems wrong.

It's tough not to, but, in finding a job, raking up past disappointments is downright debilitating of attitudes necessary to impress employers.

Bob Townsend in *Up the Organization* writes that for an executive to be successful only a third of his decisions need to be correct.

True words.

And if only a third of your interviews take off, that's more than enough—provided you generate plenty of job leads—to qualify for a couple of judgment jobs.

But I feel so loathsome unemployed and useless.

Those are the terms and conditions of finding good jobs in hard times: overcoming the natural discouragement when you miss out on a great job five yards from the goal line! And if you are not prepared to be discouraged, take my advice: stay in graduate school or belt the commonweal in a job you hate. Chances are you have some growing up to do.

It's not useless looking for a job. What you learn might exceed anything you learn on the job! And why feel loathsome for taking care of yourself—that is, looking for the job you want?

The truth is, most people feel more comfortable (and unhappy) loathing themselves than they do liking themselves and being effective. That's because being effective means giving up a sense of identity appropriate to a child but not an adult. That's why personal change is the hardest and most productive work in the world: shedding a sense of self no longer appropriate.

What can the judgment job-seeker today expect to encounter in his job search?

Most people go through four stages in searching for work.

The first stage is marked by confidence, naïveté, and optimism: the job-seeker, being inexperienced and uninformed, relies heavily upon friends, contacts, and want ads for leads.

In the second stage, if one is unsuccessful in finding a job, the job-seeker becomes pessimistic, feels incompetent, and loses grasp on his sense of identity.

The third stage, "the jobless blahs," is marked by withdrawal: the job-seeker turns inward and retires in front of his television set. It is a state of anesthesia.

Many of you who are reading this book are in the third stage, a time when you are finally forced to face the fact: society owes you nothing. You alone are responsible for finding a job.

The fourth stage is mounting a job campaign based on desire, on real objectives, on a true understanding of self.

How do I overcome the jobless blahs?

1. Call up your best friend and ask him/her to tell you what a great person you are.

2. Go back and read every flattering letter of reference, performance review, or citation you have that's collecting dust in your footlocker.

3. Take a week off and go scuba diving at Nag's Head.

4. Spend money on yourself, even if it means going into debt. (Finding a good job is the best reason I know for going into debt!)

5. Lots of exercise, outdoors.

6. Stay clear of other unemployed people (they simply tell you there are no jobs); associate only with people who are happy and effective on the job.

7. Avoid reading the financial pages or anything that retails how tough times are; most journalistic stories rarely focus on folks who find jobs. (In 1976, for example, employment jumped by three million jobs, while the unemployment rate slightly increased.)

8. Stay clear of government referral offices, which are staffed largely by people who can't find jobs.

9. Start an affair!

10. Never get between a dog and a lamppost.

Why does looking for a job cause so much anxiety?
Mostly feelings of guilt:

1. No money is coming in and plenty is going out.

2. Most people *hate deciding anything*. Better to postpone than choose. These folks don't know that we can always *change* our minds, i.e., our decisions. Nobody is "locked into a job" on a job search unless, of course, they think they are.

3. Not working at looking for a job causes guilt. Guilty people can't tolerate this condition, so they become unhappy and anxious instead.

4. Self-esteem falls precipitously as anxiety increases, thus immobilizing job-seekers. This causes them to look *outside* themselves rather than *inside*.

Antidotes to anxiety:

1. Exercise and fun

2. A friend, counselor, coach, or psychiatrist

3. Finding a stop-loss job

4. Focusing on *desire* for, not the *need* of, a job

5. Accomplishing a first-rate functional résumé.
The introspection and self-discipline this exercise requires heightens self-esteem; we become as effective as our résumés.

6. Interviewing three or four times a day—an index that we are taking care of ourselves, working at finding a job, a sure-fire way to vanquish guilt and unhappiness, although disappointment and pain are still omnipresent.

7. Allowing ourselves to become *excited* about finding a job. Protecting ourselves from disappointment by not trying to find a job means quashing the emotional thrill of looking.

8. Rejecting jobs we don't want: increases self-esteem, although it could trigger guilt.

9. Showing, from time to time, at home and away from the job search, *real* anger. The frustrations of job-hunting are real, and not showing it can cause psychological damage.

How do you break into the hidden job market if it's your first job and you're new to a city?

Never interview someone for a job *until you are sure he has one to offer.*

Interview for information if (a) you can't focus on what you *want,* and (b) you don't know where to look.

If you know what you want and where to look, skip entirely information interviews and start asking for jobs.

Nobody likes to have the bite put on him for a job—especially (which is usually the case) when he doesn't have one. That's why making doors open is so tough.

But everyone with a normal vanity quotient loves to be interviewed for information in *his* field. Do you know anyone who doesn't like to give advice?

And that's what you do when you interview for information. You ask experts about where to look for a job that interests you, latest trends in their field, where the government is spending money, who the leading contractors are, and so on.

Making appointments to pick somebody's brain is a snap. And don't leave any interview without the names of four more key people you can call for similar appointments. Phone them, drop a name or two, and then repeat the process. Before long you'll know where the action is and, without knowing it, become part of the hidden manpower pool.

The hidden manpower pool?

Did you ever find a dentist by flipping through the Yellow Pages?

It's the same with people who hire.

If a banker is someone who lends money to someone who doesn't need it, your typical employer is somebody who (a) only offers a job to somebody who already has one, or (b) to someone who apparently doesn't need one. Employers love to steal talent from competing organizations, or a whiz kid from another department in their own company. They no more rely on their personnel department to fill a key job than they phone the 7,508th person in the Boston phone book and hire him.

When you interview for information you gradually become known by people who count—the kind of executives other decision-makers rely on for help.

"Say, Judson, I'm looking for a young woman with an M.B.A.,

making no more than eighteen thousand a year, to begin work next week, helping me analyze interstate trucking rates." A hundred phone calls begin like this every day. In interviewing for information, guess who Judson thinks of first? Why, that nice young woman who spent an hour asking him intelligent questions about transport problems in the Northeast Corridor. Did she have an M.B.A.? What difference does that make? And isn't her résumé around someplace? Didn't she leave it with him or send a thank-you letter including it?

Vigorously follow this employment strategy and you become "picked up" by men and women whose referral counts. A kind of twentieth-century patronage system. And by being part of the hidden manpower pool, you tap into that great underground stream of jobs that rarely see the light of day.

Finally, ask people how they found their jobs.

Why is it sensible to ask people how they got their jobs?

First, it will confirm everything you read in this book. Second, you can test your own job-finding strategy against people who have made it work. Thirdly, you'll see how wacky the process can be. And people love to talk about how it all happened. "It was the craziest thing, but while I was deep-sea fishing at Christmas Cove, I tangled lines with a man who manages a large wine import business in New York. Well, we were both laughing when . . ."

At cocktail parties I rarely ask people *what* they do. How they found their job is my lead question. The answers are this book.

You mean instead of petitioning for a job it's better to be recruited for it?

Yes, as part of the product of interviewing about jobs in the hidden job market, you become part of the hidden manpower pool—men and women employers want to hire because they know you, know you're available, and know you're effective. You are, in fact, recruited for the job, won away from another firm (which delights your new boss), and you meet your employer on a parity —rather than on a petitionary basis. Moreover, because he wants you, the employer is prepared to pay plenty.

Sure, Mr. New Employer could find another person at half the price (and only half as good). After all, you showed you knew how to sell yourself (not a despised quality in most organizations). And, anyway, people are people. Employers no more pick their dentists, psychiatrists, or realtors from the phone book than you do. So they don't hire, as a rule, the naked and unemployed stranger.

How do you go about finding the hidden job market in your "field"?

Simple.

Let's say, biostatistics is your trade. You work for a small, wealthy, but stagnant firm whose management will never admit you to its ownership. You want to find a firm—the same size—with growth potential where you can own a piece of the company. Because Uncle Sam takes more than he deserves (and you can afford) after the first $50,000 in salary, you know a piece of the stock action is the only way you're going to survive.

So, spend your early mornings, lunch hours, or late afternoons checking out firms you might want to work with and who might need your skill. (Remember, one of your skills is knowing how to find a job.) You stake out the key people in each company, the men and women you would want to work for and from whom you can learn, and ask their advice on how to move up in your field. Always obtain the names of four more key people and companies from each person you interview, and before long you've snowballed your job campaign into fifty interviews and, I bet, four job offers.

What's happened is that you've researched your field, haven't hammerlocked anyone for a job, spread yourself (and later your résumé) around, and just happen to be the man or woman a key person first thinks of when he needs a biostatistician.

Above all, you've established what it is you *want* and asked people's help in finding it.

Are there any drawbacks to interviewing for information?

There are only two reasons to interview for information:

1. "I don't know what I want to do!"

2. "I don't know where to look."

If, however, you *do* know what you want and *where* to look and interview for information primarily to put yourself out front, become visible to potential employers, then you are in big trouble, indeed. People sense that you have *concealed* your agenda. The result is a bogus transaction. And employers become hostile; you are trading on their time and good will for carefully disguised goals and are deservedly shown the door!

How about recontacting people interviewed for information when you know what you want and where to look?
Good idea.

A nice note (and your résumé) a month later to folks who have generously given you "advice" interviews is the way to let the world know you now know that work in commodity investments in Chicago is what you want.

Yes, if these people took a shine to you the first time around, it could be they will phone you about a hidden job.

So, you're saying, it's not what you know but who you know?
Not entirely.

What's truer is knowing what you know, researching the job market (interviewing for information), and finding out who the employers are who need to know you know it!

Finding a good job is an eight-hour-a-day job.

And there is definitely a ceiling on methodology, "techniques," and cunning job-finding strategies. But there's no ceiling on competence, achievement, and the contribution you can make to an organization. You need to advise a lot of people who hire (and who can help you put your assets to work) about what you do best. You are a walking advertisement for yourself.

But surely important people can't take time to see me?
Stand around a typical business at quitting time.
5 P.M.

Suddenly, a horde of the harried salaried classes drop everything and hit that old elevator.

Calling an important person, asking for fifteen minutes of his time, is probably the most exciting and certainly the most flattering event that will happen to him that day. And what else is he doing that's so important? Everyone loves to be asked for advice.

I thrive on it.

Of course, you hear a lot of bushwa along the way. But the nuggets of information you pan from the underground job stream is not fool's gold. Treasure it and act on this information. Moreover, the technique of interviewing for information carries over on the job and makes you a more effective executive.

If you want an interesting job, find it in the hidden job market where favoritism, whimsy, and sheer capriciousness reign. Jobs frequently, as you would expect, are where the money is.

When you "interview for information," seeking out an employer you want to hire, do an inventory on where the new business (i.e., new job opportunities) is. This means asking some probing questions about your interlocutor's competition, watching the paper closely and seeing who's ripping off the system, cataloguing priority problem areas, and discovering *what* organizations are working in what fields.

Job-hunting is organized whimsy. Tracking down jobs is being at the right place, at the right time, with ostensibly the right qualifications.

What are the main reasons it's so difficult to obtain job interviews?

1. People don't want to reject you for a job they don't have.

2. Time spent talking to the unemployed is money.

3. Employers don't want to feel *obligated* to solve your problem.

So be sure, before throwing yourself on the job market, (a) you know what you want, (b) what you can do, (c) how you can help an organization. That way, you won't be "wasting" anyone's time.

Where do I find the information to conduct a job campaign?

Most judgment job-seekers, a lot of them with advanced degrees and highly refined research skills, play dumb when they think about this question. If a bright historian can research the origins of the First Bulgar War, he certainly can research how to break into investment banking. Unfortunately, he *doesn't* think about it because of the anxiety it causes.

Having interviewed a few thousand people who have found marvelous (and not so marvelous) jobs, one of the factors I check on is how the job-seeker bird-dogged the employer in the first place. What follows is a capsule summary of sources, most of which every job-seeker could use:

— libraries (the bigger, the better)
— placement offices (usually have all the standard references)
— trade associations (great for *lists of employers*).
— college placement directories
— company annual reports (the best overall view of an organization)
— Christmas card lists (use your parents' and your own list)
— Dun & Bradstreet Reference Book
— Federal Phone Book (the best single guide to finding a job in the District of Columbia)
— Poor's Register of Directors and Executives
— Congressional Staff Directory (for those with a political penchant)
— all newsletters (try to buy their subscription lists)
— listings in the lobbies of office buildings (Quickly scanning these handy directories is ammunition for the cold-turkey interviewer.)
— alumni listings (the best single source for information interviewing. A few progressive colleges and universities maintain up-to-date, computerized printouts of addresses, names, titles, and phone numbers.)
— MacRae's Bluebook
— Thomas's Register of American Manufacturers
— Moody's Manuals
— all Chambers of Commerce (often have libraries and xerox facilities)
— people mentioned in trade journals (Announcements of promotions, transfers, new accounts are lead-ins for savvy job-seekers who know that business *activity* usually means new job opportunities.)
— trustees (usually know the CEO and can arrange an interview)

— Fitch Corporation Manuals

— bankers (who know what firms are on a line of credit and expanding)

— any passenger you meet on an airplane

— listing of conference participants (an excellent way to approach the top people in a specific field)

— any Rolodex (listing of phone numbers) of someone you interview for information

— all trade newspapers

Three days' intensive researching, xeroxing, and collating should yield hundreds of organizations which deserve your résumé. Remember, the *white* pages of your phone directory are your best source. Take one letter each night, alphabetically; using a ruler and flashlight, read and record the addresses and phone numbers of a variety of organizations, write them up on 3" × 5" cards, phone and find out the name of their presidents, then send out your résumés with notes in your own hand: "I'll be phoning you Monday morning for an appointment." This strategy should double the number of interviews you receive. And remember, the better known, the bigger, and the older the institution, the more likelihood that your résumé will be minuted to the Personnel Department. The smaller, lesser known, newer organizations (which are not likely to have a personnel department) are the least likely to receive *any* résumés.

What specifically do you look for in the trade press?

Well, in addition to picking up the jargon of the industry, checking out the want ads (particularly how employers in this field describe jobs), and developing a feel for *trade trends*, the best strategy is to focus on promotional reassignments and awards.

A nice letter of muted congratulation on your part and a shameless pitch to see the great man or woman could pay off! None of us are thanked, congratulated, or praised *enough*. That includes people professedly *making it*. Recognition is important, particularly recognizing a person you would like to become!

How do you find the right person for an interview?

It's impossible to know exactly. Talk to *anyone but* the Director of Personnel.

Looking for work in designing appliances? You'll want the

Vice-president for Product Development. And suppose there is no such position. Well, try the R&D V.P. Nine out of ten times, people inside an organization will know the key individual to interview.

So asking for advice is the best strategy in finding a job?
Always ask for it.
People give it away free.
To *ask* advice is the most flattering gambit used by the jobless. The idea, of course, is that nearly everyone is part of a job network—they know of "hidden" jobs.
Now, don't go and put the make on everyone you meet. But do interview *everyone* about *where* you can find the job you want.
Interviewing for information takes the heat off those interviewed—they don't have to reject you for a job they don't have.

How do you choose people to interview for information?
By asking people you like who they admire in a field where you might want to work.
My theory, hardly original and not carefully documented, is that we learn by imitating what we admire. Learning by simulation.
So, to be consistent, learning how to function on a job is simply identifying successful people and imitating them. If what you imitate is comfortable to your style, then make it a habit, copycat.
Therefore, when "interviewing for information," stake out men and women of proven success whose style you admire. If you say to yourself, "I could be like that," then be like that.
Soon, people will start imitating you, the highest form of flattery, and won't that be embarrassing!

What about not interviewing for a job but picking out an employer you admire, respect, and can learn from?
Great idea!
Particularly for the young who want leadership. In college I chose *professors, not* courses. In the business of life pick a person you could *become,* and then learn on the job! Best education hard work can buy!
It would be great if everyone in an organization were compe-

tent and good instructors. But out of a hundred people, let's say, in an organization, about ten are likely to be effective and working at peak effectiveness. You have to find and learn from them.

But suppose I like it where I am and just want more responsibility and money?
I think I hear you saying that you like your current job and employer. But you're going broke on your current salary, right? So all the more reason to hustle up other employment and then confront your employer with the sad story of your "not being able to afford Sticky Wicket, Inc." Of course, you tell him, in your gut Sticky Wicket is your kind of firm. Nine times out of ten your boss will waste no time upgrading your job and giving you a healthy raise equal to what you found in the hidden job market.
Because your first job after going to work is finding your *next* job.

How do employers recruit to fill a key job?
How do they do it?
Simple.
They do it the same way you found *your* job. They begin the whole process by *interviewing for information,* not candidates. They make a list of fifty prominent people at the peak of their business, profession, or skill and call them cold. Flattered by being asked for their advice, they give four more leads on where to look. Pretty soon the recruiter has five good candidates (all of whom, if they're not interested, recommend others).
Then the process of winnowing the chaff from the wheat begins. It's a long process, but it's the most important function any organization performs.

What about employment agencies?
Avoid like the plague.
Especially agencies where *you* pay the fee. And don't sign your name to anything—it might mean the agency has an exclusive on your body and you can't cross the street to the competition.
Management consulting firms?
Often—if well known—they can be of real service to a client

firm and can match you against an excellent judgment job. Good, especially for industrial positions.

Career advisory services?

Most of them should be investigated by the FTC. And Ralph Nader should eviscerate them.

In brief, no one is going to find you the job you want. Best not to waste time with agencies prominently advertising their services in the want ads and business sections of your local paper. I know of one "advisory" service which charges $3,500! Well, as H. L. Mencken once said, "No one ever went broke underestimating the intelligence of the American public."

Executive placement services?

Best not to use them unless recommended by a friend with good judgment. OK for $25,000-plus jobs. But like employment agencies, executive placement firms peddle flesh for a profit. Be sure you watch out for your own interests, and don't let anyone slot you into a job until you've carefully investigated it from stem to stern.

Executive-search types, by definition, recruit only people who are doing jobs *now* the headhunters want to fill.

You can waste time, postage, and patience mailing out five hundred résumés to as many headhunters. If you're truly effective on the job, someday they will call you and you won't even need a résumé.

What if a headhunter does call?

Talk to him, dummy.

Compare his job against what you want. One warning: don't let a headhunter blitz you! You could be hustled; it's nice knowing you're *wanted*, all the more reason to review what it is *you want* (where, for whom, and how it connects with your abilities).

Doesn't the U. S. Employment Service now use computers to help professionals find jobs?

It was only a question of time (after we had computerized everything from dating to bomb strikes on Vietnam) before some scientific bureaucrats met in a smokeless room in Chicago and mapped out a way to match job applicants with jobs, using the computer.

Well, fellow Americans, the whistle hasn't been blown on the Personnel Programer—yet. Our Uncle Sam will probably waste another few million on this kind of electronic exorbitancy before the scientific approach to computer personnel placement is blown from here to the Harvard School of Business Administration.

It simply doesn't work.

I've seen employers, in and out of government, who review involuted computer printouts on allegedly available and qualified personnel.

I've never seen or heard of anyone actually contacted and hired on the basis of his background being computerized. And if you don't believe me, do, by all means, register at your local U. S. Employment Service and let Mr. Fortran and Mr. Cobol be of service.

And if they don't find you a job, tell them they've got their heads up their computer.

Why can't computers match people and jobs?

To repeat: finding a job is a whimsical, capricious, irrational, and very human situation. A human being—not a machine—is going to hire you. Computers simply can't be programed to include the hidden requirements of every job. And the good vibes that take place between the job-seeker and the employer are not mechanical exchanges of information.

I've heard that the best way to find a good job is to take the bull by the horns and simply drop in on the head of an organization and ask for a job. Is there any truth in this approach?

That's the cold-turkey contact.

And whoever told you that gave you the best advice on finding a job.

It's the most brazen and best way to find a job. Also the toughest and most discouraging.

How to do it?

Call the president of Sticky Wicket, Inc. Tell him you want a job with his organization. Or send him your résumé direct (avoiding the personnel department). Or drop in on him cold and, two to one, he will see you. And if he really digs you, his operating people are going to think just once about hiring you.

Cold-turkey contacts are direct and uncomplicated. People either say, "No, you can't see Mr. Fourflusher, he's in conference" (everyone you will find in job searching is in conference, at a meeting, or traveling) or, "Yes, will you give me your name, please?"

Not long ago a young man came to see me to "interview for information." He wanted my advice on how to secure a judgment job on Capitol Hill. After talking with him for fifteen minutes, it was clear he needed not so much advice as congratulations. In two weeks' time this hard-nosed job candidate cold-turkeyed eight appointments simply by walking through the office doors of congressmen, senators, and the chairmen of important congressional committees. Within a week of talking to me, he had received three concrete job offers. True, it meant he was "rejected" in about forty offices where he couldn't secure an interview. But by putting his own feelings first, overcoming the defeatism of most job candidates, and hazarding the slings and arrows of outrageous fortune, this young man was a walking advertisement of how to hire yourself an employer.

The president or head of an organization carries weight (or should if he's any good) down through the hierarchy. Seeing him first sets you up favorably with anyone else you see in the company; hiring authorities are predisposed to like you because you sail through a power channel.

Don't cold-turkey personnel directors—their job is to tell you there are no jobs.

Learning the cold-turkey approach is tough; it takes some brass. You'd better be effective. But, by learning the technique, it sets you up for life in making valuable contacts. Hardly anybody likes to sell himself, which is the essence of job-finding. If you cold-turkey a job, good grief, you can do a lot for your organization—because you've shown you can do a lot for yourself.

Any advantages looking for judgment jobs in organizations which are failing?

People get the wrong idea about layoffs and troubled industries. Layoffs yesterday may be today's recruitment opportunities. Organizational tailspins mean problems to be solved.

When you find a job in a failing firm, it's smart to assume responsibility, learning much where mistakes have been made.

Struggling firms need talent and brainpower. This strategy is particularly recommended for those entrepreneurs who like to turn organizations around. Crisis management appeals to entrepreneurs.

Layoffs don't solve problems. Savvy job-seekers know that employers want solutions, and proposing how to solve problems is a key to finding good jobs.

What about taking short-term employment while looking for a full-time job?

Remember in college when you waited on tables, worked in a National Park, or on a construction crew? You earned money and gained experience and met some fine people. So while looking for your judgment job, don't sneeze at taking a "grunt" or stop-loss job. It frees you from money problems while you take your time finding the right job. Better to find a job you want (and take a year doing it), than accept a job you don't want but *must* accept.

Try to find a job with variable hours: hacking, bartending, hotel and restaurant work where you work nights and weekends, liberating you for workdays to pursue your job campaign.

You say, "I have a responsibility to my employer, no matter how mundane the work." Don't be a chump! For stop-gap jobs, employers expect high turnover and plan for it. Besides, if hard times hit *him*, do you think he's going to feel responsible for you?

Is it fair to call back employers and ask for reasons why you didn't land a job?

Most employers won't level; some will, and that kind of constructive feedback is too rare. And it could sharpen your sales pitch at the next job interview. In fact, welcome criticism on your job search. But carefully weigh it too. Some people like to intimidate the unemployed and give them bad advice. Judge the advisers wisely and don't hesitate to stick to your own convictions. That's what I mean by savvy job-finders having a mind of their own.

How do you penetrate the petticoat curtain?

Secretaries are gatekeepers: they hold the keys to the kingdom, namely the time the boss has to see you. Always learn her name; *talk to her*, for Heaven's sake; don't treat her as a *functionary*.

Secretaries manage most organizations, and her opinion of you is as important as her boss's. Finally, secretaries know what's going on inside organizations, who is paid what, who is about to be fired, who has the power, why, where to find other jobs in the organization, and the personality quirks and lovable eccentricities of every decision-maker in the place. When you bag that good job, take her to lunch, for God's sake. Always memorize her *name* and use it—over and over—when phoning in for those follow-up appointments.

What about recontacting firms that have already sent you a reject?
Why not?
Organizations don't keep a 3" × 5" index card on your candidacy. You're looking for a job, not election to the College of Cardinals. Last month, sure, the Personnel Department sent you its form reject. Chances are, this time around, your résumé will surface on a division manager's desk whose budget has just been increased.

And don't hesitate to send résumés to more than one person in large organizations. (Do you sincerely believe your résumé will be read by everyone at XYZ, Inc. who has need to see it? Yes! I'll bet you believe in the Tooth Fairy, too!) Remember, résumés are junk mail; most are shredded. The few effective résumés are at least *read*, if only by a secretary. And, as we now know, secretaries control paper flow, and your résumé could be the first thing the boss reads tomorrow after the *Wall Street Journal.*

What about responding to want ads?
You'll join another hundred people doing the same, so always send a functional résumé. It stands out among the ninety-seven obit résumés and means a 500 per cent better chance of your being interviewed.

Also, study want ads for organizations deserving your résumé. While the job advertised is not your cup of tea, maybe the organization is! In addition, don't hesitate to study *dated* want ads; chances are the job hasn't been filled the first time around, or all the candidates were lacking, or money wasn't found for it three months ago and is today. In all events, want-ad reading is a part of every job-seeker's breakfast routine. And studying *how* an employer *describes* a job assists you in the vocabulary of describing yourself. In a word, appropriate key words and jargon from your line of work written to portray *a* job and use the same words to describe *yourself*. It's scary how *effective* you sound, but it's what employers mean when they say, "Jim, you talk our language! When can you come aboard?"

Why are so many want-ad jobs nothing but dead ends?
Affirmative Action in action.

That is, in order to comply with the new "liberal" ethic coming out of Washington these days, employers widely advertise a job already filled in order to comply with equal opportunity laws. Accordingly, job-seekers (who wage a campaign exclusively through the employment section of the trade and popular press) discover that a profusion of employment advertising wallpapers over plenty of concealed affirmative action discrimination: a fraud, a delusion, the degradation of democracy. Job-seekers should be *furious*.

How can replying to a three-month-old ad find me a job?
Employers don't know what they want; so, like most job-seekers, they fish. And the fish they hook help define what is wanted. Moreover, the politics of filling a job are so involuted, most organizations often blow their credibility with effective job candidates who in the meantime accept other jobs. So back-read the Los Angeles *Times*. Local libraries stock newspapers from all over the nation, and an afternoon of ad reading is a nice way to break the monotony of job-seeking.

Should I respond to blind ads?
Which employers use to conceal identity, taking themselves off the hook; employers needn't respond to a sack full of résumés sent to a box number. And it's often how employers test the labor supply. Advertising with a blind ad is one way that organizations do market research on the labor supply before making important decisions about new plant sites, or whether to relocate the home office. Finally, blind ads cover up a plethora of illegal, unethical, or shaky wheeler-dealer schemes. Religiously following up on blind ads is like kicking over a rock and watching the bugs scurry.

So, for heaven's sake, never waste a cover letter on a blind ad. A functional résumé with a note scrawled on the top in your hand, "Give me a call if we can do business," is sufficient.

Watch out, however. Ten to one, you'll receive a phone call for the "Mgt Exec's job, fine future, great pay!" inviting you to sell aluminum siding in the greater Pittsburgh area.

Does it make any sense to run your own want ad?
I don't know.

To find out, call or write someone who has done it and find out the results. That's a cheap and speedy way to find out if it's worth taking the same route.

Any thoughts on giving employers a deadline?
Why not?

After all, employers frequently ask a decision from you by Labor Day, or a month after graduation, and so forth.

Establish a *deadline*, however, if you *must* make *other* plans in case that job doesn't materialize. For example, if an investment banking firm is delaying making a decision about your employment, and it's either that job or a two-year stint in graduate school in Geneva, let them know you need to know a week before your steamship leaves Newport News. Pressing employers puts pressure on hiring authorities who really want your body. Employers will make calls during vacation to straighten out the personnel department, which is sitting on the paper. And any decision, yes or no, is better than no decision when your time (which is valuable) and your future are at stake.

What about résumé writing services?
Which cost $50 to $250. And every employer senses when a boiler shop has put its impress on you.

A résumé is a personal reflection, a self-portrait. Hiring a stranger to write up your biography guarantees a loss of personality and is a confession of impotence.

So eschew résumé writing services, résumé books, and form résumés. Play with the functional formula to mesh form and content. And never compare yours with other résumés (especially that reprinted in this book!). Try to make your functional résumé at least as "different" as you are from every other job-seeker.

Why haven't you included more kinds of functional résumés in this book?

Most folks clutch when they try to compose an effective functional résumé. And some folks are so anxious they *copy* the goals and skills of other people.

Holy Toledo, that's not why you're reading this book. Your aim is to act on your own convictions, using this functional formula to produce a résumé as distinctive as your thumbprint.

What about follow-up letters?

OK, if you haven't been interviewed.

Bad form, if you *have*. Use the phone, Tiger! Letter writing, like high tea, steamer cruises, and sherry parties, is a declining elegancy. The only letters you need write are thank-you notes. Who says you have no need for your own printed stationery?

How can I be a telephone "tiger"?

On every résumé, scrawl this note: "I will be calling you next week." A telephone follow-up won't let an employer off the hook. Furthermore, the response rate will double.

Using the phone makes the difference.

Why don't you like cover letters?

The worst are tendentious, arch, Victorian. The best are redundant and bland.

Only use a cover letter when you *know* the terms and conditions of a real job. That is, you are writing to an employer about what you know he wants. Otherwise, a mass mailing of hundreds of functional résumés, describing *what you want*, with a note in your own hand at the top of the résumé ("I'll be phoning you Monday A.M. for an appointment"), is the most effective way to raise your interview average. And check with a direct-mail expert about the "results" of your mailing: he will be impressed.

How do you find the money for seeking a new job?

Don't be afraid to invest some money into the operation. We

dun our rich maiden aunts to put us through law school, our friendly Savings & Loan lends us a ransom to restore our parents' brownstone, but we hesitate to go into hock looking for a better-paying job. If you make $16,500 per annum, find a job paying $21,000 and spend $1,100 doing it, who's ahead?

You, because you knew how to put your own feelings first.

Are there circumstances when it's best to quit a job to look for another?

Don't quit your job until you have another one! (Rule #1) If, however, you are a born risk-taker, hold a $13,000 job and are looking for a $15,500 or $17,000 job, chances are good that you'll find it. Quitting and borrowing the two to three thousand dollars to live on during the job search and finding the job you want, are cost-effective. Actually, the return on your investment, by simply staking your energy and directing it toward a good job, more than justifies the risk *if you know what you want*.

Indulge thyself!

What do you mean by self-indulgence?

Spend money on yourself. You'll feel better and interview better too. Take cabs to interviews, buy clothes, go into debt to find the job you really want. People go into debt in order to buy an education, take a vacation, or do something they enjoy. Finding a good job is fun! Enjoy! If you find a couple of thousand to invest in job-searching, don't be stingy.

If you think cheap, you are poor! Employers are impressed with interviewees who have a touch of class in their appearance and approach to life. Think prosperous. Spend on thyself. Only one out of a hundred will, and that makes you stand out!

And if you can't stand going into debt, then start saving: accumulating *capital* for your job search.

Pay yourself first!

What is paying yourself first?

The hardest thing to do is accumulate capital. One way is to regularly—once a month—write a check *to yourself*. The check may be for savings, insurance, stock, whatever will cause an *in-*

crease in capital. Pay yourself before paying the butcher, baker, or candlestick maker. This is your capital.

What remains (after paying your bills) is your "walking around money," and that's surely less than you want, but is the price you pay—the terms and conditions you must expect—if you are to find the *capital base* for your own business, early retirement, expensive job search.

Sure, finding money to find *the* job is a problem and an opportunity. The saving habit once acquired, however, *reduces* the anxiety factor (which paralyzes free behavior) and gradually makes the *means* available to do what you want.

So pay yourself *first*—every payday: another example of putting yourself first.

What about jobs in the human-service professions?

For spirited job-seekers, those who want to combine the best of both worlds—the universe of alternative employment *and* straight employment—my advice is to seek out contract or consultant work in the social-action sphere.

You must demonstrate qualities of flexibility, cross-cultural sensitivity, working often in a foreign language, and performing your job on an advisory level.

These qualities recommend you as a consultant to social programs which need (from time to time) specific taskwork or information. As a consultant (or under contract) for a specific task, you *do* the job.

The point is, you are paid well—there is every reason to demand $100 to $200 per day for your services, which is cheap if what you offer is unavailable and hard to obtain.

To be a consultant you need a specialty. You generally gain this on your *first* job. Then you market yourself as a consultant on an independent basis or with a company selling "social action" services.

Your job could be one of many: evaluating program impact, designing curricula, manpower development, advising managers of ongoing programs, upgrading administrative skills—almost anything.

Now, you will hear a lot of talk about bad consultants—"experts" who know how to rip off the system and leave nothing of value in return. If you know what you're about and sincerely care about the people you work for, you cannot help but be of help. The incompetents who crowd this field make you look good.

The point is, you can throw yourself into a tough contract or consultant job—particularly in community action—and burn yourself out. Then it's time to take your well-deserved earnings and vamoose. You've done a good job and you deserve a long rest. Give yourself a couple of months to get back in the saddle, find yourself another consultant's job, and repeat the process *ad infinitum.* That's why what you learn here and in looking for a job (your skill, remember, is finding a good job and learning from it) can be used repeatedly.

But everybody tells me I should have a "career," a specialty, a job with security?

There is no such thing as a permanent job—except a job with tenure. And if *that's* the kind of life you want, you shouldn't be reading this book.

What do the following organizations have in common?
— The Bureau of Ships
— The Sante Fe Railroad
— The U. S. Civil Service Commission
— The U. S. Supreme Court
Answer:
Everyone who works in any of the above organizations has tenure. Which is to say, they are, except in a vegetarian sense, dead. Whether they are judges, Pullman conductors, or Alfred North Whitehead Professors of Middle English Poetry, they spent a large part of their lives earning the right to a permanent job.

They cannot be fired for incompetence, lechery, poor health, or any other compelling reason.

And who suffers?

The public, that's who. You and me.

But there isn't any such thing as a permanent job. And a certain amount of job insecurity is positively bracing. Those who work in permanent jobs are punishing themselves—even more than the public they pretend to serve.

Insecurity?

A little of it makes life worth living. Its synonym is freedom (which carries a lot of responsibility).

And remember, hiring authorities are insecure too. Make them less so, help solve their problems, and you will win job offers galore.

What you offer the employer (and not what a great guy/gal you are) is what makes the difference.

Never expect a job to provide you security—even Civil Service employment. The government is always "reorganizing" and eliminating people.

The man who does not equate his job with security is free to put his job on the line, and independence of thought is what employers need most.

Any special hints on how to cope with frustration during the job search?

The toughest talent of all, on the job or off, is patience. Particularly in the proposal development approach, patience is virtue. Like a child waiting for Christmas in July, many job-seekers can't wait out their luck. The anxiety of joblessness causes them to accept the first job offer rather than patiently building a job campaign aimed at the job they want. Probably these men and women are "disqualified" for judgment jobs, because judgment jobs require people with unusual capacities to cope with frustration. And job-hunting is frustrating.

What's the proposal development approach to finding a good job?

Once upon a time, in the great long ago, this approach was how people found jobs. With the erosion of the work ethic, the growth in the welfare state, and the decline in initiative, the whole approach seems positively revolutionary.

Example: Where I work we have a street-level office with plenty of windows and lots of people traffic. One day, as usual, a young street dude walked into our offices, approached me, and said, "Hey, man, how about a job?" Three minutes later he was back on the street and I was back at my desk.

A few minutes later another young man came through our doors. He was dressed in working clothes and carried window-washing equipment, a bucket, and soap powder. Standing before me and scanning our deplorably filthy windows, he announced that he would wash every window in the place, inside and out, for fifty cents a pane. "Make it forty cents and you have a deal," I said. We negotiated a forty-five-cent rate, and three hours later he walked out of the place with a check for forty-five dollars and eighty cents . . . and our thanks.

Later in the day—at closing time—I was walking up the street and saw the same young man hard at work washing a merchant's show window. "Hey, man," I yelled, "how much did you make today?"

"Ninety-eight dollars and seventy-five cents," he yelled back. "How much did you make?"

Gulp.

What if the job I want doesn't exist?

Or no longer exists. Well, you can't know until you try to look for it. And if you can't find it and sense that the job is needed and that someone will pay for it, "invent" the job and sell it. Again, the proposal development approach.

— Two women with interior-decorating experience conceived and marketed a wallpapering business which is flourishing.

— A computer analyst structured the commuter traffic to three adjacent companies and designed a van-busing scheme which brought 90 per cent of these companies' employees to work without using personal automobiles.

— A woman with a green thumb began a chain of greenhouses and is selling plants galore through six supermarket outlets.

— An ex-clergyman established a bereavement service for the relatives of terminal cancer patients.

Most ideas fail. Some succeed. A lot depends on funding, management, and luck. But that's the free-enterprise ethic. No "system" can compete with it, since ideas which work satisfy human needs. So, if you've got an idea rolling around in your brainpan, the crazier the better, try writing it up and selling it. What can you lose? Moreover, it's a cinch seeing the most important people in an organization if you have an idea that can help them solve a *problem.* And while your idea may be tested and found wanting, chances are these decision-makers will think of you first when they want to fill a hidden job. But you need a "base" to sell concepts.

What do you mean, Everyone needs a "base" to make the proposal development approach work?
— Your husband's salary is a base.
— A small inheritance is a base.
— A second mortgage on your house is a base.
— Moonlighting on a grunt job is a base.
— A grant from the Rockefeller Foundation is a base.

Any guaranteed income, whether earned, borrowed, or otherwise, is what you need while you peddle an idea. It takes time— often years. Researching a small business venture, investigating an exposé of the CIA, developing a grant from a foundation, earning a scholarship, finding seed money—all these require organization skills, verbal and writing ability, a persuasive knack, lots of patience, and plenty of conviction.

The proposal development approach to finding what you want is the last refuge for entrepreneurs. The Department of the Interior should declare entrepreneurs an endangered species along with the bald eagle, which they resemble.

Any examples?
— An auto claims adjuster used his job to recommend an across-the-board study of a "no fault" claims payment strategy. The President liked the idea and appointed him Project Director. This man now is the head of his own division.
— An instructor at a college for women proposed an international year-abroad program. Now a dean of the University, his programs are copied nationwide.
— A Senate investigator, obsessed with human rights, created her own job by selling a key committee on the contemporary importance of this issue for which a "dream" job of her own creation was established.

Look around and interview successful people. Simulate. Adopting the mental outlook of the successful means taking responsibility for your own life. So what if your idea isn't "bought"? Most ideas *don't* work; the challenge is in habituating yourself to being open to new ideas, especially your own.

So dream jobs do exist, but you must make them come true on the job?

Or "sell" an idea—e.g., the proposal development approach—to fill the job you want.

The point is, job-finders need a base: a job. After you are on a payroll, opportunities—given the right boss, organization, and your own talent and motivation—surface. That's when people who feel good about themselves, folks who work for the pleasure it gives, design a future for themselves at XYZ, Inc. Detecting a real need at the firm, the intelligent person proposes how to fill that need. The trick is in meshing what needs to be done with what you *want* to do. Not easy, and the quality needed is good judgment.

Interview people who have jobs you want, "dream jobs." As sure as every monkey hangs by his own tail, a dream job is the product of a *single* person's initiative.

What about people looking for jobs; are they good contacts for finding good jobs?

Career counselors and placement types, please note.

Working with groups of unemployed people, job co-ops or job clubs, is the most effective method of helping people to find jobs fast. Working together with twenty other unemployed people is like hiring nineteen pairs of eyes to find jobs you want. Job co-op members swap résumés, keep the interests of their fellow job-seekers at heart, and exchange information on where jobs are, who is hiring, for how much, starting when. That's why I applaud certain women's groups who provide job-finding, backstopping services. College alumni services should emulate them for mid-career graduates suddenly out of work and out on the sidewalk. And professional associations should form job co-ops to assist members in finding jobs. The trade-off for the unemployed is tremendous. Why? Job-hunting is a lonely business and job clubs are "unoccupational" therapy for people who need the encouragement of seeing others find jobs. And, once on the job, graduates from these clubs are great sources of job leads.

If you are a member of an organization which runs a placement office, barge in, raise hell, and *insist* that its director inaugurate a job co-op. And you might be just the person to start it!

How would you rate the various strategies for finding a judgment job?

Cold-turkey interview of important *strangers* in key jobs.	A—
Interviewing important friends in key jobs.	B—
Functional résumés, widely and indiscriminately mailed within your "field," with a telephone follow-up.	A—
Obit résumés with standard cover letter, selectively mailed.	D
Completing application blanks and interviewing personnel types.	F
Using personnel agencies, executive search firms, and career counselors.	F
Acquiring another advanced degree and interviewing through the college placement office.	C
Interviewing for information in hopes that someone will like my looks and offer me a job.	F
Talking about my job campaign widely and collecting names of people to see.	B
Hunkering down at a grunt job, stopping the job search, and waiting for prosperity to return.	F
Joining a job club like "Forty Plus."	B+
Selling ideas and proposals.	A
Registering at the U. S. Employment Service.	F
Mounting a "blitz" letter campaign to company presidents.	A
Taking a "stop-loss" job and continuing my judgment-job search.	A

Any last tips on how to conduct the job campaign?

Do the most disagreeable task first thing in the morning. If that's mailing your alimony check, do it; if it's calling back on a job you wanted and are certain not to get, do it; if it's touching base with twenty employers who received résumés from you last week, do it.

Everything *else* you do the rest of the day will seem easy; you'll feel far better about yourself. But avoiding painful and necessary responsibilities leads to a decline in self-esteem and to ineffectiveness. And remember, appearing *effective* is the one condition you must satisfy in looking for a judgment job.

FIVE

Interviewing the
Interviewer

At this stage, you no longer investigate job leads and follow up on advice generated through interviewing for information. Now you're focusing on two or three *real* objectives. That's because you are sure of what you want and where to look. Now you want to qualify for a real job.

What do you mean by a "real" job?

A real job has a starting date, a salary range, definite purpose(s), specific people the hired candidate reports to and manages. Above all, there is a real commitment on the part of the employer to hire.

Genuine commitment is important. Many employers, like job applicants, can't make up their minds. They don't know what they want. They have a problem, but can't define it and have trouble delineating the kind of person who *can* solve it.

You mean, employers are as confused as job applicants?

Often.

Frequently they play games with job applicants. A confused employer, often without knowing it, schedules a series of interviews with a variety of people to educate himself on what he wants. The process is not entirely invalid. By seeing a swatch of people, the employer gradually defines a set of personal and job criteria he needs to have satisfied; he tests the manpower pool to discover if

Mr. or Ms. Right really exists; he often accidentally falls upon *the* person with the right set of characteristics.

All of this is time-consuming and frustrating for job applicants. But what employers are really doing is *interviewing for information.* That is, they are trying to decide whether a job is worth filling (or creating) by comparing it against the available manpower.

But don't employers have a responsibility to know what they want?

Well, it would save them a lot of money if they did.

Harvard University spent a million and a half dollars looking for their last president, and then found him among their own alumni.

And clients pay headhunters plenty of money to help them fill jobs.

Employers are often confused. Like job applicants, they really don't know what they *want.* A typical employer needs help, and a savvy job applicant helps the employer *think through* a job. This is part of what I mean by "hiring yourself an employer." And it means appealing to an employer's hidden agenda.

I don't understand what you mean by "hidden agenda."

A hidden agenda is what an employer hides from himself when looking for a person to fill a job. Employers won't admit it, but they *are* human. Thus, the *personal* factor, how you survive an interview as a human being, is as important as the qualifications and strengths you bring to a job.

I remember a few years back finding five candidates who fitted an employer's established needs to a T. All my candidates were rejected.

"Too old."

All five were between the ages of forty and fifty.

Now, it seems Mr. Employer was thirty-nine—a fact I should have checked out. And it's a rare man or woman who employs people older than themselves for positions of major responsibility. This is what I mean by a job's hidden agenda, which employers scarcely admit to themselves—much less to the public.

I'm no different.

I can no more be objective about people than most reporters can be objective about the news. One should try, of course, but the plain facts are that *liking* a job applicant is extraordinarily important. For the record, here are some of my prejudices about people. I generally won't hire:

— divorced men—if they can't manage their home life, what can they do for my organization?
— men with paunches and pates
— Black Power rhetoricians
— White Liberals with cheek tics
— bearded men (are they hiding weak chins?) . . . and so on, and so on

Now, my point is not to anger you because you're divorced or are balding or have a spare tire building about your middle. Plenty of divorced folks know how to face up to tough decisions, and what we *look like* has nothing to do with what we can do. It simply means that you must overcome this initial bias in order to survive an interview with me. (With another interviewer, it's an entirely different "hidden agenda." Where I work there's one fellow who won't hire you unless you *are* divorced.) In looking for any kind of job, how you fit *a priori* assumptions makes (or breaks) you in a job interview. Now, of course, hidden agendas are irrational, *crazy*.

But face it: hidden agendas are rarely addressed by employers— precisely because they *are* hidden. My only point is, as a job-seeker, your strongest suit is to know *your agendas*.

Isn't an employer's hidden agenda a formula to hire someone like himself?
Often.

Savvy employers, however, *should* hire personal, temperamental, and professional opposites—men and women who supplement their weaknesses rather than complement their strengths. Above all, employers should hire competent strangers, rather than products of the old boy/old girl network.

The mark of a first-rate executive is the quality of his staff. If they are all, in certain respects, smarter than the boss, it's a mark of genius. Strong people surround themselves with a highly competent and disparate staff.

First-rate people hire first-rate people. Second-rate people hire third-rate people.

Yes, but plenty of employers want to hire second-rate people so that they look good!

And why work for them? That's what's meant by the aphorism: "First-rate people hire first-rate people, second-rate people hire third-rate people." All the more reason to be *discriminating* in choosing an employer.

Everything you say is true about the hidden job market, but what about the top jobs in the country?

In my work, which is finding key people for a variety of organizations, the hardest jobs to fill are the most responsible and best-paying. Smart employers still recruit from the hidden manpower pool—that is, people not looking for a job but whose on-the-job reputations have spread throughout their fields. Many competent people I know often receive a covert job offer twice a year. And it's a nice feeling when the phone rings with a great job offer. So, by all means, interview in the hidden job market, but remember, the best employers with the best jobs are doing some digging on *you*. Thus, if you do an outstanding job—wherever you work, at whatever level—the job offers could be coming at you in droves.

What, exactly, does an employer learn in an interview?

Well, not much . . . and a great deal.

Sure, he can tell whether you're alert, intelligent, enthusiastic, young, old, *et al.*

But what an employer really learns is whether he likes you, whether the signals are right, whether the *human* factors are working for both of you.

Psychologists know you don't learn much about another human being in a half-hour interview.

But you learn one important thing: whether you like each other. And liking those you work with is pretty central to the hiring process.

Remember during job interviews that an organization is the sum of human beings who make it up. Two hours inside and you know whether people working there are a group you want to work with for eight or more hours a day.

So interview your employer. If the chemistry's good, chances are the job is for you. But if the vibes are bad, chalk up those interviews to experience—let it help refine what you want in an employer you do hire.

During these hopeless interviews, switch your job pitch to an "information interview." Eventually, you and an employer will light some fires. But remember, you can sometimes wade through fifty interviews before job lightning strikes.

So the climate of the interview situation is important?

The great factors in the interview are mood and atmosphere. You won't survive an interview if your interviewer:
— just fought with his spouse on the phone
— has five or more telephone interruptions
— hasn't lunched yet and it's 3 p.m.
— has seen five job applicants that day
— has four important decisions to make while he talks to you
    What can you do?

Tell your interviewer that it's a bad day for him, and you'd be happy to come back at a less hectic time for another appointment.

Will employers interview me on the phone?

Don't let them!

Your job is to bag a face-to-face interview. Nobody is going to hire you—sight unseen—on the phone. But employers are "prequalifying" you.

Switch out the interviewer and press to see him *personally*. Tough with busy employers; but if interviewed by phone *without* a follow-up interview, no business will be transacted.

What do you wear to a job interview?

Knowing what you want to do is knowing what to wear.

Another reason to interview for information is observing the sartorial splendor of the working classes. This ranges in some places, like Cambridge, from proletarian drag to Beverly Hills décolleté.

An on-campus recruiter once hired a student dressed in a chemi-

cally soiled apron and another in his jogging pants. Both sprinted
direct from lab and track to keep the interview!

Why not wing it and wear what you *want*? If your uniform fits
the environment, maybe you've found a home. If it doesn't, why
would you want to work there? Otherwise, the conventional wisdom holds: conservative dress, shiny shoes, neat appearance,
styled hairdo, striped tie, snappy pantsuit. *But knowing what you
want to do is how you know what to wear.*

Any special hints on how to start the interview?

The weather outside is still the best conversation starter,
whether interviewing for a job, picking up girls, or sizing up a
company president for a takeover bid.

Name-dropping is OK, if that's how you bagged the interview. I
tend to back off interviewees with a snappy opening gag, usually
as canned as my laughter.

Is there any way I can overcome feeling awkward in an interview?

The reason you feel ill at ease is that you're trying to *please*
someone besides yourself. You are not putting your own feelings
first. And the result is an uptight, false, and unproductive exchange.

Employers are no different. I've seen them change from genial,
put-together individuals into positive Manchurian mandarins. Or,
conversely, I've seen job applicants reduce normally tough and
productive employers to gibbering eunuchs.

What accounts for this?

Each party to the interview starts playing a role completely outside his real character. The job applicant—deferential, petitionary,
hat in hand; the employer—gruff, no-nonsense, business-is-*my*-
business attitude.

But you can block out this kind of interview situation by simply
being yourself, asking *unexpected* questions, interviewing your interviewer (asking him about *his* job)—in a word, treating your employer as an *equal*. And if he doesn't respond, why work for him
anyway? He's flunked the interview—*with you.*

Why do I feel so tense and unrelaxed in an interview?

You don't feel "free." You are trying to accommodate someone other than yourself. And whenever you consciously try to *please* someone you cause displeasure. The cliché in job interviewing is, "Be yourself." That's impossible to do if you think you are in someone else's *control*.

So in a job interview start *asking* the questions, evaluate the interviewer, let him/her tell a story. Feeling subordinate, deferential, grateful (for what, for God's sake!), is the way to qualify for dumb jobs. A practical residual of "interviewing for information" is learning "how to be yourself" while interviewing. That's warming up for the main event.

So the object of interviewing the interviewer is to control the interview?

Praise Allah and all his prophets, no!

Nobody controls an interview. You cannot turn people *on* nor *off*. People turn themselves *on* or *off*. All the more reason to listen to your *own* feelings when you answer a question. That's what's meant by the cliché, "Be yourself."

You are not responsible for other people's *reactions* to you any more than they are responsible for *your reactions* to them. That's why people trained to be sensitive to other people's feelings often seem so "unreal" and Pollyanna-ish. Don't crawfish while interviewing. What's wanted is a "business transaction," a useful exchange of views, not a policy of appeasement.

Yes, but I feel frightened and uptight when the tough questioning begins!

Intimidated.

Here's a sample of questions which cause lockjaw among job candidates I've interviewed:

1. "By the way, Mr./Ms./ ————, what are your *hard* skills?"
2. "How come you spent two months last summer rebuilding your father-in-law's summer cabin?"
3. "Why look for a job with us? We laid off ten people last month."
4. "But working on your Ph.D. for six years surely has caused you to lose touch with the job market?"

No interviewer can intimidate you unless you let yourself be *intimidated*. No woman ever castrated a man; men do this to them-

118   GO HIRE YOURSELF AN EMPLOYER

selves. So what an interviewer learns (from questions like the above) is whether a job applicant is easily intimidated, defensive, insecure, or lacking confidence. And just between you and me, who needs anyone in a judgment job who is easily frightened, can't cope with authority, can't handle constructive criticism, is defensive and lacks confidence!

So maybe your problem in interviewing is caused by some major weaknesses you must address before you enter the world of work— a need to please, an unhappy predilection for procrastination, an unhealthy desire to "fail."

Mock interviewing with friends and colleagues often reveals these manifestations. Like all mistakes, you can learn from them and improve your face-to-face negotiations if you, *one more time*, *want to!*

What happens when interviewers say I'm too young for a job?
— Ask your interviewer how old he/she was when he/she obtained his/her first job.
— Dress up in age: style your hair, wear tasteful business apparel, adopt a restrained but not undemonstrative demeanor, all of which adds five years to your chronological age.
— *Agree* with an interviewer that "the older you get, the better."
— Laugh slyly and indicate that your youth is why you are so successful with older men/women!
— Finally, don't act like a "student intern." While it's true you'll learn on the job, it's truer that you'll get the job because you show you can *do* something.

How do I evade embarrassing questions about my background in an interview?
Questions about your recent divorce, for example; or your five jobs in the past three years; or why you quit your last job?
Evading questions of a sensitive nature (Why is it that so-called delicate matters are so indelicate?) is an invitation to a beheading. Your cover-up (as if recent American history wasn't an example) is a greater "crime" than what's concealed: it causes interviewers to *suspect* much worse.
At the same time, there are questions which are downright rude

and unnecessary. The best way to handle this kind of knuckle ball is to *ask* a question: "Mr. Employer, can you tell me why that question is important?" That puts the ball back in his court. And chances are the question *is* important. I'm required as an employer to ask tough, indelicate questions. But I admire job candidates who make me give *reasons* for them.

So don't be *disagreeable* when you stonewall an employer. He is entitled to ask questions; in fact, it's *his* job. By finding out the reasons, too, you find out more about an employer's hidden agenda, and that information is golden.

What about future-oriented questions?
You mean like:
"Do you intend to go back to law school, marry, have children, follow your spouse to his next assignment, resume your artistic career, take a year off to travel in the Orient, become self-employed . . . ?"
Nobody can read the future. Don't let employers mousetrap you into thinking about future plans which don't include XYZ, Inc. And that's *not lying*. We don't know, in fact, what *may* happen; yes, we may marry, inherit money, start our own business. Don't read tea leaves in a job interview.

So answer this kind of question honestly. "I don't know. Obviously what I want to happen I've spelled out in my job objectives, and that's why I'm here talking to you. And so long as I'm effective and willing, you can count on me."

And that *is* the truth. Plenty of job-finders, however, suffer from hoof-and-mouth disease. As soon as a soothsaying interviewer probes the future, our self-destructive job candidate starts babbling like a running brook. Who is to say you won't "turn on" to Sticky Wicket and retire as its Exec. V.P. in thirty years!

Aren't most questions and answers in interviews nonverbal?
The silent language. Yes, indeed.
Raising your eyebrows, looking at your watch, staring distract-edly in the middle distance, the light in your eyes, the twitch in your left earlobe—these often convey more than words. In all events, a few mock interviews with friends constructively feed back mannerisms which could put employers off their feed. I re-

member once nearly (literally) blowing a job offer by blowing smoke (albeit unintentionally) in the interviewer's face. The poor chap, an habitual allergenic, nearly quashed the deal then and there.

Everyone knows the vocabulary of the silent language. Focus on what *you* do that subtracts from an otherwise excellent impression.

What about stress interviewers?

Professional bullies; it's why they are in the interviewing business. Ten to one, they were bullied on the playground and are paying society back. But bullies they are, nonetheless.

If someone deliberately:

— stands up in an interview and walks *around you, stand up* and follow him!

— plays games on the phone (while you wait biting your nails), open your briefcase and read *Rolling Stone*.

— offers you a cigarette (there is no ashtray), excuse yourself, stand up, walk out and fetch one from the anteroom.

— interviews you *across* the desk, stand up, pick up your chair, and place it *beside* his desk.

To repeat: people who *win* through intimidation are slobs, losers, power trippers. Game-players never win with unintimidatable people—i.e., people who know who they are, what they want, and what they can do. If you sense plenty of game-playing in an interview, where how "you play the boss" is more important than what you *do*, make fast tracks. The folks who people this place are *miserable*; they feel that power is *outside* themselves and existence itself simply a *reflection* of their organizational identity. Another example of the frightful leading the frightened.

What's the toughest question you ever asked in an interview?

Occasionally (usually the morning after hanging it up) I'll karate-chop an otherwise appealing job candidate with a question like, "By the way, what makes *you* think *you're* so *important?*"

Now, of course, you *are* important! But defenses crumble under the weight of someone who asks why you think you're so good. And people who love the pits quickly agree they are unimportant, ineffective, unemployable.

All the more reason in your job search to keep your eye on the bouncing ball. "Put down" questions are asked to find out if people can make you put yourself down.

How can people become less self-defeating in job interviews?

By building on what's *real* in themselves: reciting accomplishments with *conviction* (not humbly), being demonstratively agreeable (never appeasing), *strong-willed* (not willful), conscious of self-interests (not dumbly accommodating), and being truly open and free with an interviewer (never disagreeable and hostile).

Humble people usually have a great deal to be humble about. People who appease back off from confrontational situations and solve problems by eliminating them. Willful people are spiteful and self-destructive. And hostile folk communicate self-hatred and are unemployable (except maybe as prison guards, *Mafioso* hitmen, or art critics).

Are some questions unlawfully asked in an interview?

It's against the law to ask your age, race, sex, ethnic origin, or your arrest record.

Of course, most of these questions are obviously answered nonverbally in an interview. So, as usual, the law's an ass. And employers routinely run police checks on applicants, so while you needn't admit a police record, you can't cover it up either.

In all events, it's the worst kind of job-hunting strategy to take umbrage if someone asks your age, marital status, number of dependents, and so forth. Employers are trying to come to grips with whether your personal condition is appropriate to the job. No one is trying to discriminate *against* anybody! But employers are being discriminating; there's a big difference, and it's what interviewers are paid to do.

How about note-taking during an interview?

That's OK for student interns, Gallup pollsters, and gumshoes, but bad form for job-seekers. Keeping a handy pocket-sized notebook to jot down addresses and phone numbers is useful, but never carry a steno pad to a job interview.

How do you identify the decision-makers inside an organization?

Whether interviewing for information or interviewing for a job, make a habit of finding out who the effective people are. In any firm or department composed of one hundred people or less, you can be sure that no more than seven people are important enough to interview. Those are the people you want to see; power doesn't always match titles or a box on the organization chart. And power goes *up* (as well as down) the vertical chain of command. Trust the political judgment of people *inside* an organization to reveal the key players.

What happens when you've found a hidden job you really want and are about to interview the person who can make the offer?

Well, what you *don't* do is:

— act casual and indifferent

— gush enthusiasm and become accommodating

— sit back and let the interviewer show his/her hand, answering every question even when you don't know the answers

The best strategy is to tell him what you want, describe what he needs, show the identity of objectives and ask for the job. This means saying "I don't know" when you don't know, asking him *his* opinion, and—above all—stressing that you *want* the job. Surprise: many otherwise qualified candidates for judgment jobs *never ask* for *the* job. Remember, good jobs go to those who are *able and willing.*

You mean honesty is the best policy?

Exactly.

Next to courage, honesty is the most precious virtue. Your honesty might be the most memorable part of any successful job interview and what wins you the job.

And even if you don't get the job, an employer is likely to remember you. Because of your candor, you'll be the first to hear about another opening at the XYZ organization. Honesty will, as Mark Twain once said, "please most people and astonish everyone."

But won't candor tick most employers off?

Some.

So what. . . ?

If you know who you are, what you can do, and the kind of contribution you want to make to an employer, you shouldn't feel modest about letting your interviewer know it. But if you try to fulfill the expectations of your interviewer, if you try to *please* him, the consequence is displeasure, sure as shootin'!

So be honest in your job campaign.

Honesty gives you an instant name and organizational visibility faster than anything else. In an interview, honesty can be charming and memorable, and your job is to make an impression—even if you don't get the job. (Remember, the guy who remembers you is going to call about a job you *do* fit.)

So don't bluff. . .

It's easily spotted by sharp employers. Bluffing is a favorite ploy of PR men, commission salesmen, hucksters, and Madison Avenue gasbags, and increasingly among government executives.

Bluffing is especially obnoxious in the young. (Intergenerational conflict is no joke. Most employers over forty envy the young because they *are* young.) To add bluff to your natural—and desirable —enthusiasm, is to rub out chances of finding a good job.

Bluff is not related to gumption—the tough art of hiring yourself an employer. Gumption means you don't give up, no matter how discouraging your job prospects. Gumption is the main asset of a job-seeker who is new to a strange city, unacquainted, but *not* powerless in the face of adversity.

Bluffers seem queerly serene when jobless. They know their only chance of landing a job is to fool an employer. Underneath the polish and glitter, however, they lack self-confidence. Because bluffers don't know who they are or what they want or what they can do.

Isn't there something to be said for submitting to an employer's wishes?

That's right; there's a lot to be said for "submissiveness" training! We should *train* people to be subordinates! *Some* employers know what they want. So, if you sense real authority and competence in your employer, *submit!* That way you learn on the job.

—I can improve my tennis game if I *submit* to instruction by an expert.

— I'll save on taxes if I *submit* to advice from my C.P.A.
— I can become a better headhunter if I watch a pro in action.
— I can become a better writer if I *submit* to criticism.

Knowing when to submit (another test of your good judgment), *yielding* to superior knowledge, experience, intelligence, being *dominated* by another's ability, is a thrilling on-the-job experience. Many never taste its delight because they sense they are losing "control." No dice! *Gladly* submitting to expert leadership is a tribute to your own good judgment. And whether it's team sports, investing money, or being managed on the job, it's an exercise in subordination.

Any special "Do's" and "Don'ts" while interviewing?

If you're a woman, *do* extend your hand and shake upon meeting your interviewer (male or female). Men like me still feel awkward about the protocol, so take the initiative!

Shake hands *firmly*; no limpy, *sensitive* handclasps—this *is* a job interview.

Watch for an indication of where to sit and be seated *after* the interviewer.

Smoke only if your interviewer does, or after asking permission, and never chew gum, tobacco, or your nails.

Eye contact is desirable but can be too much of a good thing. Fixing your interlocutor under an intense stare will earn you a brief interview, indeed.

Try "listening to your own feelings" while interviewing; this is how to appear "real" in an interview and avoid seeming too bland or accommodating.

Say, "Am I giving you the information you want?" if you notice the interviewer's eyes glazing. Perhaps he needs help in asking the questions.

Say, "Can you tell me, Mr. (Mrs., Ms.) ———— why that question is important?" if it sounds irrelevant, unprincipled, or unimportant. You have a *right* to know *why* a question is asked.

Always address interviewers by their title: Ms., Mr., Dr., Colonel. If an interviewer, however, asks you to use his *first* name, don't back off, do so and ask him to do the same.

The further west you drift in North America, the more likely you are to swap first names. By the time you reach L.A., you're using nicknames!

Avoid a laid-back, play-it-cool, "no sweat" psychology—this is the mark of bluffers and con men.

Don't trash your background or put down previous employers, colleagues, movements, schools, or experiences.

Admit mistakes; admitting an error of judgment ("making a mistake") and learning from it is qualifying for judgment jobs—how are we to change and grow if we don't make mistakes?

What are some questions I should ask a potential employer? I mean, How do you "interview the interviewer"?

Job interviews are not scientific (no matter what mumbo-jumbo schools of personnel administration say).

Interviews are simply two people sizing each other up. That's why so much business goes on at cocktail parties, lunches, and even in locker rooms. The more informal both parties to an interview are, the better each judges the other.

Accordingly, conduct interviews with *your* employer on a *parity* basis. Remember, although the organization for which you work pays you, you give it your life! Time enough—on the job—to sort out your standing in the organization (who you rank and to whom you defer).

For openers, here are ten questions I would ask my next employer:

1. Why is it, exactly, you want somebody for this job?
2. Who is my boss and who does he report to?
3. Why don't you promote somebody within your organization?
4. The job sounds interesting, but can you afford me?
5. Can you draw me a table of organization? Where do I fit?
6. I like coming to work late and working late—any problem?
7. How many people did this job for your organization within the last five years? Can I talk to any of them?
8. With whom do I relate on the job? Can I talk with them?
9. You've been with this organization for five years. What have you liked *most* and *least* about it?
10. How much money can I spend? How many people do I supervise? When would I start?

Are there any questions I'm certain to be asked by an employer?

No, but once you've passed through five to ten real job interviews, a pattern of questions will establish itself. And this kind of practice is invaluable, since you've honed your answers to a fine gleam by the twentieth interview. Your problem now is glibness (appearing too confident and knowing all the answers). Still, for the record, let me list twenty-five questions most often asked of job applicants:

1. What was your rank in your college graduating class?

2. What makes you think you're qualified to work for this company?

3. What have you been doing since you left your last job?

4. What have you read recently?

5. Tell me why you were fired from your last job?

6. Do you like working with figures more than words?

7. Why did you major in canoe paddling at North Dakota State?

8. Why don't you go back to graduate school? (Why did you go to grad school?)

9. What is it you really want?

10. Draw me a table of organization where you last worked and tell me where you fit.

11. How many people did you supervise on your last job?

12. By the way, what are your salary requirements?

13. Name three people in public life you admire most.

14. I'm going to describe four kinds of jobs. Which would you want?

15. How much money did you ever account for?

16. How many people have you fired, and how did you do it?

17. Show me some samples of your writing.

18. Did you ever put your job on the line for something you believed in?

19. What men and women influenced your life most and why?

20. What do you want from a job: money, power, relevance, etc.?

21. Describe several problems you've had in your occupational life and how you've solved them.

22. What do you mean by "social problem-solving," "urban planning," "community-development" techniques, "working out-reach" (and a thousand other buzz expressions)?

23. Where do you see yourself in five years?

24. Would you rather do a job, design it, evaluate it, or manage others doing it?

25. When can you start work?

A disclaimer.
Some of these questions don't fit everybody. I particularly dislike, "Where will you be in five years?" Whenever someone asks me that, I want to punch him in the nose. Not exactly good employment strategy.

But the real hummer of a question, the one absolutely guaranteed to bring you to your knees and confess your incompetence, is, "What do you really *want?*"

That's why getting yourself together, defining your real worth, and planning realistic job goals are so important. Not knowing who you are and what you want is a disclosure of impotence. Any employer with an IQ over 90 will ask himself why you're wasting his time.

No wonder the Personnel Department is used as an organizational bouncer. Musclemen are needed to run the confused job-seeker out of the marketplace!

But what about all the alienated young people who need jobs and can't hack it?
Employers don't need them . . . and why should they?
Alienation is for failed novelists, sociopaths, and the very, very

young and spoiled. For God's sake (no scatology intended), do "have your head together" before inflicting employers with your high seriousness and precious purposes.

It sounds to me as if you have to be disagreeable to be offered a good job.

No, there's an easily demonstrated middle way between syco- phancy and hostility. It's the road of agreeableness.

Again, you and the employer are doing each other a favor if you accept a job he offers. It's a business deal and, unlike so many unproductive exchanges in life, a good business deal, renegotiated from time to time and brought up to date, sometimes survives a lifetime. So when you look for a judgment job, avoid sounding like a serf in the manor house. And don't be hostile to potential employers, because you depend on them for a living. They depend on you for the same thing.

Hostility is often found in the persevering and unsuccessful job applicant. It is the fruit of a bad job-hunting strategy, a lack of goals, or an inability to empathize with employers.

It is contagious and obvious to everyone.

Antidotes: hard work, fun, and a good sense of humor. If you look for a job, you can be almost anything—even flighty and silly, but never sullen.

OK. So a job offer is the beginning of a business relationship. How can I tell whether I should want a job that's available?

You probably have a hidden agenda too. A good exercise, there- fore, is to sit down and list those qualities you want from an or- ganization. The idea is to check out your employer before signing on for the long cruise. After all, Sticky Wicket, Inc., is checking you out!

Here's a list to help you decide whether an employer is worth hiring:

1. Does it publish and post salaries of all officers and managers? (If so, I take back everything I said about Personnel Officers.)

2. At your last interview, which concluded at 6:30 P.M., how many people were still working at Sticky Wicket? (If none, start

to worry. Sticky Wicket, Inc., is either uncommonly efficient or the hired hands stampede to hit the elevator at quitting time.)

3. Does a secrecy syndrome pervade the organization? (It does! Watch out! Sticky Wicket, Inc., is in real trouble. Maybe the top man should be cashiered.)

4. Do women, minorities, and young and old people occupy important, decision-making positions? (Yes. Then you know the organization is "fundamentally sound," as they say on Wall Street.)

5. Does everyone in the organization dress and look alike? (No. Fine! You'll feel right at home.)

6. Did people you interviewed *laugh* (particularly at themselves)? (Great God, when do you start work?)

7. Are people overworked at Sticky Wicket, Inc.? (No. What the hell do they need you for . . . ?)

8. How long before you report to work? (Six weeks. Everything is true that I said about the Personnel Department.)

9. Did the people you interviewed *like* one another? (Yes . . . OK, *if* at the same time they seemed effective, competent, and potent. Otherwise, think twice about the Sunday Breakfast Club atmosphere. Nice guys/gals and their organizations usually finish last.)

10. Must you render periodic reports, attend scheduled meetings, make decisions based on published guidelines? (If so, you might chalk up employment at Sticky Wicket, Inc., as an "unrewarding experience.")

How can you tell whether a job is worth doing in the first place?
— Ask to interview anyone who has held the job in the past five years.
— Ask what would happen if the job can't be filled.
— How many people does the job-holder report to? Plenty of people in the world of work have more than one boss. Be sure you're not the fall guy for three supervisors who aren't communicating.

—Figure out if the job is *line* or *staff*; most jobs are an interesting mixture.

—Query the criteria used to screen out candidates for the job; pressing employers about a job's definition wins you high marks in the "taking a long hard look" department.

Is it true that the first five minutes of an interview are the most important?
Half true.

That first five minutes transmits a *gestalt* which is hard to shake. Still, I've interviewed plenty of people (slow starters with good judgment) who don't reveal themselves so quickly that interviewers perceive that nothing is there! So keep in mind, when interviewing, to "psych up" before crossing the employment threshold. Warming up means some healthy anxiety. But anxiety is better than indifference or a slack demeanor. *Tension,* at the outset of an interview, is natural and desirable: it causes adrenaline to flow and brain cells to function. And it's part of the fun in finding a job—and the challenge.

How important are first appearances?
Very, for some jobs. Airline stewardesses, front-office secretaries, customer-relations types, *et al.*

But for most judgment jobs a good first appearance gets you a free pass to first base—and that's all. From then on, you've gotta circle the bases on talent. And that's what you've got plenty of. How you handle yourself in the interview, especially after it passes the uptight stage, is most important.

That's the body language of an interview.

Body language?
Eyes are important in hitting a baseball, lovemaking, and finding a job. Always—in an interview situation—from time to time look your interlocutor directly in the eyes.

Never wear dark glasses.

Body language, an infant science, is the *lingua franca* of the interview: don't sit with arms akimbo, downturned face, or prostrate before the interviewer.

Open yourself physically in the interview.

Pay attention.

Help the interviewer. Ask him about his job!

If humor comes, let it. There is, after all, nothing so structurally hollow as a job interview. The sooner you two become human beings the better.

And don't become infatuated with your own voice. Long-winded job applicants and employers deserve each other.

The economy of your speech, résumé, and person tells a good employer about your on-the-job EFFECTIVENESS.

Cultivate a passion for conscious concision. If asked a question, answer it, or say, "I don't know." In interviewing over five thousand people in five years, the incredible inability of most job applicants to answer fairly simple analytical questions is astonishing. This goes for Ph.D.s, cabinet-level officials, and university presidents. Paying attention, responding frankly and honestly and briefly, makes a far better impression than *what* you say. Convey *sincerity* in what you say (and write), and employers listen.

Answer questions, therefore, *briefly* and stick to the point.

Let the long-winded stand in unemployment lines: many good listeners there!

Should I expect to take a whole battery of pre-employment tests?

A refreshing bit of progress on the employment front these days is the increasing disenchantment with pre-employment testing. Since World War II and until very recently, employers—especially large corporate/governmental complexes—relied heavily on testing as a selection device.

No more.

Except for finding radio operators, screening out religious "nuts," or measuring mechanical aptitude, testing as an employment device is passé. Particularly for judgment jobs. Sure, tests are OK and downright necessary for pilots, lawyers, and stenographers. But for judgment jobs, tests are dumbsquat.

So if a prospective employer wants to probe your psyche, leave his office in a huff.

The real reason large employers still rely on tests is to get their Personnel Department off the hook. "Well, Mr. President, his Minnesota Multiphasic was high and our Urban Affairs people wanted to take a chance on the guy."

Test scores are great alibis for the Personnel Department. Scores mean nobody confronts a job applicant as a human being, says "no," or rejects him. But, of course, saying "no" is an employer's right *and* responsibility—if he can't bear it, he's not doing his job.

What are some of the questions I'm likely to face in a standard employment test?

There's a slug of questions (repeated in various forms throughout the quiz) on:

— how well you loved mommy and daddy (you liked daddy slightly better).

— your energy level (you never need more than five hours' sleep a night).

— your spouse (you love him/her to distraction, but you love your job *more*).

— your spare-time activities (you have none, loving work above all else).

— how you get along (people are never a problem, you love everybody).

A generation of Americans has been raised on these tests, and everyone lies. The test-givers know the test-takers lie. The test-takers know that they lie. Employers know the tests are worthless. So, yes, sometimes it's OK to lie.

Aren't these tests designed to screen in the team players?

That's my point. The last person who admitted he wasn't a team player died in 1938. It is reported that his was a full and happy life!

One of my big problems is being told repeatedly I'm not qualified for a job. What should I do?

Do you have a set of realistic job goals?

Does your résumé support these goals on the basis of your real skills?

Do you know how to disagree pleasantly with an employer when he tells you that you are underqualified?

Again, to repeat myself, most jobs are filled by people who only meet *some* of a job's specifications.

Job specs are written by personnel people who can't know the truth about any job unless it's in the Personnel Department. That's why job descriptions are to employment what political science is to politics.

Are you an educator? And somebody wants an educational technologist? List the reading you've done in the field, your familiarity with programed instruction, and how you've used teaching machines in the past. So you don't have a Ph.D.; but if you are keenly interested in the field, you'll learn *on the job*.

So in job-hunting make sure you put your best foot forward in the area where you seem least qualified. Some tips:

1. Show you can learn a job on the job. That's one of your chief skills, remember?

2. Analyze your strengths. Show your *skills* to be substantially what the employer wants. Does a job require a demonstrated record in technical illustration? Point out that you got an "A" in draftsmanship in high school, helped to illustrate a college manual, and taught elementary graph development in the Army.

3. Prepare some razzle-dazzle questions and snow your prospective employer. If you ask the *right* questions (i.e., questions he can't answer), that's leverage to qualify for the job.

4. Show that your salary expectations are *lower* than other professionals in the field. Doesn't it make sense to hire a savvy generalist and pay him less?

5. Convey a hard, charging, enthusiastic interest in the job. That's a quality for which you are never underqualified.

Yes, but I've even been told I'm overqualified for a job!
I bet it wasn't a judgment job, and what you were looking for was stop-loss employment to earn income.
Nicht wahr?
Because of a college degree, your fluent Urdu, or a Rhodes Scholarship, you'll threaten stop-loss employers.
You need a job—any job—because you're broke and "overqualified."

My advice—if it's a stop-loss or grunt job—is *not* to lie. Study what it is in your background that precludes your being seriously considered for a stop-loss position. Eliminate these factors from your résumé and consciously avoid them during interviews. In fact, don't use a résumé at all.

You're home free.

Employers, quite properly, hedge hiring those who might bore easily on a job. And since stop-loss jobs can be mind-blowing, hiring a tiger in the mailroom is not the best way to discourage turnover on the job.

But that's the employer's problem.

Some tips on acting dumb:

1. If you need a résumé, use the worst kind of "obit" style. Leave out or downgrade completely your education.

2. Don't appear too alert or bright in the interview. Let your employer coax you. Effuse gratitude if hired.

3. Dress conservatively, even unfashionably—don't appear "with it."

4. Avoid a rich vocabulary.

Before you know it, you'll have a job as a claims adjuster, bank teller, movie house manager, pizza parlor employee. Then change masks again and seriously moonlight finding the job you want.

What about the men and women who don't hire you but whom you must work for?

Ah, yes, the middle managers, the vestal virgins with brass knuckles.

Every job-seeker knows them. Thirty years ago they wore cuff guards and green eyeshades. Today you can spot them by their white socks and shiny pants. A solemn demeanor is a middle manager's certain hallmark.

You will have the bad luck many times during your job search to feel their brass knuckles. And if you are so unlucky as to work for one, there are no words to express my condolences.

That's why you should be certain—before accepting a job—that you will be working for the person who hires you. You like him/her; he/she likes you!

But in your larger organizational complexes, often you are hired at the "top" and work at the "bottom." Between you and your patron, there is a gulf swarming with middle managers ready to zap the bright and spirited.

I worked for a middle manager once. *Once.* Flies naturally hovered about him. His favorite pastime was clocking the help. Stopwatch in sweaty hand, he checked off tardy employees each morning with a bold red mark beside each name. I earned twenty red checkmarks in the month I worked for him. The matter was bucked to the vice-presidential level, where—for all I know—it still rests.

What about jobs where you pass through a whole series of interviews or face a panel?

Murder, Incorporated.

Surviving this barrage means you're in good physical shape.

It's like oral comprehensives in college, or the Inquisition.

Ten interviews in one day (which was my record) left me limp and mentally lame. My mouth dried up. My cheeks hurt, I'd been so goddamned agreeable. My advice is to eat regular meals, reduce smoking, don't drink, and read the New York *Times.* You'd be surprised how many questions are likely to be culled from your interlocutor's breakfast reading.

And don't worry too much about stress questions. There's a long-leggity beastie who is not going to like you because his bile duct was plugged that morning. His comments will be dismissed if everyone else thought you were St. Peter.

Be sure to *take your time* answering questions—a profound thirty-second lapse before you reply to somebody's soft curve across the plate guarantees high marks in the "still waters run deep" department.

And you have this advantage: You're practiced in the niceties of personal self-expression, thanks to half a hundred interviews you've had lately. Something you might do to prep for this obstacle course is to run through some mock interviews with your spouse or a good friend. Swap roles. One of you be the employer; the other, the job candidate.

How can I tell what "rank" I'll have in an organization where I might accept a job?

In healthy organizations where *you* want to work, the status symbols treasured by dying organizations are always invisible. This is tough on ex-military, ministers, and academics who come from a world where rank, title, and status are notoriously necessary.

In free-formed institutions, hierarchical authority is deliberately amorphous. But it still exists.

A mark of your sensitivity on a good job with a vital organization is to sort out where the power is, who exercises it, when and whether you should buck it. Hierarchy—even in the freest-formed institution—is necessary; the great thing about authority in free-formed institutions is its constant change. There's simply no time or place for status back-tickling. Or executive grab-ass.

Do employers ever tell you the real reasons for not hiring you?

Employers, like all human beings, loathe saying "no." So, in rejecting you for a job, the baffle gab begins:

—"We normally hire only full-time professionals with five years' line experience."

—"An M.B.A. is usually your ticket of admission to our organization."

—"We like going with younger people who have the time to invest twenty years in our organization."

—"Our organization, whenever possible, promotes from within."

And so forth. Now, none of these statements is necessarily *false*. But are they necessarily true? Chances are better than even that the organization (a) has eliminated the job, (b) still hasn't settled on a person to fill it, (c) can't decide what the person *does* in the job, (d) has decided on someone else for the job. All of which means that the other competitors for the job must be told the score. Unfortunately, employers at this point, hating to say "no," but unable to say "yes," start talking Chinese. Most won't level and come out with the truth, which generally is: "You were a fine candidate but we chose the best. I'm sure you'll qualify for a similar job elsewhere."

So don't self-destruct when you finish #2, #3, or #4 in the judgment job sweepstakes. This is constructive feedback at its best: it means you are on the right track (i.e., have realistic objectives), interview well, and are only five yards from the goal line. Therefore, ignore 99 per cent of what employers say; it's a clumsy way of avoiding the pain of rejecting people.

Crazy; but then, we act irrationally all the time. If you come in #1 or #2 behind the person who gets the job, that's a near miss; next time around you'll be on target: bull's-eye!

Why can't employers reject people?

Employers are human; they hate rejecting people. So they say, "You are overqualified," "I think, with your skills, you would do better elsewhere," "We don't have any room right now but," etc. Employers are saying "no" without seeming to reject you. Actually, the reasons are rarely close to the truth. The truth is: some other candidate was preferred, more to the employer's liking. And employers often hire for superficial reasons: personality, appearance, age, etc. The trouble is, people are upset when bites don't lead to catches. The unemployed, disappointed with rejections, retire to the seclusion of the living room and turn the TV eye to the outside world. Or abandon the job search and accept the first job that comes along.

How can I tell I'm about to be offered a job?

Lunching together, discussing non-work-related subjects, swapping ideas with an employer, are all signs: the personalizing of the encounter is a clue. Meeting the boss's boss or being invited to see the organization's wage and salary administrators, or receiving a telegram requesting an appearance for a final interview the following Monday, all testify to your being seriously considered.

The signs you discern are the "lights going on in the employer's eyes," an enthusiasm and warmth you never sensed in previous encounters, a hitherto undetected sense of camaraderie, the use of the editorial "we."

Salespeople sense a customer's mood and know when to "close." You are the salesperson, and the signs you look for in an employer's behavior are no different from customer psychology. So "close" on the employer and ask for the job!

Suppose the job for which I'm interviewing has been filled?

Disappointing, but it happens all the time. All the more reason to switch the interview into an information-gathering session. Ask for advice, secure names of other department heads, ask the interviewer his/her opinion of your employability. "Don't curse the darkness; light a candle!" (Confucius) And, for my sake, don't apologize for taking his time, thank him profusely for being considered, go into a funk and try to make him feel guilty, or interview (as if the job *hadn't* been filled) in the hopes the interviewer will change his mind.

Do you thank an employer who offers you a job you want?
    Don't!
    Would you thank somebody if they sold you a house? Would you effuse gratitude if a girl accepted a dinner date? Would you wallow in front of a college admissions board? You would!
    Go back to "Go," don't collect two hundred dollars, and try to remember, the next time around the board, that a job offer is not a gift but a business transaction.

How do you reject a job offer graciously?
    — Back off and ask for the weekend to think over the offer. Then a nice letter (you *do thank* employers whom you turn down!) in your own hand, giving reasons. If you *like* the firm, and the people who work there and what they do, enlist their assistance in looking for a job elsewhere at Sticky Wicket, Inc.
    — Take yourself off the hook at the job interview, switch the interview to an information session, ask for the names of four people who might know of a job you do want. Employers are grateful to job candidates who have a mind of their own!

OK. Do people back off from job offers—really good ones—to choose something better?
    I remember the names, faces, and background of about seven people in as many years whom I've recruited and offered excellent judgment jobs.
    The reasons I remember them so well is that all of them *turned down* the jobs, rejected what I thought was a really good offer.
    And I remember them because I admired their decision and what goes into making a tough decision like that. And three or

four of them I've since called because I know them even better for
their having conveyed to me *why* they decided as they did.

So, if you're going to turn your back on a job, level with your
recruiter, tell him *why*, and thank him for his time. If you make
sense, he'll remember you the next time another first-rate job develops and phone you.

At the same time, I bet there are two hundred people I've hired
who didn't have the guts (i.e., self-knowledge) to turn me down
when they should have.

Why?

Because I sensed they wanted to *please me* rather than themselves. My gain, their loss. Another triumph of ignorance over
knowledge. So getting yourself together for the job search and
being strong enough to resist organizational blandishments are
not of inconsiderable merit.

What about using third parties to recommend you for a job?

It depends on the clout of the third party, the timing of his
call, and the relationship between the third party and the employer.

But "using" a key person to call on your behalf *at the right
time* sways people's judgment.

So, if you are interviewing for a special assistant's job with a
firm's president (and his chief stockholder happens to be your
next-door neighbor), call your neighbor, outline the situation, and
let him godfather your candidacy.

The big problem, of course, is how much these people respect
each other. This approach has worked twice on my behalf, and
twice it was like stepping on a land mine. Again, it's a question of
good judgment, and the risk is small compared to the potential
gain.

*Won't an organization do a reference check on me before we ne-
gotiate a salary?*

Some do, some don't.

Many will actually negotiate, sign you up, and put you to work
before the reference check is complete.

Not terribly efficient.

But employers usually protect themselves with a three-month

probationary clause which permits them to discharge you without cause while the check on you is being made. That's why it's important not to fudge on any vital facts in your background and to make sure you've leveled with your employer on all matters that might have derogatory implications.

In a word, your employer is going to do a pretty complete reference check on you. Although I am astonished how many employers *don't* check out new employees.

In 1969 I fired eight people in the firm where I worked. Seven went on to higher-paying positions. No one at the successor institutions thought it worthwhile to discover why these chaps left our employ. That's what I mean when I say that employers don't always know what they are doing.

Therefore, if you hire an employer worthy of you, he's going to check you out.

If an organization doesn't check you out, it's making a big mistake.

Now, nobody by nature likes to snoop. But don't blame an organization (which is about to invest thousands of dollars on your ability to produce) if it makes some perfectly normal inquiries about your background, previous earnings, personal honesty, and on-the-job efficiency. You wouldn't buy a house or marry a woman (or a man) without some rudimentary checking, would you?

Would you?

Should I let people know I'm using their names as references?
Indubitably, Dr. Watson!

A nice note in your own hand (including a résumé) to the folks who know you best is very much in order. And if your referees happen to be on assignment in Bangkok, ask for a general *letter* of reference which, xeroxed, you can use if an employer "requests" letters of reference.

Won't my referees be contacted many times before I land a job?
Hey, remember, we are in the midst of employment depression! 6.1 million unemployed, a stagflating economy, hard times all around. But there are good jobs in hard times for effective people. And the chances of your referees being burdened with phone calls

and letters (you should be so lucky) are slim indeed! So don't be shy about including the names of busy people who can give a good report. It's what most employers like doing first thing on the job every morning: writing up a person they wish they could rehire.

Why do you call references "referees"?
Because they can blow the whistle on you.

Your referees should, therefore, be people who can give a photograph of your strengths *and* weaknesses. Good judges of how you match up against the job.

Should I ever ask an employer to lunch?
Sure, if you are interviewing for information. Bad form if there is a job at stake. At the same time, *welcome* an invitation to lunch. Chances are you'll field a host of questions between the appetizer and the main course. So don't booze; remember, it's a job interview, not Derby Day. Try not to spill the Pakistani Pilaf on your new herringbone tweed.

So your advice is never to appear desperate for a job, even if you are!
The conventional wisdom is, "Don't be discouraged." But that's nonsense. I discourage, like you, *easily.* Ted Williams once struck out three times in a row. The greatest hitter in baseball looked discouraged: a perfectly natural reaction. If you weren't discouraged, you wouldn't be human.

But the point is: desperate people are discouraging to employers and are probably unemployable. How you *bounce back* from discouragement is the key. And appearing to be discouraged discourages employers; so "with my mask, I lead" (Descartes). In ten years in business, for example, I often ask, "Say, Jim, how's business?" In ten years no one has admitted the slightest complaint about business prospects. Contrast this to the doom and gloom on the financial pages of the Chicago *Tribune!*

What does an interviewer mean when he says, "Stay in touch"?
It telegraphs that you passed muster. At the same time he's say-

ing, "There's no job *now* at ABC, Inc., so stay in touch!" And the same goes for replies to your résumé which conclude, ". . . Although there is no current position at Greater Consolidated Manufactories, do drop by if you are ever in the Cincinnati area." A nice way of saying, "We *are* interested and would like to look you over." All the more reason to generate three or four interviews in the Ohio Valley to justify a swing through the Midwest.

How about accepting a job you don't want with an organization in a field, or with a person, you do like?

This is a good strategy for people *new* on the job market or recycling into another "field," or returning to the job market after a long hiatus. It's not recommended for those who want to continue to practice their craft in the same line of work, who are in mid-career, and those past the age of thirty-five.

Looking for mentors is OK and desirable in the young, suspect in the middle-aged. Taking a grunt job in mid-career in an entirely different field suggests that you don't know, or don't know how to identify or represent, your "transferable skills" (for more responsibility and pay in an alternate field). Working at a hopeless job for an organization (which you love) in middle age is not protecting your own self-interest.

Any last words on what you don't do on the job?

— Don't look for sex on the job. "Dipping your quill in the company ink" is mistaking the board room for the boudoir.

— Don't try to be *liked* by everyone on your job search or on the job. The most popular people in organizations are generally elevator operators, guys in the traffic department, and jolly ladies in staff services.

— Don't go looking for Big Sister or Mom and Dad on your job search; search out mentors, instead. Not necessarily "nice," but they are effective. And on your first job, especially, you'll need a guide and a critic; eschew a "family" atmosphere. What you want to hear is the hum of the lathe, not a teakettle boiling over.

— Don't expect keys to the executive washroom. Those perks belong to those who were winning their first job when you were playing stickball.

In a buyer's market shouldn't you hedge and accept the first toler-
able job that's offered?

That depends . . .

Competition. Lots of it these days.

Plenty of it makes it tough on the job-seeker.

And any employer worth hiring encourages it.

Generally, anyone who hires is not going to settle for interviewing one or two candidates. If he's smart (and employers often
aren't), he takes at least a month to hire. A savvy employer finds
four lead candidates. Four solid job applicants refine what it is
that he wants.

So don't slash your wrists if you don't land the job, if there was
stiff and fair competition. Chances are good that the employer
picked the right man or woman. Because you survived to the
semifinals indicates your worth on the job mart.

And good employers remember good people.

To sum up, keep on good terms with all employers. If you handle a situation with grace and polish, it gives employers pause to
think twice about you. And that phone could ring in a few weeks
with an offer you really want.

Engineers and educators are examples of employers who stand
on one foot, then another. They can't make up their minds. They
wrestle at choosing *this* man, *that* woman. This kind of employer
is the despair of headhunters, good job applicants, and top management.

But at the same time, don't knock an organization if it takes a
reasonable time to decide you *are* or are *not* the person. They are
at least putting people before systems.

But to answer your question, "Should I accept the first job
offer?"

There's no real answer, of course; it depends on various circumstances surrounding your job search, your financial means, what
you want, how *this* job compares with *that* . . . and how long
you've tested your background against the job market.

But the thesis of this book is that good jobs can be found, that
it makes no sense to accept a job because you *must*, and that it's
better to work loose (at a stop-loss or grunt job) than to accept so-
called professional employment because it's a social necessity.
Hanging in and looking for *your* job is a far better way to spend a

year than punching a time clock in an organization you despise. Because if you don't believe *now* that you can find *the* job, you'll be postponing—perhaps forever—the possibility that a job can be more than a meal ticket.

Job-hunting is a lottery. Make sure Lady Luck is your companion. Which means treating your job search as if it could change your life.

SIX

Eyeball to Eyeball

So now you've a couple of job offers.
Well, let's be realistic, maybe only one.
Still, there's one last hurdle to jump: negotiating your salary.
Now's the time you've got to be particularly tough and able.
Honest.
You are now in the catbird's seat. Because Sticky Wicket, Inc., wants your body, now's the time to "leverage" as much money as possible.

OK. It's important that I negotiate a good salary. But how?
For those of you new to the game or who need a refresher course in haggling for more pay, this book is a guide long known to the wicked and the worldly but never before found in print except in a plain brown wrapper. Before reading further, therefore, one caveat: Don't feel *guilty* if you want more money. That's OK in Bismarck, North Dakota, where things money can buy are limited and unnecessary. But elsewhere, hustling a high salary is sustaining a life-support system. Whether you work in the steno pool, or are a $100,000 stem-winder for a growth industry, money is one name of the game.

Now, when you go out on the job market, you are the seller—your body is up for sale for forty hours a week. As a commodity you always ask for more than you're worth (i.e., more than somebody is willing to pay).

Always ask for more than you expect the employer to offer. Then the final "price" (i.e., your salary) will be more than the minimum and near the maximum the employer expects to pay.

This makes sense to your employer (who thinks he's found a bargain) and at the same time raises your real price (i.e., salary or "worth") to what the market allows.

You mean there is a "formula" for haggling a higher salary?
Exactly.

Haggling, or leveraging your salary for more pay than the job is actually worth, was first introduced into this country by the Dutch. A seagoing people, these seventeenth-century traders not only brought back to New York from the Barbary shores myrrh, frankincense, and silk, but introduced as well the bargaining mores of the fabled East. Now, when buying a house or auto, we know that there is no price tag as such. The seller asks one price, the buyer counters with another. And, as it turns out, what we pay is about two fifths more of the difference between what we offered and the seller asked, or about three fifths less than the difference between what the seller asked and the buyer offered.

For example, if I want to sell my house for $70,000 and a buyer offers $60,000, the real price of the house, which is what I'm prepared to sell it for, is $67,000. Thus do the Arabs barter in Marrakesh.

Unless you clip coupons for a living, or happen to hold the highest winning ticket from last week's off-track betting, usually your salary is all that stands between you and the high cost of living. Here in the financial seat of the Western world, a man without money is a stateless person, an atavistic relic of the extended-family system, a throwback to the barter economy and the Neolithic Garden Culture. You either join the moneychangers in the temple or are paid extravagantly for chasing them out.

What do you mean, "leverage"?
You have, queerly enough, more leverage with your employer *before* you accept the job. Once you've said you'll take the job, Mr. Employer will drive a harder bargain.

Never, never accept a job until the salary (and meaningful fringe benefits) is agreed upon verbally and clearly written out in an employment agreement. That's what we capitalists call the "sanctity of contract."

A letter of agreement?

Most small and medium-sized employers spell out terms of employment for both parties to sign. So long as the organization is free to fire you and you are free to quit, the letter serves an important purpose. It says what you do, when, for how long, at how much pay, and enumerates the conditions of employment.

The only thing, of course, which you negotiate is salary. Fringe benefits, hours of work, retirement and health provisions, are generally fixed. And it's the salary where your (and not necessarily the employer's) self-interest is at stake.

What about employment contracts?

A lot of chief executive officers negotiate, like ball players, fixed contracts: two-, five-, seven-year agreements with an organization. Poor policy: If the new president doesn't work out, the organization "buys out" his contract. And people with contracts have no incentive to *change* and need take no "risks."

So, in negotiating for a senior job in industry, if your lawyer advises you to lock up the job with a written contract (charging his usual fee of $100 per hour), he will happily accompany you to the negotiations to "protect your interests." Lawyers, however, are often deal-breakers (rather than deal-makers). Pushing for a contract and using your lawyer to thrash out its details invites an organization to use *its* lawyer to haggle with yours! And using third parties is bad employment strategy. So think through whether a "contract" is in your best interests.

What are meaningful fringe benefits for senior executives?

Foreign service, moonlight consultation, deferred compensation, organizational stock options, profit sharing, moving expenses, an annual renegotiation clause: all are considerations. Incidentally, an annual renegotiation clause means that your performance will be reviewed with an eye toward significant promotion and salary raise one year after you are hired.

A lot of my friends took jobs because of the fringe benefits.

Forget these jobs.

Only for the insecure, time-servers, and the simple-minded.

Be a tiger. What you want are relevance, responsibility, and interest in your work. Eschew organizations which give cradle-to-grave protection. They want your body eight hours a day for forty years.

Where I work, we have one fringe benefit: cold cash. We pay well. Upon your untimely exit, you receive (as a valued Associate) a handshake and 10 per cent of every dollar earned while with the company. This is a way of saying something nice to someone you can't use any more.

And it sure buys a lot more than all your corporate benefit programs!

Face it: You want the experience of growing on a job. If suckered into an organization because of its employee-volleyball program, you are in deeper trouble than I thought.

What's the most effective technique to obtain the salary you want?

Again, establish the salary you *want before* the employer tells you what he will pay!

This is a major point in hiring yourself an employer and consistent with the whole philosophy of reciprocity between you and a potential employer. Plainly, you have more *leverage* with an employer *before you accept a job offer you feel sure he will make.*

Why?

Because the employer *wants* to hire you. No, he doesn't want to hire numbers two, three, and four—he wants you, *numero uno.* In his head, the employer has hired you. And that's why you do yourself no favors when you take second place, put your feelings on the back burner, accommodate his wishes and supinely accept what he offers.

Unfortunately, most job-seekers don't know what they want ("what they are worth"), don't put that amount out on the table where both of you can discuss it, and gratefully accept what employers are apparently prepared to pay. But every judgment job is "negotiable"; there is a salary *range.* Asking for the top figure in that range guarantees a salary greater than either party "expected."

Clearly, however, you, as the job-seeker, must protect your own interests. "If the employer is on *his* side and you are on *his* side, then who is on *your* side?" Job-seekers, however, from a malignant sense of gratitude, often forget what they want (and deserve) at the most crucial time in an employment negotiation—i.e., when they sense that they will be offered a job.

If the employer establishes a salary offer *before* you have staked your position and the offer is considerably less than yours, your leverage is lost. Always establish *what you want* before the employer does.

The employer wants your body. Thus, reveal your price. Communicate your want of the job and your pay expectations. Your wanting the job and your expressed enthusiasm will ratify the good sense of the employer in hiring you. But timing is essential to gain the salary you deserve.

Any special advice on negotiating salary between the minimum and midpoint range or between midpoint and maximum?

Ask for your "maximum," prepare to yield to a "midpoint," thus avoiding the "minimum."

It's almost impossible to begin at a minimum and negotiate to a midpoint. That's uphill work; much easier to walk downhill! Moreover, employers are vexed and find you *unreasonable* when you bargain upward rather than downward. Everybody's happy: you tell your spouse that evening you've negotiated $24,500 ($4,500 more than your previous job); and your boss goes to his boss and says, "Gee, you know, that guy/gal wanted $28,000 but I bargained him down three and one-half Gs."

One final caveat: in the unlikely event you negotiate *more* money than someone on the payroll who has similar responsibilities (and five years with the firm), expect the night-of-the-long-knives. Many will make it a point to see that you "fail" on the job. So use your good judgment and wait until you are *on the job* before taking that big stride *up* the salary ladder.

How do you find out about salary structures before locking yourself into a job offer?

In interviewing for information about the hidden job market, a perfectly legitimate line of inquiry is the salary structure of the firm and the profession. Salaries are established inside organizations through a complex series of human interactions that are subsumed under the title "comparability." Which means, in plain

English, that employers cannot pay Mr. X $30,000 per annum for doing what Mr. Y is already doing for $25,000. Whiz kids recruited from the outside at higher pay for similar responsibilities jeopardize organizational equilibrium. So check out salary ranges of the men and women working at your expected level in the hierarchy and move over to the competition *only if you move up*.

But aren't salary requirements the critical consideration in being hired?

Remember, this book is about *judgment* jobs. High salary demands, far from putting off an employer, could put him on to you!

I've filled lots of judgment jobs (and been a candidate for a few), and salary was *least important* in the negotiations. Like finding your dream house, most people move heaven and earth to work out the financing.

How do you avoid discussing salary before an offer is actually tendered?

Halfway through a routine job interview, you are often asked, "What is your 'ball park figure'?" An indirect way of finding out if the organization can live with your expectations.

By all means, put out on the table what you "want" and, with elaborate nonchalance, say, "Of course, I'm flexible and everything is negotiable." And that *is* the strict truth!

Now, true, if your figure is way out of reach of the organization, no business, obviously, will be transacted. But most ineffective job-seekers back off saying, "Heck, I'll take whatever you can pay."

No joking. Knowing what you want means *knowing what you want to be paid*. Having researched yourself and interviewed for information, you should know what you want to be paid. Sure, you could be *excluded* from consideration, but it's at least as likely that you will be *included*. Employers expect your self-esteem to equal your "worth." Putting a reasonably high price on your services means a longer job search but a better job.

Figure it out: if I decline a job paying $16,550 because my absolute minimum is $19,500 (for a job I want) and I spend three months finding it, I'm three thousand dollars ahead, and *my base for my next job* is accordingly much higher. I'm far ahead of the chumps who gratefully accept less than they deserve, feel far better about myself for waiting out the job I wanted, and am twice as effective on the job because I don't feel resentment at myself or my employer. Putting yourself first means agreeably rejecting jobs you can't afford.

So never admit to low previous earnings?

In jumping "fields," taking ten years "off" to raise a couple of kids, or pursuing an expensive graduate education, there is no way you can "build" on previous earnings in your negotiations. That's building on a "weakness." But precisely because you are better educated, ten years additionally "experienced," or able to apply your "expertise" in one field to another, *is your strength.*

So, no, it's a *fair* answer to admit previous earnings. But it's fairer to say why you *deserve* what you ask. And if you have been poorly paid or were a volunteer worker, all the more reason—for the first time in your life—to establish *real* worth based on ability. That's putting your feelings first, not succumbing "to the disease to please" and saying to employers, "No more Mr. Nice Guy."

Why is it better to beat the employer to the punch?

You have one-upped the employer. Most employers are ready to one-up you. They establish, if they can, a salary level. By your moving first, you automatically increase the amount of money you are offered.

How do you know when to make your demand, or to "one-up the employer"?

Timing: Once you sense that the job will be offered.

You might say, "Now, pending a job offer, let's talk about money. I want $33,000 to start, and let me tell you why!"

Give reasons: education, experience, acquired knowledge, accomplishments. Your talent and motivation—all ammunition to justify demands.

In brief, it's a question of *timing and judgment.* And knowing *when* to ice the cake is another qualifying factor in being chosen for a judgment job.

Do job-hunters ever double salary in changing jobs?
It might happen once or twice in your life.
The *level* of responsibility is the key to doubling your pleasure. So, if you are capable enough to qualify for a job twice current earnings, press to be paid at least what the previous incumbent was paid.

How about an example of someone with no salary history who negotiates a decent salary?
Say a graduate student, twenty-eight, with a history of grunt jobs: summertime work in construction and teaching assistantships. He has a degree in systems analysis and applies for an entry-level job in a company's Operations Research Department.
The crunch comes when the employer asks, "By the way, what are your previous earnings?"
Given what he would have been paid had he worked upon graduating with a Bachelor's Degree at age twenty-two, meritorious pay hikes, cost of living increments, and citing his Master's Degree, he establishes his monetary "worth," taking into account "opportunity costs" in pursuing his M.A. (this strategy works *if* an advance degree supports a job he wants).
Some employers do back off from candidates because of low previous earnings. More reason to negotiate the highest possible *base* salary on your first and second jobs. That's protecting yourself against unimaginative next employers who "know the price of everything and the value of nothing." (Wilde)

So previous earnings are important in negotiating salary?
Another obvious breakdown in personnel systems is their predilection to pay on the basis of previous earnings.
This is an outrageous injustice to divorced women suddenly in the job market, subsistence professionals—like Nader's Raiders—who must work for little pay to be effective, men returning from the military, and international types who might live on much less abroad.
If you fit any of these categories, come on like Gang Busters and ask for what the market allows. For a good man or woman, an organization budgets to pay him/her well.

In your negotiations, a fair salary demand (plus stubbornness on your part) makes most institutions yield. The others you don't want to work for anyway.

And if you're an "entry-level professional" (to use the jargon of the trade), starting salary *is* important—not for the now, but for what you're paid ten years hence. Not your salary, but your *salary base* is what's important.

Some rules of thumb: If you have no "experience" and have just graduated from college, you should receive no less than $13,000—anyplace. Add another $2,000 if you have an M.A., and $3,000–$5,000 if you're a Ph.D. without previous work experience.

Don't clutch if you don't have degrees. "Equivalent experience" is worth $2,000–$5,000 in most work. And every year you work adds a grand or two to your "worth."

Nobody, not even psychiatrists, is able to figure out what we are "worth." The point is to become a productive human being. The money awards follow as an inevitable concomitant of ability.

Does it ever make sense to stress why you need more money?

Say you bought a house you can't afford, are still paying on last year's winter vacation to Catalina Island, and bought season tickets to the Bruins—but that's *your* problem, not your employer's.

The biggest mistake in negotiating salary is talking about *your* problems, not the employer's. I remember once being confronted by a chap on our payroll who had just bought a new oriental rug and wanted a salary increase in order to make his payments. Well, sports fans, he struck out in three straight swings of his bat. And, for all I know, he is still trying to make some employer pay for his home furnishings. For all I know, this fellow *did* deserve a raise; but my judgment was so clouded by his patent hamhandedness that neither of us ever addressed the issue of his augmented contribution to the firm.

So don't talk about your "needs" (school debts to repay, a down payment on a vacation cottage, your $2,000 stereo system). Bargaining from weakness is a strategy of incompetence and brings into question your personal judgment on important matters, hardly a winning strategy in qualifying for a judgment job.

What if an employer refuses to budge from his original offer?
Stonewalled!

Suppose salary is non-negotiable (fixed), which often happens if:

— a number of people are hired to do the same job.
— entrance-level inductees are all paid equally.
— industrywide "averages" are used to establish threshold salaries.
— fixed compensation, based on industrywide labor agreements, is negotiated on behalf of professional engineers, professors, computer science types by union officials.

So, normally, you expect to know this information *before* a job offer. If not, press employers for the reason *why* salaries are fixed. More often than not, the reasoning is sound; often, however, you can negotiate a substantial increment on the basis of simply proving that you deserve it.

Fixed salaries are usually negotiated with experts, technicians, craftsmen; negotiable salaries are associated with judgment jobs which are difficult to define, evaluate, and "quantify." That's your latitude of negotiability.

Check out the reasons for the employer's frozen position, and if you find justification, be reasonable and yield. There's something to be said for submissiveness training. There are limits in negotiations. An employer is signaling to you that this is his final offer. Don't be mulish.

Should I fib about my previous earnings?
Never!

Savvy employers always check out a person's past employment *and* earnings.

But friends of mine have lied about salaries and gotten tremendous raises!
Sure, it works.

So you lie again, and again, and then "gotcha." And shaking a history of lies is the hardest job of all in looking for a job. Smart employers, headhunters—yes, even personnel departments—*check up* on you. Lying will get you to second base, but you'll be picked off going to third and hate living with yourself ever after.

What about a woman long out of the job market?

An example would be a suburban housewife who has not worked since the early '70s. Then she was a secretary. She has a degree.

As a college graduate, she should not ask for less than ten thousand. Add a couple of thousand for age, a couple more for the special skills picked up in the past decade.

Employers put a high price on flair, talent, and one's contribution potential. Paradoxically, asking for a high price instead of $9,500 is more impressive. No employer wants to buy cheap goods.

And women, especially, should press to be paid at the *level* of a person doing equivalent work.

In a word, it's the same old game. And haggling is *not* petty larceny: it's the only way to stay alive while Uncle Sam prints monopoly money driving prices up, up, and away.

Any simple formula to determine how much you should be paid?

The only simple (and simplistic) method used by many mid-career people is to multiply your age times $1,000. Are you forty-nine years old and a candidate to manage the Western Region of your organization's marketing department? Well, according to this formula, you're now making $49,000 (salary plus meaningful fringes, or profit sharing) with prospects of making (in constant dollars) $65,000 when you slink off to your sunset years.

For many men and women hooked on this formula, however, the anxiety caused by being ten or fifteen thousand dollars shy of this hypothetical figure forces you to play catch-up ball in a line of work you no longer love. And it ignores what should be the goal of every man and woman: self-fulfillment. Many people who switch fields, change careers, pioneer new endeavors, face a drastic reduction in compensation. My strong feeling is that those who find fulfillment in "new careers" recover earning power rapidly and *exceed* their highest previous salary.

Are some organizations easier to negotiate salary with than others?

If you're thinking of government or one of the *Fortune* five hundred corporations, there is a narrower latitude of negotiation. Most competing organizations in the market economy, however, are "open." It's good sense to negotiate for more than you expect.

Is it really better to wait for a couple of job offers?

Yes, unless the anxiety is unbearable. If two months elapse and you have two tentative and two concrete job offers, the time has come for a decision.

Now, *you* are in the catbird's seat; play one employer off against another. Compare salary, job responsibility, personal growth, and job interest of one job against the other. Keep in mind those two jobs which *might* develop. Do you have the means and patience to wait them out?

A bird in hand is worth two in the bush, to coin a phrase—so don't be so clever that you reject all your job offers!

Let it be known that you are being wooed by another organization. If it's a competitor, your value on the marketplace escalates. By skillful negotiation you raise your starting salary.

Don't be shy in keeping one employer a secret from the other. After all, they sought a good man (and found him in you) and rejected five other candidates. So play it from strength: weigh one offer against the other.

It doesn't hurt to keep employers waiting. Besides, they spent two months keeping you on the hook; they can wait a couple of days while you make some discreet phone calls.

Lastly, should you be so affluent, thank all employers who offered jobs that you declined. They represent good future contacts (and possible jobs). Besides, you might not work out at Sticky Wicket, Inc. It'll be nice to phone someone about your problems.

Can you leverage a higher salary from your current employer by using the same mousetrap techniques?

Yes, if you have a job, make it leverage you a better salary where you *now* work, or use your job as a base to find a better position elsewhere.

Now, how to accomplish these grand goals? Well, you can't be raised in pay unless your employer augments your responsibilities and changes your title. Accordingly, make it easy for your employer to give you a raise. Are you in charge of the mailroom? Rename it the "Production and Distribution Department," assume some important new tasks that nobody else is doing, then call yourself "Chief, Communications." Are you a Special Assistant to the President? Well, be a leader and plot to become an "Executive Assistant to the President," with responsibilities you alone can assume. The point is to upgrade your job, change your title, confront your boss, and come on strong for a raise in pay. Before you can say "Jack Spratt," you've qualified for a boost in pay.

What if my current employer doesn't bite?
Then it's time for you to move on.
In other words, start job-jumping.

Job-jumping?
As soon as you have a gig, start looking for your next job. Job-jumping, the art of finding another job with more pay and responsibility, is a downright necessity in our fast-moving economy. The rewards are to the restless job-seekers. And don't worry about organizational loyalty. This is your last priority. Who in his right mind feels a warm glow inside working for Consolidated Conglomerate, Inc., anyway? Your real loyalties, on the other hand, are to your talent, your craft, and your field of work. To survive on salary means moving up on the job at least once a year, or jumping over to the competition for a 15 or 20 per cent increase. Every manpower study on executive employment trends bears out the rapid rise in salary, the heavy turnover in jobs, and the fluid mobility of the high-salaried classes. Many people at the top of their form and at the top of their firm didn't start at ABC, Inc. Rather, these men and women learned early the fine art of finding the job they wanted, expanding that job into something more responsible and better paying, and then job-jumping to the competition.

What are the important points to remember in negotiating salary?
   1. Never accept a job before you know and agree to the salary.
   2. Don't hesitate to sleep on a salary offer—two or three hours' reflection and a few phone calls to knowledgeable friends should convince you whether or not you are being euchred.
   3. If you have no previous earnings, invent hypothetical salaries you might have been paid. And—on top of those salaries—cost of living increments and merit increases.

4. Always say, "It's not the money that's important, Mr. Employer. I'd hardly be a good representative for Sticky Wicket, Inc., and represent its best interests if I can't represent *my own*."

5. Try, delicately, to find out the salaries of people doing equivalent work. If your salary is lower, ask for a review and an upgrade to their level after a three-month probationary hitch.

6. In hard-nosed business organizations, push hard for equity in compensation. In nonprofit organizations, don't push so that anyone doubts your commitment to the purposes of the organization. Nobody working there will admit it's the money that keeps him; the organization has a hammerlock on "commitment" greater than Corning's on glass.

7. Be tough on federal, state, and city employers. They are point conscious: 10 points for being a veteran, 5 points for being an ex-Peace Corps volunteer, 10 for being blind or a hunchback, 15 for having a master's degree. "Equivalent experience" is the big buzz word here. Demonstrate that your "experience" is equal, as it is, to two years in grad school. And you've got 'em by the short hair.

8. Ask employers for an employment letter spelling out details of employment. Be sure a provision exists to review your salary after three months or (at least) after the first year.

9. If hired as a consultant on a daily basis, be sure to calculate your daily worth (divide 280 days into your annualized highest salary) and then add 30 to 50 per cent. Consultants are often unemployed, and the added amount is insurance against the wolf at the door.

10. If you are a contract-hire (hired for a specific length of time for a certain task), ask to see your organization's budget to manage that contract. Some employers might be miffed at this brazenness, but it's simple fact that the employer put a price on your head before he saw you. You have a right to know what that price (i.e., salary) is and to get it.

11. On your résumé, after salary, write "Negotiable." This means you are prepared to talk about anything—or nothing.

12. Remember, in bargaining for salary forget fringe benefits. Only in special cases, where benefits are actual compensation—free travel privileges, paid health insurance, rent-free housing, board—do they count. Compute the cost in cash for these items, add to the salary offered, and calculate your real take-home pay.

13. Women, since the law is on their side, need to press to be paid at the appropriate "level" of responsibility. Avoid falling into "what are your previous earnings?" trap.

14. Research what other organizations in the same field pay for a comparable job. Be certain that your salary requirements *match* dollars paid to people with equal responsibilities and functions. Back off and negotiate *downward* if your salary demands *exceed* compensation paid to key players performing at an *equal* level.

15. Establish your highest previous earnings—whether hourly, daily, weekly, monthly, or annually—and focus on the figure that works out to the highest annualized earnings.

16. Out of the work force to pursue a graduate degree? Calculate the rate of inflation, and *add* the result to your highest previous earnings.

17. Consider leaving a *margin* between what you are paid and what you "expect" as a negotiating point at your first performance-review session. This means the possibility of a meaningful jump in pay after your "probationary" period, dependent on productivity. Employers like rewarding performance on the job, not potential to fill a job.

18. Does your Ph.D. in the New Math *support* this job? Give yourself an additional three to five thousand dollars.

19. Establish with your new boss a process for evaluating what you do, and schedule regular performance-review sessions to provide for regular merit increases based on *productivity*.

20. Focus on the special abilities, talent, or flair you bring to the job (because *you are you*) in order to support your salary demands.

21. Make sure your final agreement is in black and white, thus

avoiding misunderstanding six months hence. Offer to do the first draft, let your employer edit, and agree on the third and final draft.

How can self-employed consultants justify adding at least 30 per cent, or even 50 per cent, to a daily rate of pay?

Most self-employed professionals are "unemployed" a great deal of the time. One of their qualifications, therefore, is availability. Any self-employed person—writer, lawyer, management consultant, accountant—must consider "downtime" as an important factor in negotiating a transaction. "Downtime" to a self-employed person is what "overhead" is to a company. It is the money paid for personal upkeep so as to be "available" for "assignment." A fee (hourly, daily, weekly, or even monthly) should reflect this "overhead." A 30–50 per cent "add on" is normal. Finally, time to "market" your services is lost when you accept a consulting assignment. Pay yourself back for these "expenditures."

Is there no ceiling on an "open" salary?

No. Sorry about that, but the sky isn't the limit!

Salaries are truly "negotiable" if a new job is created, or when the job is central to the organization's "core mission," or the job is *so* important (and talent so rare) as to require a headhunter's services.

But no job's salary is without a ceiling. Knowing what you want, what you can do, and where you want to do it, circumscribes how much you will be paid. Interviewing for information is the way to establish the high/low range of salary you can expect.

What if I'm independently wealthy and really don't need a salary?

Press for it anyway.

Salaries, to repeat, are how organizations *rank* you, and working for less than you deserve means having less power than you want.

Furthermore, most employers, wrongly, want to think that an employee *needs* his paycheck. To acknowledge *you don't* could cause unimaginative employers to back off from your candidacy.

Isn't the job title important?

Once upon a time I needed a full-time man to repair a hundred commodes at a summer camp I managed. I had no luck advertising for plumber/janitor/maintenance types.

So, when I rewrote the ad, I said:

"WANTED: A HYDRAULIC MECHANIC."

Four applicants called the next day.

Well, it was my first experience in playing games with titles. And if God is just, I'll pay in the hereafter. Be sure you make prospective employers define your title before accepting employment.

Is there any benefit in the probationary period for the job candidate?

There's something to be said for it.

The probationary period means that you can back out with grace if the organization or your job doesn't pan out. For years now I've been trying to convince my clients and the company I work for never to hire anyone on a so-called "permanent" basis without at least a three-month look-see period. Employers shouldn't, normally, go out on the limb. And as for employees: well, marriages aren't made in heaven, and neither are jobs.

A healthy organization never hires until employer and employee share the same bed for three months. "Jack, I want to hire you, but quite frankly you might not be the guy for the job. I want to make you an offer contingent on your ability to perform and our ability to plug you into the right situation. We'll make you an offer of three months' employment, and—if everything else is equal—you're on board after that time subject to your performance and business activity. Now, this is what we would like you to do . . ."

What about the four-day work week?

It's found increasingly now—in police departments, publishing houses, investment advisory firms.

A ten-hour day; a four-day week.

It's surely the best thing since striped toothpaste.

And in a free-formed organization, where you want to work, come salary-negotiating time, you might bring up the four-day week. It could save your marriage, improve your health, and replace war, commerce, and crime as America's number-one institution.

What's the Department of Wage and Salary Administration?

That's where the man who hires you might send you to negotiate your salary.

In the best organizations, the chap who hires you should have the power to negotiate your salary in conjunction with the controller. After all, he's the responsible party. But, alas, some organizations are so large now that a whole department is necessary to administer the compensation plans of the people who work there.

Most organizations usually designate the company flub to work out "equitable" wage and salary policy. In larger organizations, this fellow has five spastic clerks with M.A.s in Personnel Administration working somewhere in the bowels of the company. In a vital organization, the first people fired are in the Department of Wage and Salary Administration.

So, if you go to work for a big organization, you'll deal with these people. Remember, if your organization is fair, they pay people well who (1) bring in the business, (2) manage the business well. Those who bring in the bacon make it. Everyone else is a functionary.

What department should I work in if making money is my main object in a job?

As Samuel Johnson once remarked, "No one is more harmlessly employed than in the making of money." So, first of all, don't be ashamed of it, and make damned sure your interest in money is conveyed to your potential employer.

If you want to make a lot of money, it's for sure that you're going to make money for the organization that has the good sense to hire you. My suggestion is that you advertise yourself as a marketing man, the man or woman who can bring in the business and fulfill the objectives of the organization.

Cynical?

Not in the least.

Without people out front "selling" whatever it is your organization does, nobody else has a job. So back up ten steps and rethink your prejudices about "salesmen." If they are any good, ten to one they are more than salespeople: they are analysts, experts, and leaders in some technical field. They do sell pots and pans and encyclopedias, but they also sell *to* the Congress of the United States, a government agency, a hard-nosed accounting firm. The point is, *they* must sell before anyone works.

So, to help yourself and the organization, become a "marketing" person. And since the first thing you do is sell yourself, job-hunting is good practice for a lifetime.

Remember, whatever you do, the man justly compensated is he who brings in the business. The accountants, production men, "administrative assistants to" . . . ad infinitum, subsist wholly on someone's ability to find work for the organization. If you are a marketing man, you are the most important element in an organization's ability to survive.

So searching out a high-paying, money-making position is OK?

Sure, if you know what you want—which, we have seen, is tough work.

Money, in the abstract, is meaningless; it's how you intend to spend it that counts. What are your objectives? The man or woman who says, "I won't accept less than $45,000," is not necessarily rating quality of work *second* to compensation. The nub of the problem is that money alone is never a satisfactory objective. Nor is self-fulfillment an end in itself (*poets must eat*). Reconciling these twin objectives, making compensation and "career" congruent, while tough and tricky, is not impossible.

Moreover, most natural "money-makers" are rarely materialists. Means, not ends, are central to those who are beneficiaries of great wealth (i.e., *earned* wealth).

Yes, but I'm looking for a lot more from a job than just a good salary.

Psychic compensation. It means rewards other than material.

Except for work in New York City, where $60,000 minimum is required to keep you and your family in the upper-middle class, the plain truth is that most people-of-plenty prefer modest salaries (given taxes) if a job pays off in "meaningful" ways. It could be a thousand things: the satisfaction of improving the lives of retarded children, the rewards of pure research, the happiness of working on real problems, the companionship of vital people, almost anything besides salary.

You seem to be saying, on the one hand: Bargain for every penny you can get; and, on the other: Money really isn't important.
Agreed.
There is a contradiction.
But my dialectic, while it might appear rather too Hegelian, does make sense—depending on the individual situation of each job-holder.
Toby Tyler ran away to the circus and worked for *nothing*, and he did the right thing. But if Toby took a job with IBM tomorrow, as its assistant publications chief, he should bargain for $28,000 minimum, meaningful fringes, and a corner office!
My observations support the following generalizations:
— "Glamor" jobs pay either nothing or everything.
— Public service positions pay more than the public suspects.
— Technical jobs pay well to start, but tend to sag in salary later on.
— Grunt employment often pays very well, but is the work steady and is it what we *want?*
— Industrial jobs often pay well, but it's the profit sharing, stock options, and incentive bonuses that count.
— International employment pays well-to-good, but it's the travel that hooks us in the end.
— Subsistence or expenses-only employment for a "cause" is a wacky life and usually a full one.
— Entrepreneurial jobs are dangerous (and fun), but the money goes back into the business!
— Senior management jobs pay the best, but the responsibilities can be crushing.
— Consultants are well paid but work is intermittent, and consultants miss seeing the impact of what they do.
Negotiating compensation finally depends on whether the institution that wants you *has the money available.* Don't take less than the best because you're grateful for the job in the first place, or because you want to make a good first impression on the boss. Ask and it shall be given.
On the other hand, your next job might mean a substantial cut

in pay. But if it's doing what you want and you've obtained the most lucre you can, who's ahead?

What about taking jobs in New York City? Don't you need a lot more money to live there?

Just living in New York, for instance, makes you worth twice as much as elsewhere because it *is* New York.

This is no jest.

I've spent a good part of my time these last ten years trying to convince some of America's top executive talent to take jobs with my clients in New York. Out in the provinces, in case you didn't know, New York has earned a bad name for itself. Being posted to New York by your company is roughly the corporate equivalent of a tough Peace Corps assignment or submarine duty. Accordingly, most firms are having a devil of a time finding the right men and women to staff their New York headquarters. The competition for top jobs in New York is far less than legend allows. While Americans like to move up in their jobs, nobody wants to walk the plank. That's why you double your income requirements the moment you drive through the Holland Tunnel.

Are you making $20,000 per annum as a C.P.A. in Pottsville, Pennsylvania? And your employer wants you in the accounting division in the White Plains plant? Then you need a bare $40,000 to maintain your high standard of living out there in O'Hara country. So, the next lesson is to double your price if you are New York City-bound.

If you already have a job in New York and haven't been looking for another, then you are in deep trouble. Oh, sure, unemployment is terrible and masses of talented people are crawling through those canyons of commerce. But don't forget, they—the unemployed—are jobless. And you, a corporate gunslinger, are on a payroll. And employers are always more comfortable with the already employed.

Can you give some examples of a successful salary negotiation?

From whose point of view?

Since I usually sit on the opposite side of the desk and play yo-yo with job candidates, let me change seats with you and moxie us through an imaginary negotiation that takes into account some of the important points made here.

You are hired as a Foreign Student Adviser at Benedict Arnold College. Before you sign on, however, you meet with Mr. Silas Stringsaver, the executive assistant to the president of the college, to sign your papers and arrange your salary. Before you see him consider the following:

1. Phone a good friend on the faculty (who told you about the job) and learn what the salary range is at the college.

2. Let's say the lowest professional salary at the college is $9,000 per annum paid to grad students who carry full-time undergraduate teaching loads.

3. You meet Stringsaver armed to the teeth with hard information about yourself and what you're worth.

4. You ask what your predecessor received. Told it was $14,000, you ask for $14,500.

5. Stringsaver blanches, figuring to get you at $9,000 to $9,500.

6. You counterattack, telling him—nicely—that you are super-qualified: you speak fluent French, spent two years in Africa, sponsored foreign students while an undergraduate, and served as an escort interpreter for the State Department at $75 per day. (That works out to a little over $18,500 per year.) You figure you give Benedict Arnold a break at $14,500 because you really dig the job.

7. Impressed and a bit puzzled, Stringsaver explains that the budget permits him to pay no more than $9,000. You wonder aloud, quite innocently, how the college afforded $14,000 last year. "Is it because I'm a woman?" You look him straight in the eye and wear a winsome suspicion of a smile.

8. Stringsaver curses silently and reflects that his starting salary in 1941 was $2,500. And he's only making $17,000 in 1973. "These goddamned spoiled kids," he thinks (with some justice).

9. Stringsaver recovers, makes a couple of phone calls. It seems that Harvey Wallbanger, last year's Foreign Student Adviser, also

assumed certain teaching responsibilities. And since he was a member of the faculty and a Ph.D. besides, the college felt justified in paying some of his salary from faculty (rather than the administrative) budget.

10. "Great! I taught English as a Second Language in Africa. I feel sure I could teach foreign students English while working as their Adviser." Stringsaver, who knows Wallbanger was fired for being the faculty flub, is slowly won over by your insouciance. You remind him of his daughter.

11. Stringsaver tells you to interview at the Language Arts Center. If they think you qualify, you come aboard at Benedict Arnold at $14,500.

12. You thank him, then commiserate about the financial plight of the private college. You imply that, without first-rate administrators such as one sees at Benedict Arnold, most colleges would fold. He agrees, modestly. After you leave, Stringsaver calls your boss and tells him what a great gal he hired for that Foreign Student Adviser position.

A few final words of advice to all of you fighting your personal battle with the rising cost of living:

1. If money is your object in the job search, say so. Don't talk about "a challenging career with a new firm" or "wanting to be where the action is." I hear this bushwa every day. Flat out, say you want more money, deserve it, and can show any employer why.

2. Insist, in any new job (or in your current job), on an annual salary-and-responsibilities review. This puts employers on notice that you intend to earn your way to the top.

3. A low salary and interesting job might be OK if it's relevant and encourages personal growth.

4. If your boss is fair and just, you obtain your just deserts. If not, seek another organization.

5. Salaries are important *only* compared to other salaries paid out in the organization. They are invidious symbols of rank.

6. Lastly, a salary is *earned*. It comes if you do a good job, an effective job, a better-than-average job. *Nobody but slobs works solely for money—let it be the thing that follows outstanding performance.*

What happens if I begin a job, and the job I really want is offered two months later?

Quit and take the second job.

It's crackers to be "obligated" to employers. Betcha he/she will congratulate you on your good luck.

Rejecting the job you want out of a malignant sense of obligation or loyalty is eliminating yourself. Martyrdom hardly befits anyone who wants to become the person he/she can be.

SEVEN

The People Game

The name of my business is really the people game: a professional labor exchange where employers and job-seekers alike discover one another, bid for each other's services, and purchase a product based on their respective requirements.

If you accept a job, therefore, you really *do* hire yourself an employer. In return for your service, the institution owes you certain dues and services, like a salary. Study the feudal system. The similarities between corporate, institutional America and the manorial system of Central Europe is astonishing. The ancient barons —the counterpart of today's corporate managers—exacted specialized services from their vassals: the hewers of wood and haulers of water, the sheriff, the wardens, and the knights. For these services, which were largely economic and military, vassals demonstrated loyalty to their masters and performed certain social acts of obeisance. The nobles, in return, guaranteed the livelihood (i.e., income) of their vassals and protected them.

Well, times have changed, but not *that* much.

We still owe our employers loyalty—though only eight hours a day, and only so long as our services are not outbid by a competitor. We still make social obeisance, though we generally don't admit it—we view our employers with a kind of American deference best defined by an anthropologist.

Of course, the state has assumed control of the military. We now owe it, rather than our lords and masters, this particular duty.

My point is essentially that the employment relationship, while at best tentative, mutually beneficial, often more social than we think (How many of our best friends happen to be also our working companions?), is based on a reciprocity of dues and services. In other words, it's still feudal.

Are you saying that organizational loyalty is largely outdated?
Not entirely.

If the purposes of the organization for which you labor suit your craft, talents, and beliefs, then your relationship is healthy, although still tentative. Tentative because organizations and the individuals who comprise them are constantly changing. One continually renews, readjusts, or terminates employment relationships because changing conditions no longer make the relationship healthy. Learning how to find a new job, switching fields, job-jumping, are skills which should be taught—even at business schools, which are the last strongholds of the organizational-loyalty syndrome.

Yes, but employees are dependent on employers.
That's the trouble.
Employers are equally dependent on employees.
And that's the trouble too.

Without wanting to make too strong a psychological case here, let me simply say that any kind of a dependency relationship—whether between mother and child, wife and husband, or employee and employer—breeds resentment and hostility. That kind of atmosphere permeates the employment relationship of twentieth-century America. How many people do you know who really *hate* their employer? Why? Because they need that paycheck. They feel *forced* to work. They call it their duty, and they say it's for the wife and kids, but in truth, they despise their employers.

Now, nobody who wants a reasonably healthy mental life wants that. To hate what you do and for whom you do it eight hours a day breeds psychosomatic diseases and kinky neuroses.

So what do you do?
Well, if you can help it (and most job-seekers don't know how to help themselves), never accept employment based purely on need. And many employers—believe it or not—often retain people on their payroll based on that person's needs rather than on organizational requirements.

How many clergy, academics, military, business executives are being kept on somebody's payroll for pathologically compassionate reasons? And I'll bet in the gut of every time-server who knows Big Brother is watching out for him, there's a terrible hatred masquerading as gratitude.

So when looking for a job, treat potential employers as *equals*. What you want is a reciprocally respectful *business* relationship in which compensation is based on *contribution*.

That's why the best employment relationship is the commission-sales type. You are paid on a performance basis. You can measure your productivity, and you and your employer work *together* rather than hierarchically in reaching your objectives.

Performance contracting is possible and desirable in most employment relationships.

In looking for a job the secret of a healthy relationship is to demonstrate how you can *help* an organization.

From then on, it's up to you and the organization to bargain with each other to determine what your contribution is worth.

What is the ideal size of an organization?

I like smaller organizations. If you do too, don't work for an organization where you must relate to more than fifty people. Nervous systems overload when dealing with too many people. If under fifty people, chances are good that it will be a humane organization. Many large outfits are, thus, opting for smaller profit centers, which takes into account a natural predilection of people to know (as well as work with) each other.

In plain fact, most people are not occupationally happy in departments of more than fifty people. In larger organizations, *effective decentralization* can postpone giantism (or elephantiasis), but not eliminate it entirely.

So hire yourself an organization where you learn the job on the job. (Your skill is learning *how* to get jobs and learning *from* them.) Be sure the organization is *human size*.

We read that executive productivity on the job has dropped. Why?

People don't work as hard as they did once upon a time. Socializing, coffee breaks, luncheons, downtime, etc. are substitutes for work. They are especially evident in the executive suite. Twenty years ago, you found an executive, an assistant, and one clerical staffer. Today, there are several assistants, and even assistants to assistants. More and more people cause each other work. That's why the government is irradiated with "co-ordinator" positions.

In other words, many people on the job today are doing "busy" work but are less productive. The fancy word for this disease is "entropy," and it's epidemic in the executive suite.

Yes, but there's a variety of jobs where performance evaluation is strictly qualitative and subjective.

True.

Then it's between you and your employer to establish indices of measurement which calibrate your contribution. In a word, how do you know what a judgment job is worth?

All management jobs are subjective. Still, these jobs should be evaluated.

Usually the marketplace governs what these jobs cost an employer by way of salaries to people who perform them. It's up to you to find out what the range of compensation is in your craft. Then bargain to obtain the highest possible figure.

So even on judgment jobs you are always being evaluated.

"What have you done for me lately?" is the attitude of my boss.

And that's worth remembering. Healthy organizations never pay you on the basis of past performance, but rather on present prospects or future expectations. Pick up the sports page.

Ball players' salaries are based on what their owners expect them to do next year. Who cares if Johnny Backstop hit .350 in 1980 if he can't hit his weight today? Remarkably, the same kind of psychology is at work in the job market.

What you can do *today* for your organization is what counts. That's why I deplore elimination of the grading system in college. The Antioch plan. Most graduates can't abide grades. But, goddammit, everybody worth his salt is being *graded* all the time. Fairly or unfairly, somebody is keeping score.

Thousands simply can't recognize that organizations don't pay their help on the basis of good looks, philosophical purity, high IQ, or social connections.

"What have you done for us lately?" is management's toughest question. And the one they should be asking everyone, from the executive vice-presidents dining on the expense-account circuit down to the squaw and men working in "administration."

Isn't that a pretty cynical and hard-hearted attitude?
Not in the least.
There is unemployment insurance.
There is public welfare.
There is Social Security.
All are shields against the slings and arrows of outrageous fortune.
Work is an honorable estate.
Those who feel *forced* to work because it's their duty, who feel grateful to employers "for keeping them on" while others pull their weight, secretly die a cubit every working day.
You do no one a favor by making him *labor against his real wishes*. That is truly hard-hearted and cynical. To keep a man or woman in bondage because an organization's retirement program is too attractive for you to dismiss them is cynical and self-destructive.*
There's both bribery and blackmail at work here and a sickness unto death.
And it's bad for organizations and people.

So you recommend quitting a job once the business relationship fouls up?
That might be in a month . . . or after twenty years. The relationship may sour because . . .
— your boss is fired and the new man doesn't cotton to your personality.
— the organization takes on new purposes different from when you were hired.
— there's a roadblock between you and the job you want: the boss's nephew.

* See *If Things Don't Improve Soon, I May Ask You to Fire Me* (Anchor Books).

— you've grown bored, out of touch with your own job.

All of these are signals that you should seriously consider leaving, or sit down and frankly talk out your problem with the boss.

What is a real job search like?
It's an adventure.
It means being free to find that *good* job!
But most people fear freedom. They take a job, any job, based on its availability instead of as a positive choice. Big mistake.
Competent job-seekers have no such problem. Taking a job they want, they stay as long as it satisfies. Once this feeling is gone, they grapple with what they want to do *next*—either inside or outside the organization where they work.
Job-seekers are free to live the adventurous way, free to go hire an employer. That's what looking for work means.
It does take time—the way a shopper cost-compares items to determine value. A purchase is made when one chooses a job that comes closest to what one *wants*.

But suppose you've invested fifteen years in the same organization and the same job. Who wants you . . . or needs you?
It means you've got to analyze what you did best where you worked, break that job down into functional components, assign each part of the job a name, and then advertise your abilities based on an inventory of accomplishments, rather than organizational affiliation, salary level, or job title.
Ex-foreign service officers, clergy, military, academics, and other specialists have this problem. The first step in its solution is breaking out of the stereotype your institutional affiliation assigns you.
It means smashing, if you will, your own self-image.
It means, above all, an act of imagination.
It means a conscious act of discrimination: judging who you are, what you do best, and translating that into a broad spectrum of occupations you might want to follow.
Be a person of discrimination.

Don't employers discriminate too?
Yes. That's human.

Where your discriminations and a potential employer's coincide is the point of sale in an employment relationship.

Anyone who hires discriminates by definition.

It's not necessarily a bad characteristic (with no apologies to the Equal Employment Opportunities Commission). A person who discriminates is a person who judges.

The best employers judge long and hard before they choose an employee. At the same time, all judgment reflects prejudice. No one escapes.

In running the interview gamut, a thousand prejudices might be working *for* or *against* you. To show you what I mean, the following continues my earlier list of employment prejudices carefully nurtured over the years:

— No man wearing a diamond ring ever found employment through me.

— Women in white gloves I tend to knock myself out for in finding a job (something Oedipal here).

— Women libber's note: many men, including me, look askance at women job-seekers who have under-school-age children.

— Women with freckles often get the employment nod from me.

— Persons who combine scientific and humanistic backgrounds I favor for important jobs.

— People who successfully switch fields find me a mooch for their services.

— People who write in their résumé ". . . managed a 3½-million-dollar program to co-ordinate . . . etc." are never invited to interview.

— Those who use the word "swinging" in any but a facetious sense leave me with a case of chilblains.

— Professional clergymen, engineers, teachers, lawyers, and military who suddenly "want to be where the action is" never find it where I work.

My "hidden agenda," however, is no worse or crazier than other employers'. So if you are "lucky" in your job search, it's usually because of a mesh between your hidden agenda and the employer's: the rocks in his head fill the holes in yours!

I've hired hundreds of people in the last four years and made thousands of dollars selling good horseflesh to client firms. I know what I'm doing; otherwise I wouldn't be writing this book. But occasionally, in the darkness of my soul, I admit that my raft of prejudices won't withstand scientific analysis. That's why the business of headhunting is an art rather than a science.

Doesn't industry put a high premium on "getting along"?
It was truer in the fifties than now.

The "Organization Man" is still with us, however, complete with button-down brain, gray-flannel mouth, and lockstep locomotion.

It's not all his fault.

My observations confirm that most people hate working in very large organizations. But since most employment opportunities are found, obviously, among huge organizations, the price we pay is a diminution in personality development—hence, the Organization Man.

Studies of men and women at work in these industrial/corporate /governmental/academic octopi suggest that the great problem is interpersonal relationships—in a word, getting along. The motto of the Organization Man is: "Don't Spit in the Soup; We All Have To Eat."

Countless manpower studies bear out this truth. Thus, in looking for a job, your SIR (Smooth Interpersonal Relationships) factor is carefully evaluated—even by the Personnel Department.

Why don't people make it on a job?

Because they can't make it with people. Now, this doesn't mean you become part of a homogeneous mass, the specific gravity of most organizations. Just the opposite. It's your job to become a visible, productive, and vital part of the organization, and *at the same time* make it with the people you work with, over, and for.

This is not an easy art, and nobody bats perfect in the human-interrelatedness department.

But if you can become effective on the job, win the loyalty of your subordinates, the admiration of your peers, and the gratitude of your superiors—you have a great future.

You think you have the potential?

Think again. Repeatedly in my experience in many types of organizations I see organizational heroes (ranging from the tiger in the mailroom to the Executive Chairman) unravel during "people" crises. People crises are a thousand things:

1. Your secretary suddenly feels oppressed working for you.

2. Your boss doesn't have lunch with you any more.

3. You are dead wrong in something and can't admit it.

4. Your job is dissolved, your ego liquidated.

5. You do a good job and somebody else gets the credit.

6. You suddenly lose your sense of humor and find titles, job descriptions, and status-standing in an organization important. You are in grave trouble and about to quit.

Like the guy who just can't make his marriage work, a divorce seems called for. You solve a problem by eliminating it. Until, of course, you are re-employed and the same difficulty surfaces again. While I can't document this argument, I'd wager a month's pay that chronic job-hoppers quit every organization for the same reason.

Do all employers share some characteristics in common?
Yes.
A few.
They all have hidden jobs, hidden agendas, and find people in the hidden manpower pool.
They love to talk about themselves.
They all have problems.
They come in every shape and size. The more you know about what they do, the better chance you have of landing a job.
A good ploy after writing and sending off your résumé to a prospective employer is to ask him to send you information on his business. Use this material to guide your interviews.
Everyone loves to talk about what they do—especially employers. Flattery and pertinent questions make favorable impressions. A thousand job-holders are working today because they got the hiring authority to talk about *his* job. So be sure to interview the interviewer.
Finally, an employer wants to hire someone because *he* has a

problem. When he talks to you, he's thinking, "Can this person solve *my* problem?"

So, when you interview, find out what your interlocutor's problems *are* . . . a bevy of potential jobs might develop for you!

Sharp, analytical, and probing questions on your part convince employers—usually harried by a flock of problems—that you are just the man or woman to whom he can hand over this particular prickly pear.

In some of my job interviews I've been given the run-around.

That's because a lot of employers don't know how to employ *people*. If people would just stay put on a Xerox résumé and not betray human characteristics, some institutions—like the phone company, the U. S. Army, Anaconda Copper—would all feel better. These organizations minister to every need—except one: individuality. (They compensate for this by a heavy advertising program denying charges that they don't treat their help as individuals.)

So, it's true that on a job campaign you're subject to the games employers play.

Games employers play?

1. *"Now I have a job, now I don't."* Henry Hoax didn't line up his ducks. He has no approval from the controller on a job he wants filled, no idea what qualifications he seeks, and is vague about specifics.

He is incompetent.

You don't want to work for him (unless he's looking for someone to straighten out his atrocious hiring techniques).

2. *"Would you mind—as part of your job as my special assistant—doing a few clerical chores?"* You are about to be hired as a secretary. If you've accepted, you've been had.

Make crystal-clear that you are a professional applicant. Let your résumé and person show it.

3. *"I'm looking for a young man with a Ph.D. in statistics, with five years' progressively more responsible experience in a research organization, married with children, a fine publications history, a*

minority member, and speaks fluent Urdu." An employer of unreasonably Utopian vision. In two months—when his own job is on the line—he'll take a second look at you.

4. "*Say the job you want won't open up for about two months —would you mind terribly coming on as an administrative assistant until the urban-planning job becomes available?*"
"Oh, yeah, what else is new?"

Why is the Personnel Department to be avoided at all costs?
The reasons: (1) The Personnel Manager is swamped with job applicants; (2) his organization keeps him too busy doing things your teachers made you do after school; (3) he carries no clout with the people who hire.

Robert Townsend in *Up the Organization* writes: "The trouble with personnel experts is that they use gimmicks borrowed from manufacturing: inventories, replacements, recruiting, selecting, indoctrinating-and-training machinery, job rotation, and appraisal programs. And this manufacturing of men is about as effective as Dr. Frankenstein was . . . the sounder approach is agricultural. Provide the climate and proper nourishment and let the people grow themselves. They'll amaze you."

A lot of organizations have been talking to me about their training programs.
Organizations which prominently advertise training programs for "entry-level professionals" are on the downward trend of a Bell curve. Only departments of Personnel, Wage and Salary Administration, and Public Relations compete with the Training Department in superfluity.

Training departments are the first signs of an organizational disease well known in corporate and governmental America: elephantiasis.

The bigger an organization is, the larger its training department —then the harder *you* fall.

Don't lobby for a slot on a training program *anywhere* (no, not at the Bank of America or HUD) where you spend a year reading mind-blowing tracts, attending "executive" seminars (which wouldn't burst the brain of a Harvard professor), and playing kindergarten hopscotch with your fellow "management interns" (known by their betters, who do the work while the management trainees play organizational tic-tac-toe, as "crown princes"). Don't be a crown prince; work at being an elected monarch.

These training programs, which any trainee—if pressed—would admit are not worth a pitcher of warm spit, are found at the highest level (the White House Interns) and at the lowest (Sticky Wicket, Inc.). Training programs spawn like guppies.

Why?

I'm saving the answer for my next book: *The Decline and Fall of the American Republic.*

I really want a job, but I don't like the politics on the job. Am I being unrealistic?

Unless you want to be a stack librarian. And I'm not so sure about librarians any more.

Politics is as much a part of life as sport, sex, illness, or in-laws. Found anywhere where two or more people gather. Where you work, there you find it. Don't fight it; accept it.

Politics is compromise, trading one idea for another, acting out responsibilities and dreams.

In any organization, the politics of the place can be ruthless and claustrophobic. But politics also enlivens and changes your work environment overnight. If you care about yourself and what you do, your job on the job is to find allies: people who think like you. Conflict, the drama of politics, results as opposing forces collide.

Nothing wrong with conflict: it causes sparks and lights fires, and with light an organization sees its way.

So be an effective politician; if you believe in the organization, put it and yourself *first.* By doing so, you steal a march on everyone else who puts only *himself* first.

And if the organization's not worth it (and you and your allies can't change it), start another job campaign. Hire yourself an employer for whom you can be effective. In other words, where you can play politics.

Your politics.

What are your guidelines about promotion on the job?
If after nine months on a job you haven't been promoted, something's wrong:

1. Every year you should receive a cost-of-living increment, 7 to 20 per cent.

2. You should be generously compensated if *you* bring in new business or responsibilities to an organization, or if you manage what you do so well that organizational capability is augmented.

3. If you work for a good organization, you should not have to ask for a promotion. If you do, do so by written memo to your boss—then his boss, if there's no action.

4. Avoid being promoted to your level of incompetence (the Peter Principle). You might be a tiger as a programer, and a bomb as a controller. Don't let an organization push responsibilities on you which you *cannot* handle.

5. Again, get yourself together and define what to do *next*. You are a better judge of your own capability than your boss is.

6. Think twice if offered a raise. Does someone else deserve it more? Push to have him or her promoted; that's putting the organization and your own feelings *first* and winning a helluva ally.

7. So if promoted, ask yourself, Do I deserve it? Justice is important—as important as your ego. So spread it around, like money and manure. A lot of justice makes living things grow.
Namely, human beings.

What about job-jumping before you're fired?
Not a bad idea.
Most people are fired for *political* reasons. Once the weather vane is blowing in the wrong direction, you know it's time to jobjump.
After nine months on a job, if you're not moving up, then think . . . maybe some other organization needs your talents.
Job-jumping is OK—if you jump up!
Job-hopping, however, is bad. When you job-hop, you don't jump up—you jump sideways.

Beware. Most job-hoppers don't leave one job *for* another: they flee one job and take any other.

Job-hoppers are kith and kin to shelf-sitters: these are middle-management drones who never quit their job. Of the two, the job-hoppers are less deleterious to society—they often don't survive on any job long enough to do permanent damage. But the shelf-sitters lobotomize organizations.

Job-hoppers move sideways all their occupational lives, usually at the same salary level, and always with an appropriate story of woe. In the trade they are known as losers. So don't be a loser.

Before you change jobs, be sure it's a step up for you in salary, responsibility, and relevance. Otherwise, ten years hence you'll have a lot of explaining to do in hundreds of awkward interviews.

What should job-hoppers do who go from job to job?
In the trade they are called grasshoppers.

More goats than lambs, I bet, among ticket punchers.

Clearly, employers are wary of those who can't *become expert* in anything, drifting from one occupation to another. The main reason is the confusion in the minds of grasshoppers, an inability to focus on goals, "a need to fail." But nobody *wants* to fail. Unfortunately, a pattern of behavior develops which makes termination an inevitable product of some people's work experience. Clearly, at the point someone is aware that this *is* the problem, clinical help is in order.

Is it really true—what you've been saying—that older people face the most heartless discrimination on the job market?
Maybe only one group suffers worse: fat people.

The plain American truth is that this country is infatuated with youth, beauty, whiteness, WASPness, and status. Nothing less than a transvaluation of our value system (which is beginning) will change the situation.

But people over fifty who might otherwise be acceptable face a horrendous problem. All the worse, if the employment world was their oyster up to that time.

For people over fifty, they could do worse than think seriously about starting their own business, becoming self-employed consultants, or commissioned salespeople—in other words, letting their time and effort govern their income. Straight-salaried jobs—judgment jobs—are often reserved for the middle-years people, those people an organization wants to invest time and money in. The tragedy of being over fifty is the presumption that older people can't "grow." Stronger yet is a presumption that older people can't cross generational lines and communicate.

Nonsense. But caprice is often the name of the employment game.

So, if older, steal a leaf from the young—all of whom want to do their "own thing." The problem with the young is that they have the imagination but not the experience. My impression of older people is that they have the experience but not the imagination. Either way, whether young or old, you are going to need courage. Turning your back on the organizational syndrome is an act of both defiance and redemption. While this approach is often an invitation to failure, those who remain behind, secure in the bosoms of institutional safety, are only hiding the *possibility* of failure.

You haven't said anything about racism. Is it still as bad for Blacks, Chicanos, Puerto Ricans as always?

Any minority member with an M.B.A. from Harvard can practically write his own ticket anywhere for salaries 20 per cent higher than his WASP competitors.

In the middle-management regions there has been enormous improvement. In my judgment—remember, I'm white, middle class, and forty-five years old—things are looking up for *educated minority applicants*; downstairs in the kitchen, it's business as usual.

This is not the time or the place for me to develop a long exegesis on the race problem. But one word of advice:

If promoted or transferred on your next job, recruit your replacement from a minority group. If we all practiced this kind of enlightened racism, occupational discrimination would disappear before you could say Jackie Robinson!

So long as you focus on talent among classical minorities. This kind of reverse racism/sexism *works*. If, however, people are hustled, recruited, and hired for judgment jobs primarily *because* of race or sex, it will cause resentment. Plenty of capable women and

Blacks are suspicious of being hired for *who* they *are* rather than *what* they can *do*.

Aren't teachers in oversupply in today's job market?
Back in the late fifties, the country panicked about our educational system.
Now the hens have come home to roost.
The result is the biggest glut of teachers in history. Every kind of teacher, from pre-elementary to postdoctoral, is swamping every personnel office in the country.
Here are some suggestions:
— Start your own private school.
— Manage a day-care center.
— Obtain specialized training for a specific population: retarded children, juvenile dropouts, underachievers. Demand is still there for the special-education teacher.
— Think about Job Corps camps, Neighborhood Youth Corps programs, and counseling as alternate careers.
— Work in a "knowledge" industry with an organization that develops, markets, and implements new teaching techniques, curriculums, and subjects.
In brief, teaching is a field with broad applicability to curriculum development, sales, management. Study what elements in your "teaching" personality make you an effective teacher. Is it leadership, research, organizational ability? Then translate those skills into another "field." If you can teach, you have by definition a lot to contribute to any organization you hire as an employer.

How can "hiring yourself an employer" help placement counselors?
Counselors need to persuade individuals to get in touch with their feelings.
Routinely bringing employers to campus, managing useless "career seminars," providing job-placement information (usually written by some organization's PR department), compiling résumé books—are *not*, repeat *not*, being a counselor.
— Effective counselors make students focus on themselves, not on the job market.

— Counselors help students *research* themselves before they research *jobs*.

— Counselors don't rely on aptitude tests or life-planning guidebooks—they want to get inside a human being's head by becoming involved with him/her.

— Effective counselors are coaches and players. The best have "switched" careers two or three times in their lives!

— A counselor never says to students, "Do what you want." This is the kind of noninvolved comment they hear from parents.

— Effective counselors are not afraid of sharing painful information with students ("Do you really think you can hack medical school if you *failed* anatomy?").

— Effective counselors focus on jobs (not careers), assignments (not "work"), next steps (not last steps), tomorrow (not the day after tomorrow), desires (not duties), reality (not romance), accomplishments (not diplomas).

— Finally, finding out what one *wants next* in life can't be done *alone*. The effective counselor *cares* about his clients, stays in touch with them, and learns from them.

Well, I've always told my children they should do what they want!

Tomtit.

That's no help to a child. What's usually missing is any parental emotional involvement with a child. And middle-class parents today cop-out by muttering, "Your mother and I want you to do what you want!" Big deal.

What children need is a sense of caring, intense caring about the scary problems of becoming independent. A lot of *dis*couragement, criticism and investigation (as well as loving encouragement) is what a child is crying out for from his parents. Far, far better for a parent to announce that junior is *expected* to take over the family business. That kind of caring at least gives the child something to *react* against, helps him sort out if he wants to go to law school as much as his father wants him to. But leaving a child abandoned, to cope with his future alone, is intolerable. Career counselors, placement people, and yours truly see the victims of this philosophy of nonconcern every working day.

What do you mean, "You can't look for a job alone"?

The brave are lonely (and usually ineffective).

Unemployment is a crisis. Like most personal crises—divorce, bankruptcy, bereavement, loss—it can become a time of enormous personal growth. Like a "challenging" job, personal crises *test and push us,* compel us to rise and challenge the gods.

So the meteoric expansion of group therapy (the "self-awareness revolution") is a harbinger of a widely shared belief that people *together* can solve problems. Theology, as you would expect, is not my department; but my observations are that those who believe in God are never *alone* on or off the job.

So you can't become the person you want to be alone?

That's why job co-ops, like Forty Plus, are important; why prayer is efficacious; why therapy can help; why spouse, parents, even children, are central in helping you and me in our job search.

Plainly, people frustrated in finding what they want need a "coach." Otherwise, how explain the proliferation of career advisory services? But you needn't lay out thousands of dollars for advice if you have a relationship with one other person (or God). Becoming the person you want to be cannot be done in isolation. And this help might be criticism: good coaches are critics. People we trust love our weaknesses because they sense that "our deficits are the defects of our virtues" (Montaigne). So, in your job search, don't be ashamed to admit that you need help. Needing and giving help are definitions of our humanity. And we are not "islands" unto ourselves unless we hate the mainlands. We are people living in communities.

So the aim of effective "career" counseling is to teach people how to conduct an independent job search, not place them in a job?

Exactement!

Many people think they have no power. It's a banal complaint favored by spokesmen for groups of people with a grievance. That's because power in the minds of most people is exterior; it acts on them, thus they feel unfree. And unfree people are unhappy.

Other people know they have power and use it to help themselves but are unable or unwilling to help others. They, too, are unhappy, since human happiness is a result of feeling free together, i.e., with another human being.

And then there are people who have and use power *for others,* never for themselves. They are often spiteful, resentful, and unfulfilled because power benefits everyone but themselves.

Finally, there are those who use power for both themselves and other people. These folks are generally freer, happier, and more self-fulfilled.

"Career" counselors need to show their clients that they have *power* to change themselves and the world.

But shouldn't "career" counselors focus on "majors," "fields," "organizations," and "professions" to assist their clients in discovering where to look?

That's the conventional definition of *placement* counseling. But job counselors who want to do the job need to focus on a client's abilities and persuade the client to do the same.

Finally, "career" counselors should drop the word "career" entirely. It's a worthless expression. Call yourself a "Job Counselor," "Occupational Therapist," or "Job Coach". I call myself a "Job Shrink"—it's as close a definition as any.

What else can a coach or a professional counselor teach me?

That you are a *free* person, that you needn't accept any job because you feel you must, that unfree people rarely qualify for judgment jobs, that freedom in the job search is likely to be more self-fulfilling with a consequent increase in personal self-esteem and happiness, that you can't control the future but you can plan for your next job, that people are "lucky" who plan for it, that you do have *choices* and that choosing the third-best job (because the first two weren't offered) doesn't mean you are "locked into this job for life," that you are not a *victim* powerless to control your environment, that you act as much on your environment as it acts on you, that good jobs go to those who want them, and that "the size of a dog in a fight is less important than the size of the fight in the dog" (Woody Hayes).

So don't focus on a career; zero in on skills?

On my trips to colleges I'm often asked what my "field" is! And out in the business world people want to know what organization I represent! And my prospective mother-in-law wanted to know my *profession!* And in my youth I sought a *career.*

These words no longer suffice. Sure, there are professions and organizations and fields of study and, allegedly, *careers.* But, as we have seen, most people will have two or three fields of study, four or five careers, work for a score of organizations, and increasingly pursue a variety of professions.

Why?

Because talent is mobile, skills are transferable, and the world is changing every day. And this crazy quilt congeries of abilities inside everybody is the synergy that drives the modern world.

Few of us "realize" all of our "skills," nor does schooling induce "skills" so much as refine them. What we do well is applicable in many "fields."

What happens if I'm fired?

"Yes, Virginia, there are people who are fired, but who don't necessarily fail."

If it happens, make tracks as soon as possible and find yourself another berth. But be careful of accepting any job; plenty of good reputations fade away in rebounding from a bad job situation.

If fired, our propensity to rationalize comes into play: we make up a thousand beautiful reasons why we haven't worked out on the job, nine hundred and ninety-nine of them untrue. Do yourself and your boss a favor: if you are not working out, confront him with this fact. A long discussion follows and clears the air.

The best test of a manager is how he fires people.

The best test, if fired, is how you handle it (which says a lot about you).

Let's face it, almost everyone loses a job for a variety of reasons: a political reshuffling, a departmental merger, the new boss doesn't fancy your long hair, a clash of principles versus pragmatics . . . and on and on and on. The best thing to do is set aside an hour, write out the reasons you think you should leave, and ask for an appointment with the boss.

By taking the initiative (making sense in a tough situation), a frank exchange takes place and clears the air. You took your boss off the hook and showed some mettle. That's why he'll think twice about keeping you on at Sticky Wicket, Inc.

Lastly, if you've been fired for outrageous reasons and nobody levels with you, dip your quill in the nearest pen pot and write the boss (or his board) a nice, pointed little note. It won't help anything but your ego, but that's the most important thing you've got.

I think you're saying there are no dream jobs, but I've known and heard of people who really seem to have terrific opportunities.

Far be it from me, humble reader, to destroy your dreams. That's the point of writing your obituary, remember—to ignite that old dream mechanism.

Yes, indeed. Dream jobs *do* exist. But you make them happen. How good a job you do is the leverage you need to *expand* your current job into something with greater scope. You do this by changing the attitudes of your peers, subordinates, and superiors. You define a new *objective* for your department, you take on new responsibilities, you're a bear for more work—you make your humdrum, pedestrian job into the dream job you've always wanted.

That's because you know yourself so well, you are so put together, you know how to put your feelings first, you can show your boss how this helps him and the organization, and Presto!—you've worked yourself out of the common rut and staked out a new job, the kind of job everyone always wants and never finds. Because that's the job you truly must make yourself.

What do you mean, that you can learn from the job search and apply it on the job?

Let's face it: You learn more about business (negotiating *one* contract), more about "personnel" (hiring ten people), more about sales (making five sales), than from all the textbooks ever written.

Make your job hunt an experience in sales, learning your field, idea mongering, self-management. The carryover on the job is astounding.

I want work with an institution that I can change. Is this necessarily a naïve notion?

And you want to change it into a more democratic, just, and humane working environment. If you succeed, you'll be doing the institution for which you work a good turn.

For those who want a career of changing institutions, working in the Establishment—anyplace—offers a fertile field for socially constructive change.

Making the "system" work so that there is a little more distributive justice is not an ignoble calling.

Many people are "fired" on "principle" from their first job. Before you quit, or are fired, give the organization a chance to change—quitting is often the easy way out. Try to find allies within the organization and present your demands collectively and with dignity. Ill-mannered demonstrations provoke irrational response and do little except massage the egos of those challenging the system. And if you change the system some (and are not cashiered), you live another day when you can change it more.

Don't wear a whistle around your neck. But carry it on every job—and blow it for the country's sake.

EIGHT

The Working Woman

If you happen to be a woman, a forty-plus, a highly trained specialist, a B.A. generalist, terribly young, an ex-con, a noncollege graduate, or a member of a minority group, everything written up to now applies to you. I mean, all jobless people share certain problems; and I hope what you've read has helped.

Finally, however, you—the unemployed—are a great deal more than simply jobless. You usually belong to a specific *class* and share within the confines of that group special problems not common to other classes of unemployed.

So, if you're a woman, there are special strategies in the job search. However, the fundamental approach to hiring yourself an employer remains, regardless of race, sex, occupational status, and so forth.

Well, I'm a woman, and that's a problem in itself when you confront a society of male dominance in the job search. Any special advice?

Plenty.

And take it from me, as a woman you are different. And *vive la différence!* And on the job market it is, as philosophers are wont to say, in the nature of things for you to be perceived differently. That will *never* change, unless unisex sweeps all before it.

Thanks to Gloria Steinem, Bella Abzug, and Betty Friedan, I know I'm not necessarily a sex maniac—just a male chauvinist pig!

Well, men are slowly changing, incrementally to be sure. For example, in interviewing a woman these days I no longer . . .

—look at her legs before I study her face. (I do *that* second.)

— ask why she isn't happy as a suburban housewife. (There are no happy housewives in suburbia.)

— calculate how much my company saves hiring her (rather than some grasping, male oppressor.)

— expect her to act like a "lady." (The last lady I met was in 1964; and she emigrated.)

— treat her as a "sex object." (She should be so lucky.)

As a practicing male chauvinist, I join thousands of American men who, while professing a philosophy of equal pay for equal work, sometimes fail to practice it. My problem (which is what professional women grapple with everywhere) is believing that women are truly *serious* about judgment jobs. So many people, most of them young men, want *jobs*, but back off from hard work and responsibility. And judgment jobs require a greater commitment than many people are prepared to make in terms of time, emotion, personal relationships, children, and recreation.

Don't you agree that women are treated unequally in terms of salary, job definition, and responsibility in most employment situations?

But men, for example, have trouble landing jobs as receptionists, chambermaids, fashion editors, gossip columnists, Head Start directors, elementary school teachers, travel advisers, research assistants, secretaries, and dental assistants.

And the last ten years has seen huge improvement in the employment status of women in the military, medicine, academia, government, and the law.

But for the *top* jobs in every walk of occupational life, men still hold the reins.

So, there's the rub: Decision-making jobs, the kind of jobs you want, are unconsciously reserved for men.

But that's occupational sexism!

A few years ago I thought a "sexist" was someone who made untoward advances to the prettier secretaries in the supply room. No more.

So women have a positive *duty* to insist on egalitarian treatment in the marketplace. For no other reason than that the economy of an affluent society necessitates a job. Women who don't *need* to work are rare exceptions these days; many women positively must work to keep their families economically afloat.

Moreover, the millions of highly educated, underemployed, or unemployed women are one of America's least recognized social problems. And the children of unhappy mothers are making America's psychiatrists rich beyond anyone's dreams of avarice.

Aren't women made to feel sexually subordinate on the job?

Men are naturally the aggressors with women when it comes to sex. That might carry over on the job too. Men, for example, might be too protective of a woman on the job, too considerate (or completely inconsiderate), or come on like Valentino.

Women need to straighten us out pronto. For when this happens, men are confusing categories with environments. Company mashers, board-room Lotharios, and Daddy-Knows-Best types are effectively dealt with by an intelligent working woman if she knows who she is, what she wants, and what she can do, and if she makes it clear that a workplace is not a love nest.

Women do not become less womanly when they refuse advances (fraternal, paternal, or otherwise) of men who are an easy touch to the wiles of a seductive woman. And women need to de-escalate men's expectations. Accommodating men's expectations of you—except on-the-job performance—argues for a less than serious attitude on *your* part.

Any special hints for women?

My special contribution to the subject is that women are not *special*. That is, how they act as job-seekers, on the job, and terminating from a job is in no wise different from their male counterparts.

For openers, women who seek important work, judgment jobs, a place in the organizational sun, should:

1. quit feeling sorry for themselves.

2. recognize that most younger and middle-aged men are stronger advocates of equity between the sexes on the job market than are many women (according to a recent national poll).

3. know that—as a class—they are making enormous progress,

far greater than any other "minority" group, in the organizational world.

4. realize that bad luck on the job market (i.e., the promotion you missed, the job that fell through, the contract you were not awarded) is not necessarily happening to you *because you are a woman*.

5. realize that taking on the shibboleths, dress, and manners of males is nonsense. (Women from the better business schools, for example, are interviewing in three-piece tailored suits!) Androgyny might be fashionable, but paying males the compliment of imitation is not building on your strengths.

6. guard against swapping the boredom of suburbia for the boredom of the board room. Boredom is inside every one of us, not a product of our environments.

7. face the fact that 10 per cent of jobs in America are judgment jobs—tough to find, tough to qualify for, and tough to hold on to. Women who want them must be effective. No, not "nice" or "aggressive" or "cunning" . . .

8. realize that balancing the roles of mother and wife with "career" is a difficult and tricky art. *Some* women succeed at combining all three; most people (men, particularly) fail. All the more reason to think through whether *it's a judgment job you really want*.

9. face it: 90 per cent of jobs in America are not *decisive* inside organizations. Are you prepared to pay your dues in qualifying for a judgment job?

10. realize that economic independence, having a job, project, cottage industry—a talent you can exercise—is crucial to becoming happy with yourself. Also, it makes people (namely your husband, children, in-laws) *happier* with you.

It is a fiction that men want women to be *dependent* on them. That's OK during the first stages of courtship, marriage, and procreation, but a drag as a marriage/relationship moves into its second stages (husbands welcome a second income or a tax shelter). So whether it's a vocation or avocation, a special project or a regular job, a mad hobby or place in the corporate sun, an *outside-the-home* project (i.e., where you invest your emotions), a "job" helps the people around you, particularly your children, who see far too much of you anyway.

Children become far more independent and self-reliant when Mommy *stops* keeping them dependent on her. Many women deliberately tie hubby and children to their apron strings. That way they needn't face up to personal (and occupational) problems. Conversely, wives often work outside the home in order to *escape* personal problems with hubby and kids. At all events, women workaholics are as pitiful as domestic drudges who have no life outside the home.

Whether you are recycling back into the job market (after a twenty-year stint bringing up baby) or a young woman new on the job market (burning with a cold gemlike flame), the Walls of Jericho won't come tumbling down because you happen to be the new girl on the block. Men are not likely to give up their jobs because you want them to. Most working women today must sweat out time "on the line" before employers pass out the plums.

So it's arithmetical nonsense to cite spurious statistics (e.g., 90 per cent of the highly technical managerial positions are men, etc.) as proof of conscious discrimination. That women want these jobs is OK. But no man or woman wants people picked for jobs because of *who they are* (a woman); employers should pick people because of *what they do*. To think otherwise is illiberal, illogical, and probably paranoid.

If current trends continue—a big IF (plenty of women today are returning to motherhood)—by the end of this century, parity between men and women in judgment jobs is a certainty. A long time? But a blink of God's eyelash!

Finally, now that women are breaking down the doors of law, business, and other professional schools, it's worth repeating that the major jobs in America today are technical. And in high technology, engineering, and applied-science organizations women are as rare as a Swedish heatwave. So, if your daughter has a knack for math and likes science, give her a lot of love and encouragement. Engineering schools are the last bastion of male exclusivity. And we can't have too many of these guys, and now gals.

OK. What should a woman do to find and keep a judgment job?
Be assertive: Fly solo and be yourself. Men don't know it, but they really want independent women.
Work Saturdays: Steal a march on all those lazy male drones.
Think analytically: This trait impresses organization men. Logic is no more a man's province than intuition is a woman's.
Welcome conflict: Particularly with men who frighten easily.
Take your boss to lunch: You'll both be better for it.

Why do women seek out male approval on the job?
Ask your local headshrinker.
People on the job naturally *want* the approval of authority. Most authority exercised in the world of work is male. Accordingly, whether you are a woman working for a man, a man working for a man, a man working for a woman, or a woman working for a woman, it's healthy to want his/her *approval.*
So, it's not strictly true that women seek male approval. It's far truer that people want the approval of their boss.
Period.

If a woman follows her husband from place to place, drops out of the job market to raise children, or takes a grunt job to finance her husband's medical school education, how can she represent this effectively in a résumé?
By telling the truth.
Trying to conceal these laudable objectives, or even omitting mention of them altogether in your résumé, makes interviewers think, "She is covering up."
Don't eliminate yourself. Raising children, working to improve a family's earning power, negotiating eleven corporate transfers in eighteen years, are accomplishments every woman should be proud to report in a résumé. No employer *with a mind of his own* expects you to have done all of this and simultaneously pursued a career with an earnings record equal, say, to the Executive Vice-president of Union Carbide. Raising kids, arranging the sale and purchase of eleven homes, and bringing home the bacon (not to mention being five times President of the local PTA!), while Dad

learns why F=MA, means that you know how to manage time, money, and people: a definition of a manager.

Yes, but why are women so prone to follow the rules?

Well, if you mean the conventional "rules" about finding a job, are women any less savvy than men? Women, as a class, seem, in this respect—job-hunting—to be as dim-witted as men. If you mean that women tend to be "nicer" and more respectful toward institutions, well, that's surely changed in the past decade. If you mean that women on the job tend to be less assertive, more inclined to protect other people's interests, more ready to obey than command, then that's also true of *most* men.

That's because 10 per cent of the jobs in any place of work *count*. Women have these jobs in less proportion than men. But there are more men than women working, and accordingly, far more men (than women) who have jobs that don't *count*. At all events, be you man or woman, being "nice" while looking for a job (or on the job) is nowhere near as important as being *effective*. That plenty of ineffective men manage institutions should encourage effective men and women alike to go after their jobs.

Another definition of a judgment job is that the fewer "rules" that govern it, the fewer criteria used to fill it, and the more difficult it is to evaluate, the more likely it is to be a true judgment position. Tolerating ambiguity, taking some elementary risks, knowing how to *reduce* risks, not knowing how well you are doing, are elements of every judgment job. These kinds of jobs are not likely to attract either "rule-makers" or people who want and need excessive structure and supervision on the job.

But don't men really want women to become subordinates?

For *non*-judgment jobs. (Reread Chapter One.)

That would be true, too, if they were interviewing men for the same position.

If you *feel subordinate*, then why try to qualify for a judgment job? And subordinating—that is, *submitting* to expert authority—is a necessary ticket to enter the world of work. So, maybe, if this is your first time around in the job market or the first time in twenty years, *the job after this next job* should be a judgment job!

What are some appropriate questions women should ask male employers?

1. "Why do all the men sit in offices and all the women in little cubicles?"

2. "Could you describe to me the day-care facilities at Sticky Wicket, Inc.?"

3. "Do I have to be especially tactful to men who work under me?"

4. "What's your company policy on pregnancy?"

5. "Why aren't there any women vice-presidents at Sticky Wicket, Inc.?"

6. "Why is it, exactly, that only women are hired for the routine jobs?"

7. "Could you draw me a table of organization and tell me where I fit?"

8. "Would you mind describing similar positions you've filled here and tell me something about the qualifications of the candidates."

9. "As my boss, would you mind sharing some of the office duties, like Xeroxing, greeting visitors, making coffee, taking notes at important meetings, going to the deli, and arranging the department's Christmas party?"

10. "Am I expected to engage in a lot of witless intramural flirtations on this job?"

Are women more hesitant than men about becoming the boss?
Increasingly less so, but still a problem for plenty of talented women.

For the past ten years, I have been in the business of paying attention to successful people—mostly men, I'll admit—who want to move on to the Top Job. At the same time, the women's movement has been sending seismic vibrations through corporate/governmental/academic America, giving more than a few men a bad case of abdominal bends.

That brings me to my first point: Women who make a habit of success don't worry about "The Man." For a woman to withdraw from competition for a job, to finish second out of some misguided gesture toward the protection of some man's ego, is in itself enough to disqualify her from holding an important job. Would you hire a woman as a university president, or a cabinet officer, who believed her success meant the failure of some man? Of course not. Sensitivity to other people's feelings is fine, but sensitivity and consideration of your own feelings are more important.

Second, women who sincerely want to be the boss must give up the role of Victim. The martyred, long-suffering housewife is a stock character; her career counterpart is, frankly, a pain in the derrière. You will have to take responsibility for what happens to you. Knowing that, and knowing that the dues leaders pay are steep, take three steps back, look long and hard at the situation, and ask yourself, "Do I sincerely want to be the boss?" If the answer is still, "Yes, yes, a thousand times, yes!" the chances are better than ever that you'll make it.

But not if you feel sorry for yourself. A major quality in successful candidates for the Top Job is the capacity for disappointment —the bounce-back ability, the refusal to fail.

A third point: Do you understand what the consequences of real organizational leadership are? Are you prepared to make trade-offs between your personal life and your professional objectives? Do you who aspire to wield the executive scepter know the score?

If you answer yes—with conviction—to all the following questions, chances are that you're an Exceptional Woman, someone who really is grooming herself to appear someday on the cover of *Business Week*.

1. Am I willing to be called a bitch behind my back once I'm in the Top Job?

2. Will I work weekends to get on top of my job?

3. Am I prepared to take a chance on my rich relationship with my husband/boyfriend/friends/children/professional colleagues?

4. Do I have it in me to fire an ineffective man (late forties, three kids in college)?

5. Am I prepared to be judged by organizational results—quotas met, sales made, people hired/fired? In short, am I a bottom-line person?

6. Am I willing to give up my reputation as a Nice Person?

7. Can I admit I'm wrong, hire a staff all of whom are smarter than I am in certain respects, and make crisis decisions based on insufficient information?

8. Am I ready to go no faster than my slowest organizational runner? In other words, do I have the patience, sheer grit and capacity for frustration and painstakingness that is the common lot of organizational leaders?

9. Am I equipped to put organizational goals before personal feelings?

10. Do I have my own control problems under control; that is, can I resist manipulating people when what's needed is leadership?

Let's say that you scored 100 per cent, that you're prepared to pay your dues, that you really know the personal and professional consequences of being an Exceptional Woman. Do you still want that Top Job? Well, if you do, that's a great qualification. Really wanting any job is half the battle in qualifying for it. You'd be amazed at the number of qualified, trained, experienced people who've blown the final interview because, deep down, they didn't really want that important job.

The reasons are many, complex, and probably unconscious. If you don't really want a job, you'll communicate that to a prospective employer in a thousand ways. So, if you once blew a chance for the Top Job, the chances are that your motives were sound. Cheer on the person who did land that job. Sour grapes are for losers. Don't play the Victim.

By now, you should be rethinking the risky business of being the boss. And that's my fourth point. Are you a born risk-taker? If the answer is yes, then you qualify in the last important respect for the executive suite.

But what about the Exceptional Women who have made it? Are they winners on the job and losers on the home front? Probably many of them are, like successful men whose personal lives suffer. But plenty of successful women are effective both on and off the job. Here's why:

1. They are unafraid of personal involvement, a primary factor in successful marriages. These women really know how to get into a person's head, and that carries over onto the job.

2. They are effective managers: At home they know how to keep things running, and if they're mothers, how to raise independent children.

3. They feel free with people on or off the job and don't hang around people whose chief burden in life is resentment.

4. They aren't hassled by control problems.

5. They welcome success, love, and responsibility. They know how to set limits and wield authority with conviction, feeling, and equity.

6. They are cheered by support, approval, and applause. Recognition of work well done is appreciated.

7. They know how to cope with frustration, and they can teach others how to as well. That's why they have reputations for being effective executives and excellent mothers—there's little difference.

8. They make a habit of being assertive. People who can't watch out for their own interests are Nice People—and hardly ever effective on the job or off.

9. They want to be vulnerable, open. It's a myth that successful women conceal their feelings, "control" their emotions.

10. They aren't afraid to fly solo. The Exceptional Woman understands that people who know what they want and do it are admired.

It's tricky, but there's no contradiction between being effective and happy on the job (and off the job). But women do need to make a habit of success. My hunch, documented by a few thousand interviews, is that women shy away from taking major job responsibilities, hesitate to outperform men, and back off from going after the Top Job. Why? I'll risk saying that I think many women self-destruct on the job out of fear of wrecking their relationships with men off the job.

That does happen. There are a lot of weak men who envy success. But who needs a relationship with someone who measures his self-worth against yours?

Nobody succeeds in business without really trying—and that is the only path an Exceptional Woman wants to follow.

NINE

The Government Gig

OK.

So much for distaff problems. Let's examine the special problems of government employment. (Uncle Sam is now the nation's largest employer.)

I've been in the people business here in the nation's capital for twelve years—both in the government and in what humorists call the "private" sector. And after all this time, I can no more distinguish between government employment and private industry than I can tell the difference between offensive and defensive missiles. From where I sit—except for a few downtown and suburban merchants, a bond salesman or two, and the flower vendors—the District of Columbia seems populated mostly with bureaucrats dependent on Uncle Sam. And that goes for ex-bureaucrats who are retired from, selling to, consulting with, reporting on, or seeking re-employment in the federal system. We are all, every one of us, sometime civil servants.

The time is long overdue for some plain talk on how to survive, nay prosper, while in the service of our government. What follows, therefore, is my modest contribution to the science of public administration. And don't blame me if your College Placement Counselor never breathed a word about it or it wasn't taught in "Pol Sci 3A."

What are my credentials to help you cope with the bureaucracy?

Well, for openers, I recruited overseas and Washington staff for the Peace Corps back in those heady days when we were all very young and asked not what our country could do for us but what we could do for our country. Then I spent one disappointing year, 1966, outside my craft, lobbying for progressive arms-control measures and an end to the Vietnam War. It was not an especially vintage year for peace, arms control, and the brotherhood of man. But it was the year when all the big guns were fired in our War on Poverty. Every harried bureaucrat in town was either programing social action in East Harlem or systematizing food-stamp distribution in Mississippi.

So, for the next five years, I belted the commonweal with a newly established social-consulting firm. I hired nearly eleven hundred people, "sold" one hundred or more professionals to similar social-action enterprises, and herdhunted groups of specialized personnel under contract for a couple of government agencies.

As a consequence, I grew knowledgeable about the curious rites of government hiring and a trifle uneasy about the soundness of our civil service system. As the Englishman said: "If at night we knew in our hearts how badly we are governed, who of us could sleep?"

So, to ease *your* passage through the Washington maze, I've assembled some useful information on the "people" game and how it's played on the shores of the Potomac.

A few elementary facts about working for the Feds:

1. No one ever got a judgment job in the United States Government through the Civil Service Commission (unless he was applying for work in the Civil Service Commission!).

2. The Commission was established in 1883 and has never been "reformed." Next to the Bureau of Indian Affairs, E.E.O.C., and the GSA, it's probably the worst place in town to work (if it's real work you want).

3. The average number of people who seek work every working day with the Civil Service Commission at the Federal Application Center averages, *nationwide*, in the thousands! In Washington, D.C., the average number is 800 per day!

4. Of 300,000 official applications, give or take a few thousand, every year, only 10 per cent are hired. Of these, only 1 per cent represent judgment jobs.

5. GS-5–GS-7 jobs (entrance-level professional positions) for college grads require a written exam (PACE: Professional Administrative Career Exam).

6. Around 2,000 GS-5–GS-7 jobs are filled each year. Of these, half are "name requested." (More on this later.)

7. Many of these jobs are based on "quotas" from each state in the union. Accordingly, if you are from Nevada, the chances of your actually getting a job offer are greater than if you are from New York State.

8. Thus, 50 people compete for each PACE job.

9. Of 15,000 GS-9–GS-15 jobs, 80 per cent are filled on a "name requested" basis. That means that somebody needs to request three names from the registrar, one of which is yours, to get a job offer. Thus, only about 400 jobs per year are really "competitive."

10. Of GS-13–GS-15 jobs, 95 per cent (!) are filled through Agency promotion.

11. Of the remainder, 80 per cent are filled on a "name requested" basis.

12. Even super-grade and schedule "C" jobs (presidential appointees, so-called plum jobs) are 90 per cent filled by the bureaucracy itself.

13. The odds, therefore, on your finding a judgment job in government by the accepted means are about 75 to 1. The Civil Service Commission, thus, has 3,500 employees to fill 4,000 jobs throughout the government! As you can see, the Commission has never been reformed!

14. Grade "creep" is a national scandal and accounts for a major part of the increase of the national budget from 170 to 400 billion dollars. In other words, we have far too many GS-11s–GS-15s crowding the halls of government. A 60 per cent increase since the early sixties.

15. The "average" salary in government exceeds $13,000; in

private business it's about $11,000. So much for the starving civil servant.

16. Steps in grade are *automatic*.

17. M.A.s automatically receive a GS-7 rating.
Lawyers automatically get a GS-9 rating.

What's this "name requested" business?
Job-seekers find jobs in the "public" sector the same way as in the "private" sector. The major difference is that in the federal government you:

1. complete a government application form,

2. take an exam for middle management jobs, and

3. receive a "rating" from the Civil Service Commission.

Millions have accomplished all of the above and never been offered employment. That's because they "satisfied" government conditions for employment but never had a face-to-face interview for a job that was truly open.

So in your job search with the Feds *do* take the exam, fill out the application, and qualify for a "rating." The point is that your name can then "be requested" from the Commission as a viable candidate for a "real" job. In the absence of your being listed on the Civil Service Register, you would lose time (and maybe the job) trying to complete these first elementary steps.

At all events, however, you cannot possibly wage a judgment job campaign in government by merely satisfying conditions of employment. Someone must have a job and offer it to you; your job is to *find* that person. Then your potential employer, if he likes your looks, can "request your name" (along with two others) to consider for the opening. As the figures show, for judgment jobs in government, there really is *no* "competition." It's still a question of being at the right place at the right time with half the qualifications.

What about "freezes" on federal employment?
There has been more or less a "freeze" on employment since the second term of Grover Cleveland. It's meaningless.

Sure, it's tougher to find employment in the District now than in 1968, but that's true every place else too. And, as a breadwinning bureaucrat, you are necessarily concerned when . . .

— an Eisenhower announces that 50,000 Defense Department civilians must be "riffed" to balance the federal budget.

— a Kennedy rolls back government spending overseas to improve our international balance of payments.

— a Johnson freezes spending across the board to repel aggressors in the Far East.

— and a Carter clamps down on government employment to fulfill a campaign promise.

But, as President Kennedy once quipped about the bureaucracy, it's worth seeing if the American Government "intends to cooperate."

You mean, the President, by himself, can't stop the government from hiring people?

The President might order a 5 per cent reduction in workforce, but his bureaucracy really decides.

In other words, business as usual.

The hiring policies of most government agencies are the same as a decade ago, because the actual business of hiring, promoting, reassigning, and retiring bureaucrats goes on unabated. The President proposes, but the agencies themselves dispose. In fact, I can't remember a time when some sort of spending or employment crisis wasn't wracking Washington. The favorite personnel "put off" in town is rejecting job applicants on the basis of such high-level policies, which are, at best, unevenly applied.

Isn't there a personnel ceiling?

There is.

It's a simple reporting device for the convenience of the Office of Management. As far as you, the job-seeker, or the good bureaucrat is concerned, it bears about as much resemblance to reality as campaign rhetoric.

Why?

Because the "personnel ceiling" conceals the teeming activity, the sheer Machiavellian scheming, which transpires under its cover. There simply can't be a "freeze" on employment. Too many civil servants are retiring from government service, job-hopping from one agency to another, dropping out from the job scene altogether, returning to school, being reassigned—*all of which means open slots for enterprising job-seekers.*

Why does the President announce a freeze on employment if, in reality, it means so little?

It does mean *something.*

It means the government is holding the line on inflation. And the policy reflects changing, but often unadmitted, new national priorities. For example, the National Aeronautics and Space Administration is reducing the aerospace staff, but the Environmental Protection Agency is hiring pollution-abatement experts. And it does cripple the psychology of what has always been the best game in town: job-jumping.

Job-jumping? In the government?

Job-jumping, as elsewhere, is the art of finding good jobs in government service.

For Washingtonians, job-jumping is the only practical strategy for fighting inflation until Uncle Sam learns to live within his budget. The players range from the GS-1s and GS-2s in the mailroom to the GS-18s, who cavort at the deputy undersecretary level and lunch in private government dining rooms.

Don't let all the scare talk about widespread professional unemployment shake you. Comparatively, Washington, D.C., has an unemployment rate of about 6 per cent. The best people in government today are continually on the occupational move, as with executive employment in the private sector.

No one is going to raise an eyebrow if you've had three jobs in the last five years so long as you grew in salary, competence, and responsibility.

Is there much job-jumping back and forth between the government and the private sector?

Yes.

That's my main point.

Let's follow a career civil servant, the type that zaps back and forth, like the New York City shuttle, between the private and public sectors. A hydrologist by training and fresh out of college, our man finds federal employment with the "Department of Waterways and Canals." After advancing to GS-7 and during a brief stint in the general counsel's office of this mythical agency, he becomes an expert on riparian rights. And advances to GS-11.

Our man on the make is offered a high post with an engineering firm which apparently does 75 per cent of its business with the Department of Waterways and Canals. After accepting a position and becoming a "key" man (as we say in the private sector) with this organization (remember, he knows all the plays and players at DWC), a sudden longing to serve his Uncle Sam surfaces after a new administration takes office in Washington.

Back in the government as Chief, Domestic Operations, at a GS-18 level, our friend in a year or two bears all the trappings of a successful civil servant: plush carpet on the floor, autographed picture of the Secretary of the Interior on the wall, thermos of hot coffee permanently atop his desk, verdant drapes that match the latrine-green walls. Our man even attends senior staff meetings as a nonparticipant observer.

Alas, another administration takes power. But a sympathetic committee on Capitol Hill, controlled by the opposition, offers our man its staff directorship during the interregnum. For the next four to eight years, he coasts in this job at a salary in the mid-30s, awaiting his return to power—after the next presidential election—when he triumphantly becomes the chief of R & D at the Transportation Department—an undersecretary position.

Before the age of fifty he retires from government, working, because he wants to keep his hand in, as a consultant to his old engineering firm. A generous government pension, a corporate-stock payout, and an annuity (which he took out as an insecure GS-5) richly compensate him in his sunset years for his services to Uncle Sam.

Whether you work in the military-industrial complex or the peace-poverty axis, the ping-ponging between the public and private sectors is notorious. So, if you move out of government, you are likely to land on both feet with (a) a congressional committee monitoring the agency for which you worked, (b) a "management-consulting" firm which exploits your friendships, connections, and knowledge of the agency's business. Washington is really a small southern town. The intimate, unrecorded personal relationships you develop link you with your future job.

Well, job-jumping's OK in the private sector, but surely you can't do that in the government?
   Oh yeah . . . ?
Let us follow a good friend of mine as he wends his way through the labyrinth of government employment. Back in 1964 my friend was a comparatively underpaid civil engineer with a well-known electric-appliance manufacturer. A man of energy and intelligence, he sought volunteer service with VISTA, answering his government's call to wage war on poverty. After a brilliant stint as an extension worker in the Southwest, he found a GS-9 slot open with the General Services Administration before switching back to the VISTA staff in its fiscal department. Six months on the job and at a GS-11 level, he job-jumped to the General Accounting Office (the congressional budget arm) and rapidly scaled to Olympian heights as a GS-15. Undaunted, he pressed on and won a berth at the Commerce Department, whence he became a Congressional Fellow. Jumping to HUD, the youngest and highest-grade government employee in the history of that governmental conglomerate, he took "off" a year to work in private industry (through a special government program), then was on two one-year stints overseas with agencies where he was on "loan."
   Who says government service is boring?

Is there any one place to look for government jobs?
   The best publication I know of is the Federal Phone Book.
   Tracking down government jobs is being at the right place at the right time with ostensibly the right qualifications. Ask yourself: (a) Who are my friends and what jobs do they know of? (b) What are the nation's priorities and what agencies and contractors are working on them? (c) Is that where the money is? You can find out more about judgment jobs in government service the same way you do in the private sector: interviewing for information.

Should a job-seeker use his congressman for agency employment?
   Hundreds do.
   This kind of political clout is largely overrated. No government

man in his right mind is going to hire anyone based on his recommendation by a Strom Thurmond or a George McGovern. If an agency *does* hire on this basis or caves in to pressure from Capitol Hill, it is an agency in irreversible decline.

Congressional referrals should be treated like any other job applicant: courteously. Occasionally a good man or woman is hired via this route. But the practice does cast doubt on a job-seeker's capacity to wend his way into a job stream.

Well, if political connections are not as important as one supposes, what element is decisive?

The decisive element is the character and quality of the comments of the people who recommend you.

Past performance, rather than education, experience, salary level, or political chums, is what counts.

Choose your references wisely. People in government who can take a profile of your strengths and back up what you say about yourself make good references. One phone call from a respected bureaucrat to a potential employer is worth fifty job interviews.

And since none of us walks on water, be sure you include references who can speak to your next employer about the kind of things you *don't* do well. Surprisingly, a balanced view of any job applicant is worth a hundred times more and is twice as effective as a blurb recommendation.

Is it necessary to fill out a Form 171 (Government Application for Employment)?

Yes.

The Form 171 was designed during the height of the Cold War to throw confusion into our bureaucracy. Next to the fine print in *Robert's Rules of Order*, the works of R. D. Laing, and the later novels of Gertrude Stein, it ranks high in the Obscurantist Department.

In addition to a Form 171, prepare a résumé that is *so* good it opens up doors in the bureaucracy. That's the only value of a résumé. It's a sales document, an advertisement for yourself. The Form 171 has about as much sales appeal as an income tax form. And it tells the Feds nothing worth knowing about you. Slap your functional résumé on top of your Form 171 as a sales device.

I know a GS-11 who reproduced a hundred copies of his Form

171 and mailed them out to key bureaucrats in seven agencies. Only three of his applications were acknowledged; he gained only one interview: a job with the Coast Geodetic Survey located on the North Slope in Alaska. Each of his Form 171s with attached amendments weighed a half pound, and was as thick as the Sunday *Times*.

How do you get ahead in government?

The same way as in the "private" sector: Do a good job, a productive, visible job, and stake out the men in your agency who are real achievers. These men—like you—will move up (or over to other agencies) and invite you along for the ride. You have now reached that enviable plateau in government service when you no longer must hunt for a job, but are actively sought after, recruited within the government itself. I know one able Black civil servant who feels badly if he doesn't receive at least one good job offer each week.

What's the best time of year to find a job with the government or one of its contractors?

October 1.

That's the end of the fiscal year, when agencies spend wildly so as to justify next year's fiscal request.

The result is that wholesale hiring goes on inside and outside the government; the rest of the year, government employment is a backwater.

I've heard that government employment is badly paid?

Don't believe it.

The plain facts are that, except for grunt laborers at GSA, clerks and secretaries, and foreign service officers, federal employment is—relative to industry—more than holding its own, and at many levels often exceeds pay standards in the private sector.

Of course you won't become rich in public service. But after the latest spate of pay raises for government employees, the poormouthing civil servant feeding at the public trough is no longer a sympathetic figure.

How committed should I be to an agency's goals?

In Washington, D.C., everyone is committed to something: antivivisection, guarded railroad crossings, gun control, income tax reform, and so on . . .

Thus, without knowing it, every job interview in the District of Columbia is a political litmus test.

Of course you don't read about *that* in any job description!

Commitment is a staple of life to Washingtonians. If you're opposed to cigarette smoking, don't work to subsidize tobacco farmers at Agriculture; if you think migratory labor is a national disgrace, don't work at Labor. But the Surgeon General is fighting tobacco and the CSA wants to eliminate the migratory stream. The point is to match government agencies against your politics. Government policy is not consistent; you can find some agencies whose goals contradict others. Who ever said government was logical?

How serious are bureaucrats about their jobs?

Deadly.

Sure, you can laugh at anything in Washington: the devalued dollar, prospects for a thermonuclear exchange—but *never* a person's job. You'll earn a lifetime enemy.

Here in the nation's capital every bureaucrat thinks he works in the powerhouse. I knew a fellow who, while working on a task force to manage the war on poverty, burst out laughing when a high-level bureaucrat predicted the elimination of "poverty, disease, illiteracy, and injustice" by 1976. My friend now works in Des Moines selling an interesting line of casualty insurance.

How do you avoid bureaucrats who tell you that you're under-qualified?

Don't try to get around this objection. Meet it head on and prove you *are* qualified.

Sure, you need to type to qualify for the steno pool. College degrees for some obscure reason are required for most entry-level professional jobs. But the government usually provides a convenient loophole through which you could drive a Mack truck. The buzz expression is: "or equivalent experience."

I wager that in nine out of ten judgment jobs I've filled the hired bureaucrat did not meet all (or even most) of the unreasonable qualifications outlined. So if you hear of government jobs in the hidden job market and you meet half the "qualifications," chances are good that your application will carry the day.

Everyone says government employment is secure.
Another glittering half-truth.
It's nearly impossible to be fired from government service. Boozing, lechery, and politicking on the job are about the only charges that can be made to stick if the government wants to fire you. I have never heard of someone being cashiered for *incompetence.* (The last man fired for inefficiency was during the administration of Chester Arthur.)
However, for entirely different reasons, government employment is far more insecure than you would think.
The reasons: Winds of change blow and change directions in Washington, D.C., depending on the country's mood. A new administration with new plans takes power, intra-agency competition undermines your agency, the country's priorities are whipped about by political fashion to the consequent discomfort of those public servants who are working on *this* problem and not on *that.* Between riffs, freezes, rollbacks, and reductions in force, the fast-moving public servant must continually job-jump to stay even with where the judgment jobs are.
In a word, you can't be fired, but your job can be eliminated. Since your boss can't fire you, he'll probably promote you, eliminate your job, or take away your responsibility so that you'll quit.

Is the government loaded with deadwood?
At the middle level, yes. But so is private industry. Except that business recessions force periodic housecleanings in the private sector, to which the government, because of the terms of tenure, is largely immune.
In 1964, Congress tied a rider to an AID appropriations bill which would have removed a swatch of AID fat cats whose elimination was essential to the vigorous administration of our overseas-assistance effort. But the U. S. Employees union lobbied long and hard, and the rider was at last dropped. Government service, it was shown, meant punching a time clock. And the morale of hundreds of truly able people was wiped out by the victory of the drones and time-servers.

But surely there are some imaginative men and women in government service.

Yes, there are.

Among government people you will find some truly fine public servants. Men and women who are flexible, imaginative, purposeful, and hard-working. You will find such people in about the same proportion in a government agency as you find teachers with the same characteristics in a public educational system. Nobody in government or outside it has figured out a way to give them the recognition they need and deserve.

What about civil service registers?

You register by taking a government test: The Professional Administrative Career Exam (PACE).

College graduates should be able to pass the test easily. High school grads shouldn't forego a shot either. But don't expect a job on the basis of the test. Millions take them, and when the jobs turn up—about nine months later—you're presumably already well-employed. And the jobs are usually with the Bureau of Ships at a supply depot in Escondido, California.

But by all means do take the test; otherwise some spastic clerk in "personnel" will veto your job offer on the basis of your not having met civil service requirements.

For those of you who have trouble computing your income tax, be sure to study advanced arithmetic. For reasons wholly unclear to me, the PACE is chock-full of questions like: "If a canoeist is paddling downstream at 10 miles an hour and a steamboat is moving upstream at 30 miles an hour and both are 80 miles apart, how soon will they pass each other if both begin at 8 A.M. in the morning?"

As for the Military, that's the best economic bargain going in the United States. Since my days in the mid 1950's, when I was a PFC, salaries have quadrupled, benefits have vastly improved, and the Military has an unbelievable retirement program: twenty years of service to be eligible. Many ex-military, thus, have plenty of time to pursue a second career.

What is grade "creep"?

The federal job you have is redefined and you move up one, two, or three grades.

Since 1963, there has been a noticeable, progressively deterio-
rating standard of work in the government. Many mid-level jobs
have been upgraded far beyond comparable positions in private industry, making the cost of government prohibitive. It's not the
number of federal employees that's shocking, but the salaries paid,
which is costing the taxpayers.

*Is anything being done to reform the terms of tenure in govern-
ment service?*

No, but it's not too late to start.

It has been done before. President Garfield presided over a
thoroughgoing reform of the federal service late in the last century
and eliminated the "spoils" system. But of course, in its place we
introduced into the government bloodstream the fatal bacillus of
tenure and protected employment.

Why not try to reform once more the terms of government
service? Now that civil servants are well paid, isn't it time to let
the bracing winds of change blow through the government's rab-
bit warrens. A simple law restricting all federal employment to
five-year hitches, applicable to everyone and nonrenewable before
another five-year term has expired, would vaccinate us all against
the civil service mentality. Giving government executives the right
to "fire" people would, also, help enormously.

Such a reform movement is best led by those dedicated public
servants who understand better than anyone else the need to upgrade the quality of government services. It is in the interests of
all groups which *depend* on the quality and quantity of government services to expect those delivering the services to have *their*
interests at heart. I mean the students, the working mothers, the
welfare recipients, the sick—all those whom government vitally
touches.

A movement to reform the terms of government employment
would be best, however, for those who now work for, or want to
work in, the public interest. The insecurity of employment would
attract the self-secure, the limitation on government employment
would appeal to the conscience of public-service-oriented Americans, and the substance of government would at last be in the
hands of those who are truly the people's servants.

TEN

Ten Things I Wish
I Had Learned
on My First Job

Teaching people how to find jobs is a cinch; finding *any* job, relatively easy; finding a really *good* job, quite difficult. But hardest of all is *learning* on that first job and making a habit, from that point on, of taking responsibility for your own occupational life, staying in touch with your own deepest feelings, and focusing continually on *what you want to do with your life next*.

Maybe a lot of what I preach is what you have already learned in Sunday school. The trouble is, you don't believe it because you learned it in Sunday school!

What follows is a ten-point guide on what you want to learn on the job. So herewith the gospel:

1. Learn on the job to *feel free!* "Feelin' free," as the Pepsi slogan has it, simply means you are more *effective* than folks who consider work a pain, a joyless occupation. People who work because they feel they *must*, self-destruct; for them, work is an obligation, a duty, a burden. People who work out of a sense of duty (did you ever see *anyone* enjoying himself when he was doing his *duty?*) complain, put themselves down, blame the "system." They work because they *must*, not because they want to. . . .

Work is a joy!

So on your first job, ask yourself: What do I *like* to do? What gives me *pleasure?* What makes me *feel free?* Feeling free is an essential precondition to job satisfaction. Human happiness is a result of feeling free. Feeling free and being happy on the job is a sure-fire formula to being *effective* at what you do.

2. Learn on the job to *feel free to leave it!*

In other words, a good job is knowing you can be fired at any time and feeling free—at any time—to quit.

Many people, however, take a job . . . and think it's for life! And a life sentence, whether in prison or on a job, is sure as shootin' not feeling free! Most professional people today have four or five "careers." They feel free to leave a job they do well to take another. And there is no great secret why they do it; these men and women know what they *want*. And how we admire the person who knows what he/she wants! It might be the highest compliment paid us during our short lives.

Younger people stay at jobs they don't like because (a) they *panic* at the thought of finding another job; (b) they don't know what to do *next;* (c) they feel "loyal" to the person or organization they work for; (d) they don't feel free to do what they *want.*

Loyalty to organizations is the most misunderstood and confusing of all values in the workplace. More crimes, beginning with Watergate and its cover-up, are committed in its name than any other so-called virtue. People who "quit" organizations feel that they "betray" their (a) boss, (b) colleagues, (c) customers, clients, parents, students, target populations, stockholders, and so forth. But, remember, your first loyalty is to yourself. If unfaithful to your own wants, you betray both yourself and the organization. As you grow older, you change. If your changing objectives don't fit the objectives of your employer, your "duty" to yourself is to leave the premises . . . pronto! Hanging around the bullpen because of some misplaced and malignant sense of loyalty is bad form, terrible politics, and self-destructive. Focus on what you do next, establish a job campaign, and go after what you *want!*

3. Learn on the job what gives a *sense of fulfillment.* People want to overcome difficulty, take pains, *work hard!* People don't want big salaries, ideal working conditions, cradle-to-grave security —it's what they want when they feel no sense of fulfillment on

the job. Money is not the most important thing in a job; that's what follows becoming truly *expert* at some *skill*. So for your first job, aim for one that taxes your imagination, physical stamina, intellectual capacity—a job that stretches you as a human being. That's what we mean by a "challenging" job—you are challenged on a job when you are pushed, *stretched*. And, in the process, it causes some manageable anxiety, some pain, and a good deal of disappointment. That's why good jobs cause pleasure *and* pain, why people who succeed know how to bounce back, why we openly admire a person who does what he/she wants *despite all the setbacks*. It is our setbacks—the idea rejected, the report unread, the books unbalanced—that give us that sense of achievement when, by God, the idea *is* accepted, the report *is* read, and those pesky double entries *do* balance. That's what we really mean by a challenging job.

4. Learn on the job that doing something over . . . and . . . over . . . and . . . over . . . and over again is not, repeat *not*, a big bloody *bore!*

Yes, what I do might bore *you* and it might bore *him* and it might bore *her*; but if it doesn't bore me, then, baby, I've got a good job! Many younger people are terrified of boredom. "I don't want to be chained to a desk all my life" . . . "I don't want to do equations for a bank all my life" . . . "I don't want to edit copy forever . . ." And so forth, and so forth.

Practice does make perfect. Whether you are competing for the Olympic Games, preparing for your 148th root-canal job, or doing for the umpteenth time another international credit survey, repetition is the essential condition of mastering a *skill*. Why else hire anyone? For their good looks, fine feelings, high intelligence? No, I hire someone because he can *do* something (and wants to do it). And doing something well means doing it over . . . and over . . . and over again.

So on the job, study what *doesn't* bore you. Let that function, skill, expertise—call it what you will—lead you to the job you want. And that job is one where constant repetition, far from turning you off, turns you on! Every good, growth, judgment, knowledge job—the kind of job you want—contains a high quotient of repetitive action. If you really like yourself and care what happens to you on the job, search out what bores everyone else but makes you feel effective. You have found your niche in life, as my maiden aunt was wont to say, and you're a lucky guy/gal.

5. Learn on the job not to *compete* with anyone except yourself. No matter what you do, you alone are the best judge of how well you are doing. If you measure up in your own eyes, chances are good you've got a good job. Don't be, in David Riesman's phrase, an "other"-directed person, who measures his progress against a group, not his own standards; accepts received opinions as his own; moves no faster or slower than the mass about him. "The masses are asses" someone once said. And you're an ass, a jackass, if you let your boss, your peers, or your investment counselor decide how well you're doing! That's something you'll know if you are in touch with your feelings. Life is not a race—there are no winners and losers. There are simply people who love what they do and those that don't. Don't be a winner. Be a lover! And the world loves a lover!

6. Learn on the job to invest your emotions in it. People who care about what they do, do so because what they do touches their feelings; they are involved, they care about the consequences of their actions. Whether you work as a claims adjuster, a bank clerk, a teacher, or bridge-toll collector, get involved. People who care about their jobs feel anger, joy, distress every working day. That's because their emotions are engaged. And that's the kind of job you want.

7. Learn on the job how to cope and co-operate with all kinds of people.

A lot of people are going to resent you on the job. Especially if you are young, educated, ambitious, and they are older, not so well educated, and maybe no longer ambitious. On the job, you might be surrounded by people who no longer care, those who wrongheadedly perceive life to be a "race" which they have "lost."

The world has more people of this unfortunate disposition than people like you. As such, "middle managers" will put you down, try to intimidate you with their experience, age, occupational "street savvy."

Your job is to win them over to your side. And that means hear-

ing them out. There are a lot of good talkers on the job; few good
listeners. Be a patient person with those who are less fortunate.
Suffering fools gladly is not my message. My message is that the
world of work is composed of more people who hate what they do
than love it. Working with them and not becoming like them is a
full-time job in itself.

At the same time, it's also your job to stake out people within
the organization whom you truly admire. Make them your mentors, learn from people who are effective. Pay them the compliment of imitation. As for the rest of the ineffectives, remember:
When you're the boss, what you learned in coping with them will
be worth a lot to you as a manager. Managing people for effectiveness means working with people of every condition and cir-
cumstance.

8. *Learn to be like a boss who presses you beyond your limits.*
There are not many men and women who really *care* about what
they do, care enough to teach you to do your job better, push you
beyond your ability, ask a day's work for a day's pay. Such employers are often *not* nice people; but they are effective. On your
first job, look for that man or woman who is tough, demanding,
and from whom you can learn. It's worth a graduate degree in
Business Management. And you will learn to care about your
work and push people who work for you.

9. *Learn on the job not to be afraid.* A lot of people fear failure. "How am I doing, Mom?" they ask. People on the job who
never run risks run a far greater risk of never being considered for
risky jobs—i.e., jobs in line management where qualities of leadership are demanded.

But before you take risks, you've got to feel free. And what's the
worst risk you can take on the job? Why, being fired, of course!
And what's so wrong with that? It's men and women who risk
being fired from time to time who keep organizations alive and
well—because they care enough about themselves, what they do,
and the organizations that employ them (and its objectives) *to
make waves and raise rows!* Chances are you won't be fired, but
spotted as a young person with leadership potential. And if *fired*,
what's so bad about that? Who wants to sustain a bad working
relationship? Now you are free to go out and find the job you

want. You are *free* to leave one organization for another. In many countries around the world, freedom of occupational choice is unthinkable. The State *assigns* you a position; it's yours for life. And yet life on the job in those countries seems so dreary, so bleak . . . *so secure.* No wonder. People are *not* free and cannot *pursue* happiness, which, as an American, is our constitutional *right.* And that's the thing about human happiness: It's a matter of feelin' free. Nobody and no organization can *guarantee* you happiness. That's not a constitutional right, nor ever should be. What is promised is the chance to feel free and happy on the job, and therefore be effective. But the responsibility is yours, *not* the organization's.

10. Learn on the job how to *separate* life from work. Part of feelin' free is feeling separate. Sure, it's great to throw yourself into a task, invest your emotions, see a project through to completion, and feel pain and pleasure in the process. But while work is a joy, so is the rest of life. Many successful men and women put *the* job before everything else in life. My hunch, not carefully documented, is that workaholics have *no other life!*

The politician consumed by public office, the teacher who always finds time for his students, the "company man" always willing to "bear any burden, pay any price," are, from a distance, admirable characters. We read about them in the better business publications. Up close, however, they are a tedious breed: they have no conversation, no family life, no mad avocations.

So on your first (and second, third, or tenth) job, beware of becoming nothing but a worker bee. There is world enough and time to accomplish a great deal before you die in your traces. And let's give as much to life as to work.

My last point: You can't really learn about yourself by reading. You can learn by doing. So, finding a job and learning from it is the job of everyone.

Making mistakes on and off the job is certain—how else are we to learn except from our mistakes? The challenge on the job is learning from your mistakes . . . and that means being conscious of them in the first place. Verily, I do believe most men and women in the workplace repeat their mistakes over and over again. Why? Well, it has to do with what psychologists inelegantly call our "character structure." So if you find yourself repeatedly making the same mistake—taking jobs you don't want, being intimidated by authority, refusing to reveal your feelings—it could be *you* need to change. So think twice before you blame your on-the-job woes on the "system," your boss, the nature of work itself. The enemy is usually in our own head. And the way to attack and defeat him is to acknowledge him in the first place (i.e., you admit mistakes). Then you ask yourself whether you really *want* to stop making that mistake (plenty of people don't). Finally, you must become practiced in substituting another action —looking for a job you really want, standing up to your boss, involving your best feelings in a job—before you can be sure your "character structure" is changing.

People hate change. But people hate making mistakes too. So, while personal growth (which is what I mean by change) is tough and slow and disappointing, it is also the only game in town if you want to be happy and effective on and off the job. May we all change into people we want to become.

Write, when you find work!

INDEX

226   INDEX

Business relationships (interpersonal relationships). *See* Employment relationships
Business schools, 12–13, 14, 170

Cab driving (hacking), 97
Calling(s), stress on, 6
Capital accumulation, 3, 102–3
Career guidance counselors (career advisory services), xxi, 76 (*see also* Consultants); as coaches and players, 185, 186, 187; effective, 184–85, 186–87; proliferation of, 186; teachers as, 184–85
"Careers," ix, xxi, 8–14, 72, 163, 194, 218; counseling and, ix, xxi, 185, 186–87 (*see also* Career guidance counselors); dropping use of word, 187; focus on skills in place of, 187–88; stress on calling instead of, 6
Careers Today, 72
Caring, 39; parent-child relationship and, 185
Carleton College graduates, 11
"Challenging" jobs, 18, 70, 186, 219; judgment jobs as, 42–43
Chambers of Commerce, 90
Change, personal (personal growth), x, xii, xiv–xv, 82, 170, 186 (*see also* specific aspects, jobs, kinds, situations); education as, 8; feelings and (*see* Feelings); learning on the job and, 217–23; and organizational change, 170, 189–90; self-knowledge and (*see* Self-knowledge)
Character structure (character weaknesses), learning from mistakes and, x, 223. *See also* Strengths and weaknesses
Chicanos, 183
Children (*see also* Adolescence): caring parents and, 185; working mothers and, 193, 194, 195, 196, 201
Christmas card lists, 90
Civil Service Commission, 79, 204, 205, 206
Civil service employment, 203–16. *See also* Government employment
Clergy, the, former members of, 174, 175
Clothing. *See* Dress
Cold-turkey contacts and job search, 95–96
College alumni services, 108
College placement directories, 90
Colleges and universities, xii, xvii, 2–3, 7–14 (*see also* Education; Graduate schools; specific aspects, degrees, developments, institutions, kinds); degrees and jobs, 7–14, 153, 155 (*see also* specific kinds); and government employment, 205, 206, 213, 215; grading system and, 172; and job market, xvii, xx–xxii, 2–3, 7–14; "overschooled" society and, 8–14; placement counseling and, 184 ff.; and résumés and transcripts, 63, 69–70, 71; and salaries, 151, 152, 153, 155, 158, 159; starting salaries and, 153, 155
Commission-sales type relationship, 171. *See also* Sales
Commitment (*see also* Loyalty, organizational): government employment and, 212–13; judgment jobs and, 192
Communal syndrome, 2
Community-action employment, 18, 21, 51, 104. *See also* specific aspects, jobs, kinds
Community-development work, 51. *See also* specific aspects, kinds
Company annual reports, 90
Comparability, salary, 149–50
Competence (incompetence), xiv, xv, 174. *See also* Ability; Effectiveness
Competition, 18, 143; job search and, 44; judgment jobs and, 20–22 ff., 220; women and, 199
Computers, use in job-seeking and hiring of, 94–95
Computer science schooling, 9
Concealment. *See* Secrecy
Conciseness, importance in job interviews of, 131
Conflict situations, x, 121, 196. *See also* Employment relationships; specific aspects, kinds
Congressional Staff Directory, 90
Congressmen, government jobs and use of, 210–11
Congruence. *See* Job congruence
Consultants (consulting jobs), 67–69, 103–4 (*see also* Career guidance counselors; specific jobs, kinds); fees, 158, 160, 164; as judgment jobs, 20, 67–69, 103–4; strong and weak points of, 68
Consulting firms, management, 93–94. *See also* Executive search specialists
Contract-hire, salaries and, 158
Contractors, government, 212
Contracts, employment, 147
Control (leadership) problems, women and, 200
Convictions (arrests, ex-cons), interviews and résumés and, 67, 121

and job-market revolution, 7–10; and "overschooled" society, 8–14; and salaries, 152, 158, 159
Grinnell College graduates, 11
Group therapy, 186
Growth, personal. See Change
"Growth" jobs, judgment jobs as, xv n. See also Judgment jobs; specific aspects, jobs, kinds
Grunt jobs, xiv, 13, 75, 97, 134, 143, 196; pay for, 164
Guidance counselors. See Career guidance counselors
Guilt feelings, 43–44, 83–84 (see also Anxiety; Fear; specific problems, situations); success and, 24–25

Hacking (cab driving), 97
Haggling, salary negotiating and, 146, 155
Hair styles, xviii, 113, 118, 188. See also Beards
Hamilton College graduates, 11
Happiness (discontent, dissatisfaction, unhappiness), x–xi, xvii, 3–4, 18, 22–23, 24–25, 26–27, 43, 121, 171, 222 (see also Self-fulfillment; specific aspects, jobs, problems); effectiveness and work and, 201–2, 217 ff., 222–23; feelings and (see Feelings); freedom and, 187, 222 (see also Freedom); goals and (see Goals); human will and, 3–4 (see also Human will); and job search, 82–84; judgment jobs and, 22–23, 24–25; nature of work and specialization and, xvii, 217 ff., 222 (see also Alienation); success and, 24–25; wants and (see Wants); working women and, 194, 201–2
Harvard University, 112
Health status, listing in résumés of, 49, 57
Help-wanted ads. See Want ads
Hero-worshiping, 39. See also Achievers
Hidden agendas (personal factors), job campaign and offers and, 112–14, 128–30, 175–76, 177–78. See also Discrimination
Hidden job market, 75, 79–81 ff.; breaking into, 84–85 ff.; finding in specific fields, 87; good jobs (judgment jobs) and, 79–81 ff., 114, 122 ff.; hidden manpower pool and, 85–86 ff., 91–92, 114; interviewing for information and, 85–89, 91–92, 93, 96, 122; and job offers, 122 ff.; meaning of, 79–80; recruitment and,

85 ff., 114, 122 ff.; salaries and (see Salaries)
Hidden manpower pool, 85 ff., 91–92, 114; interviewing for information and, 85–89, 91–92, 93, 96, 114; recruitment from, 86, 114
Hiring yourself an employer, 78 ff., 191 (see also specific aspects, jobs, situations); employment relationships and, 169 (see also Employment relationships); hidden agendas and, 128–30; interviewing for information and (see Interviewing for information); meaning of, xxii, 78, 112; negotiating salaries and, 148; placement counselors and, 184–85
Hobbies, résumés and, 49, 50, 55
Honesty (candor), interviews and, 122–23. See also Secrecy
Hostility, x, 128. See also Agreeableness; "Getting along"
Hotel jobs, 97; management schools, 9
Housewives, 192, 194–95, 196–97, 199. See also Women, working
How-to-find-a-job systems, xi–xii, xv
Human-service fields and professions, jobs in, 12, 51, 103–4. See also specific jobs, kinds
Human will (free will), xii, xiii–xiv, xvi, xix, 4, 10, 12, 19 (see also Feelings; Wants); and job search, 29–44 passim
Humor (laughter), interviews and job offers and, 128, 129, 131

Ideal (dream) jobs. See Dream (ideal) jobs
Ideas, selling. See Proposal development approach
Identity (self-identity), xiv, 17, 23, 24–25, 82. See also Self-esteem; Self-knowledge
"If I had a million dollars" exercise, 3–4, 38
If Things Don't Improve Soon, I May Ask You to Fire Me (Irish), xiii n, 173 n
Imitation, success and, 39, 92, 221; biography-writing exercise and, 39
Independence, xxii, 15–16 (see also Dependency relationship; Freedom; Self-employment); women and, 194
Industrial jobs, salaries and, 164
Inexperienced, job search and, xviii, 9, 24. See also Experience
Inflation, 2, 5, 208
Information, "inside," 72. See also Interviewing for information